Browning and Wordsworth

Browning and Wordsworth

John Haydn Baker

Madison • Teaneck
Fairleigh Dickinson University Press

Associated University Presses
2010 Eastpark Boulevard
Cranbury, NJ 08512

The paper used in this publication meets the requirements of the American National Standard for Permanence of Paper for Printed Library Materials Z39.48-1984.

Library of Congress Cataloging-in-Publication Data

Baker, John Haydn, 1972–
Browning and Wordsworth / John Haydn Baker.
p. cm.
Includes bibliographical references (p.) and index.
ISBN 0-8386-4038-9 (alk. paper)
1. Browning, Robert, 1812–1889—Knowledge—Literature. 2. Wordsworth, William, 1770–1850—Influence. I. Title.
PR4242.L5B35 2004
821'.8—dc22

2004000211

PRINTED IN THE UNITED STATES OF AMERICA

Contents

Acknowledgments

I would like to thank the following for their help in preparing this book: the Armstrong Browning Library, the Browning Society, Philip Kelley, Michael Meredith, Adam Roberts, Robert Woof, John Woolford, and the Wordsworth Trust.

Portions of this book have previously appeared in a slightly different form in the following articles: "Wordsworth's 'The Warning': A New Source for Browning's 'The Lost Leader'?" *Notes & Queries* 242, no. 3 (September 1997): 340–41; "Did Wordsworth Drink Browning's Health?" *Notes & Queries* 243, no. 2 (June 1998): 214–15; "Browning's *Sordello*: A New Source?" *Notes & Queries* 245, no. 3 (September 2000): 329; "Browning's Apology: Robert Browning, Wordsworth, and William Knight," *Review of English Studies* 54, no. 214 (2003): 220–37. They are reprinted here by permission of Oxford University Press.

A Note on Texts

The Wordsworth critic faces a baffling variety of texts. Wordsworth was an enthusiastic and thorough reviser of his poems, and each new collected edition he published during his lifetime contained numerous revisions. The Collected Edition of 1849–50 must be accepted as Wordsworth's last word on how he wished his poems to appear; most editions of Wordsworth's poetry since 1850 have reprinted this text.

There are several objections to the argument that scholars should refer to this particular text. Aside from the aesthetic argument that many of Wordsworth's revised poems are plainly inferior to his earlier versions, one must remember that contemporary readers of Wordsworth would not have had the option of using what they knew to be the final authorized text. To these readers, until 1850, Wordsworth's poems were in a continual state of flux.

Since this book focuses on Browning's attitude toward Wordsworth, it is vital to discover precisely which *version* of Wordsworth's works Browning was thinking of whenever he alluded to a Wordsworth poem, commented on or criticized Wordsworth, or grappled with issues raised in his work. John Maynard has demonstrated how Browning was reading Wordsworth from his youth—perhaps, startlingly, even before 1820—and, during Wordsworth's lifetime, while Browning was actively contending with Wordsworth in several of his own poems, nine collected editions were to appear.[1] To which version of Wordsworth's text was Browning referring? He continued to engage with Wordsworth until his own death in 1889—which text was he using during this period?

Browning had access, at least from his marriage in 1846 (and maybe before), to a copy of the 1836–37 collected edition of Wordsworth belonging to his wife. In a letter of November 10, 1885, to William Knight, president of the Wordsworth Society, he declares his intention to consult this edition, "marked" by his wife, as part of his attempt to construct a list of favorite Wordsworth poems.[2] However, it is by no means certain whether this was a genuine intention or a ploy to make his selection seem less personal.[3] Browning certainly had no access to his wife's copy of this collection before 1845. What edition was he using *before* then, and, in particular, while writing *Paracelsus*, a profoundly Wordsworthian poem, in 1835?

In a letter of July 9, 1880, to William Knight, who was editing a Wordsworth selection and had asked for Browning's advice, Browning said that he believed the *first* text of a Wordsworth poem was usually the best; in fact, he went on to say, he found many of Wordsworth's revisions aesthetically displeasing.[4] Browning disliked the whole practice of revision. The revisions Tennyson made to his earlier poems when he republished them in 1842, for example, infuriated Browning; in a letter of July 13, 1842, to Alfred Domett he sternly describes Tennyson's alterations as "insane," the result of "mental infirmity."[5] In the light of these declarations, it can be assumed that Browning would have sought out and read Wordsworth's poems in their earliest published forms, and, furthermore, that his engagement with Wordsworth would have had these texts in mind. Therefore, the Wordsworth texts from which quotations are taken are in all cases the earliest published versions. Spelling or punctuation have not been modernized. For the purposes of reference, line references for the poems in the authoritative De Selincourt and Darbishire edition of Wordsworth's poems are quoted. In cases where the versions of the poems that appear in the De Selincourt edition differ from Wordsworth's earliest texts (which are numerous; De Selincourt uses Wordsworth's *final* edition as his copy-text) De Selincourt prints the original readings of the lines at the foot of the page upon which he prints the extract in question. Nevertheless, *all* quotations from Wordsworth have been taken from the earliest *published* editions; quotations from *The Prelude* are therefore taken from the 1850 edition, the only version of the poem Browning could have read.

In Browning's case, the question of texts has a simpler answer, since he was not anywhere near as extensive a reviser of his own poems as Wordsworth. Nevertheless, he did give some attention to revision when new collected editions of his poems appeared in his lifetime, particularly in 1849, 1863, 1865, and 1868. Most of the corrections were connected with punctuation, but *Paracelsus* and *Sordello*, in particular, were extensively revised. At the end of his life Browning revised all of his works for a collected 1888–89 edition, which has remained the copy-text for most subsequent editions. This edition has not been used, for two reasons. The first objection is to the reliability of the 1888–89 text itself. In particular, one should avoid using the 1888–89 text of *Pauline*, except in a very few circumstances. *Pauline* was very extensively revised for the 1888–89 edition, and it is thus extremely misleading to print the 1888–89 text as the *first* of Browning's productions in a chronological collection (as Pettigrew and Collins do in the Penguin Browning). For work on *Pauline* it is vital to use the 1833 text, unless one is specifically studying the way Browning rewrote his first published poem at the end of his life. The 1888–89 edition is to be used with caution for other reasons as well. Browning noticed a number of errors in the 1888–89 text; as Mary Campbell wrote in a memoir of the poet, he asked her husband for a copy of the new edition so he could make the necessary corrections, and Browning made corrections to ten volumes (which are now in the British Museum) before his death.[6] Some, but not all, of these corrections would be incorporated in a partially corrected reprint (known as "1889," though it was in fact issued in 1890). Browning, unlike Wordsworth, died before he could leave the world with a "fully authorized" final edition; "1889," though it contains numerous corrections of the 1888–89 text, *adds* other misprints. The 1888–89 text cannot, therefore, be regarded as textually reliable, and cannot be regarded as Browning's final word on how his poems ought to be read—if, indeed, one is seeking such "instruction."

Quite aside from this question of textual reliability, there is another reason why the 1888–89 text has not been used. Since this book's intention is to examine Browning's fluctuating attitude toward Wordsworth, which changed radically several times during his lifetime, it was decided to focus on the earliest published texts of the poems, in the belief that they reflect "the work's most active engagement with its historical moment."[7] As John Woolford and Daniel Karlin argue in the Longman edition of Browning's poetry, "[A]n author's earlier intentions may have as great a claim on a modern reader's attention as his final ones. A poem, or any other literary work, on its first publication emerges from, and enters into, a particular historical and biographical context which determines important elements of its identity."[8] Subsequent revisions do not therefore create necessarily *superior* texts, with value slowly accumulating cumulatively. They create *different* ones, which may well be fascinating in themselves, but are not necessarily somehow more "authentic" or "valuable." Woolford and Karlin therefore decide—as do I—to print the earliest versions of Browning's poems, in order to reflect the importance of the "historical and biographical context" of their original composition and publication.

It was decided, therefore, in Browning's case as much as in Wordsworth's, to focus on the texts as they first appeared. Browning's relationship with Wordsworth is not, by and large, affected by his revisions. Only in the case of *Sordello* and "The Lost Leader" do some revisions clearly indicate a change of opinion, rather than expression, when it comes to Wordsworth; the use of later editions of these poems is clearly indicated in the text. Otherwise, as with Wordsworth, all quotations from Browning's poems are taken from the earliest published versions. To aid the reader in locating these quotes, line references to the texts as published in modern editions are added, as follows: for *Pauline*, *Paracelsus*, *Sordello*, and "The Lost Leader" the Longman edition, edited by John Woolford and Daniel Karlin, which reproduces the earliest published versions of the poems, has been used; for "Transcendentalism" and later poems other editions have been used, since the Longman Browning has not yet reached *Men and Women*. Therefore, for references to poems in that volume, the Oxford Browning, edited by Ian Jack et al., has been used, since it is more extensively annotated than the Penguin text. For later poems, the Penguin text has been used; though it reproduces Browning's revised 1888–89 texts, it is largely reliable, and from it one can clearly, if one wishes, "re-create" Browning's earliest published texts (Browning's revisions of his later poems are not extensive).

Browning and Wordsworth

1
Why Browning and Wordsworth?

ON SEPTEMBER 6, 1889, THE ELDERLY ROBERT BROWNING, HAVING RECENTLY ARRIVED in the small Italian town of Asolo on a visit to his friend Katherine Bronson, wrote what would become the prologue to his final volume, *Asolando*. In this poem he describes the not-uncommon way his return to a much-loved place has failed to live up to his earlier experience; in particular, the landscape now lacks the extraordinary qualities he had seen in it as a young man over fifty years before. He begins with two stanzas whose placement in quotation marks gives them the appearance of a quotation from the work of *another* poet—a "poet" who seems to share Browning's melancholy feeling that the landscape, perceived in old age, lacks the lambent qualities it seemed to possess to a younger eye:

> "The Poet's age is sad: for why?
>   In youth, the natural world could show
> No common object but his eye
>   At once involved with alien glow—
> His own soul's iris-bow.
>
> "And now a flower is just a flower:
>   Man, bird, beast, are but beast, bird, man—
> Simply themselves, uncinct by dower
>   Of dyes which, when life began,
> Round each in glory ran."
>
> (lines 1–10)

Browning answers this poet with a determination to face up to "truth ablaze," asking his "friend" whether he would rather gaze at the world through a colored "optic glass" or through a *clear* glass that will aid rather than distort or blur perception, revealing "the naked very thing" (lines 19, 11, 16). He prefers such a "glass" to "falsehood's fancy-haze" (line 20). His return to Asolo fails to provide him with a "lambent flame," but this does not depress Browning in the same way that it depresses the other poet; he rejoices, instead, at his newfound ability to distinguish "fancy from fact" and see the world as it really is: "hill, vale, tree, flower—they stand distinct, / Nature to know and name" (lines 31, 36–37). He concludes by linking this newfound "realism" with his religious faith:

> No, for the purged ear apprehends
>   Earth's import, not the eye late dazed:
> The Voice said "Call my works thy friends!
>   At Nature dost thou shrink amazed?
> God is it who transcends."
>
> (lines 41–45)[1]

The "Voice" of God instructs Browning to avoid the temptation to seek "transcendence" on earth, through veiling the natural landscape with metaphysical qualities it does not possess. One's relationship with nature ought to be one of friendship, rather than one of self-abasement, which should be reserved for God. The poem is an exhortation to a "realist" view of the world—a view that lacks the awesome qualities of the distortion of the inexperienced eye, but is ultimately healthier and more conducive to a profitable relationship between man and nature. Truth is "ablaze" in its own right.

The poem is ideally suited to serve as a prologue to *Asolando*—a volume much concerned with the conflict between "Fancies and Facts" (the book's subtitle). However, it also has its relevance to a conflict that had troubled Browning since the very start of his poetic career. Several critics have pointed out that the poet "quoted" by Browning at the start of the poem sounds like Wordsworth: the lines are, in fact, a fairly accurate pastiche of the opening lines of the "Immortality" Ode.[2] Browning is mounting an optimistic riposte to his predecessor's well-known mourning for "the glory and the dream," implying that the "celestial light" Wordsworth saw about himself as a boy was illusory and thus pernicious. In the words of Lawrence Kramer, "at the close, the 'Prologue' to *Asolando* wants to have things both ways: to purge the self of feeling the burden of visionary loss and to compensate the loss with a more than visionary gain . . . this awkward maneuver testifies to the quality of desperation in Victorian dealings with the Wordsworthian pattern."[3] Browning is also engaged with another Wordsworth poem here: the "Elegiac Stanzas" Wordsworth wrote on the death of his brother, in which Wordsworth recognizes that the remembered beauty of Peele Castle on a calm day was an inaccurate depiction of the realities of life:

> A Picture had it been of lasting ease,
> Elysian quiet, without toil or strife;

No motion but the moving tide, a breeze,
Or merely silent Nature's breathing life.

(lines 25–28)

In depicting this scene in paint, Wordsworth recognizes that his younger self would have added

the gleam,
The light that never was, on sea or land,
The consecration, and the Poet's dream.

(lines 14–16)

Now, however, he has a new perception of the world's bleak reality, and Beaumont's painting of the castle in a storm seems to him a more appropriate depiction of existence—it is only through a refusal to let oneself be blinded by fantasy that one can begin to cope with life rather than deny it.

The "Elegiac Stanzas" prefigure Browning's message in the "Prologue." Both poems serve as exhortations toward realism. In the "Prologue," Browning's attitude toward Wordsworth is ambivalent; on one hand, he is criticized for his nostalgia for the fond illusions of his youth, but on the other, the poem's repetition of the message of the "Elegiac Stanzas" indicates an awareness that Wordsworth did not allow his nostalgia entirely to cloud his realism. This double-sided view of Wordsworth is not as baffling as it may appear. Though critics have noticed that the "Prologue" is engaged with Wordsworth, they have not put this into context; the poem is in fact the last flaring-up of an old conflict with Wordsworth, in the light of which the ambivalent attitude Browning displays becomes understandable.

Why is the relationship between Browning and Wordsworth worthy of study? The relationship was almost all one-way; Wordsworth influenced Browning, not vice versa. Though Wordsworth did not die until Browning was thirty-eight years old, there is no evidence that he paid any attention to Browning's works; even if he had read them, he was writing so little poetry at this late stage of his career that it is extremely unlikely that Browning's poetry had any influence at all on his writing. Wordsworth's library, upon his death, did contain a copy of *Paracelsus*—the only one of Browning's volumes Wordsworth is known to have owned.[4] The copy, sold at auction at Christie's in 1976, has vanished; but according to one of the bidders at this auction, who examined the book before it was sold, it contained no dedication—no inscription at all, in fact, apart from Wordsworth's own name.[5] How Wordsworth obtained this volume, and whether he ever read it, are difficult questions. Browning himself would surely have inserted a written dedication. A mutual friend (perhaps John Kenyon) may have presented it to him, and he may even have taken the trouble to seek it out himself, but however he obtained it, the vanished volume is no more than a tantalizing spur to speculation.

Neither is there much evidence as to the personal impact Browning made on Wordsworth; they met several times, but, to the elderly poet, Browning would have been no more than one of many minor literary figures who swarmed around him every time he came down to visit the capital. The two men never seem to have corresponded, and Browning never visited Wordsworth at Rydal Mount; indeed, he never went to the Lake District at all.

This study will therefore focus on Wordsworth's influence on Browning. What is meant by "influence"? The most obvious influence Wordsworth had on the younger poet was personal; Browning's encounters with the older poet left him with a negative opinion of Wordsworth as a man. More interesting, and almost entirely unexplored by critics, is the question of Wordsworth's *aesthetic* influence on Browning. In relation to the idea of poetic "influence," it will be useful to keep in mind the works of Harold Bloom, whose best-known theory—that of "influence"—is most clearly described in three books written in the 1970s: *The Anxiety of Influence*, *A Map of Misreading*, and *Poetry and Repression*. He contends that "strong" poets (as opposed to weak poets, who never move beyond imitation of their predecessors) are acutely conscious of the "influence" of the "strong" poets before them; this consciousness torments them. They feel what W. J. Bate has called the "burden of the past"—a phrase by which Bate describes the accumulated weight of the achievement of one's predecessors.[6] Bloom describes "poetic influence" in *The Anxiety of Influence* as "the sense . . . of *other poets*, as felt in the depths of the all-but-perfect solipsist, the potentially strong poet. For the poet is condemned to learn his profoundest yearnings through an awareness of *other selves*."[7] The "potentially strong poet" is faced with a dilemma. He can surrender to his predecessor's influence and collapse into the "belatedness" of imitation. Alternatively, he can *struggle* with his predecessor and turn his relationship with him from an imitative to an "agonistic" one. How, though, is he to do this with a long-dead predecessor? Bloom contends that the strong poet reaches out to take control of his predecessor's *works*, through a process he calls "misreading."[8] He believes that the youthful poet—or "ephebe"—begins his career in imitation of a predecessor, but is soon forced, if he is to become "strong," to "misread" the predecessor's works in order to escape their influence.[9] Bloom suggests that the strong poet "misreads" in a total of six different ways, or "revisionary ratios," which he terms *clinamen*, *tessera*, *kenosis*, *daemonization*, *askesis*, and *apophrades*. Some of these "ratios," in the present context, are more useful than others; particularly relevant to Browning's relationship with Wordsworth are the first two, clinamen and tessera. Bloom defines clinamen as "poetic misreading or misprision proper."[10] A clinamen is a sort of swerve; this "misreading" allows the poet to imply that the precursor somehow made a wrong turning in his or her own poem—a wrong turning that is corrected in the new poem. Tessera, meanwhile, is "completion and antithesis."[11] Bloom takes this term from certain ancient cults; it originally meant a fragment—of a vase, say—by which one could recognize an implied whole. The poet uses tessera to "complete" the predecessor's poem, thus implying that the predecessor had, rather than taken a wrong turning, stopped too soon and left his or her work incomplete.

I contend that this relationship can principally be illuminated through an application of clinamen and tessera. A change of attitude toward Wordsworth in Browning's poetry after 1840—a movement from imitation (as most clearly demonstrated in *Paracelsus*) to rejection and scorn—can only be fully understood if one uses a revisionary ratio that combines clinamen and tessera in a fundamental "misreading" of the precursor.

Bloom has written extensively on Browning, though not, except in one isolated instance, on the relationship between Browning and Wordsworth.[12] Bloom concentrates on the relationship between Browning and Shelley, as evidenced in "Childe Roland to the Dark Tower Came," though he also writes on "Thamuris Marching" and "Cleon."[13] In these analyses Bloom presents Browning as a strong poet struggling against the influence of a predecessor—in this case, Shelley—through "misreading." Bloom seems to have allowed his consciousness of Browning's struggle with Shelley to blind him to an equally intense struggle with Wordsworth. He is in error when he announces that Browning was not *personally* conscious of the struggle in which he was engaged; an examination of Browning's correspondence with William Knight indicates that Browning found his relationship with Wordsworth deeply troubling.[14] Nevertheless, an application of a Bloomian model—in this case—reaps rich dividends, and offers a convincing explanation for some otherwise baffling transformations.

It will be objected that using such a model excludes any historicist reading of Browning's relationship with Wordsworth; one of the most vulnerable points in Bloom's theory is its antihistoricism, which has been seen by some critics as reactionary and naïve. Graham Allen, for example, specifically points out the antihistoricist nature of Bloom's theory: in his words, "[P]oetic history is valorized at the expense of a historical understanding of poetry."[15] Bloom himself is aware of this problem, but is not concerned by it: as he puts it, his only concern is with "*the poet in a poet*, or the aboriginal poetic self."[16] Bloom's exclusive concern with the "aboriginal poetic self" leaves out the entirety of external influences—historical, cultural, political—that both old historicist and new historicist critics acknowledge have influence over the writing of poetry. Bloom's unfashionable status at present has a good deal to do with this deficiency. This study, though it employs a broadly Bloomian model of influence in order to illuminate Browning's struggle with Wordsworth, should not be taken as evidence that its writer believes such a model can be profitably employed in examining *any* such relationship. Bloom can help us to reach some useful insights in this case, but it would be foolish to maintain that this—or any—relationship was *purely* the product of "influence anxiety," and, indeed, some possible historicist explanations will be examined in due course. This study *uses* Bloomian theory as a tool, rather than allowing Bloom's "influence" to dominate it. It agrees with Bloom when he maintains that his theory, whether true or not, is nevertheless a *useful* tool for poetic analysis.[17] It is profitable to use a variety of literary theories much as one might use a variety of keys to open a door; the key that eventually opens *this* particular door may not open many, if any, others—we will not know until we try. In the meantime, we should concentrate in exploring the room the key has opened up for us, and avoid the temptation to reach for an ax.

Applying this model of the poet's struggle for self-definition to the relationship between Browning and Wordsworth is extremely illuminating. Browning was faced in Wordsworth with a predecessor whose influence could not be avoided. Critics (including Bloom) have tended to focus on Shelley's influence on Browning, at the expense of that of the other romantic poets, Wordsworth in particular. Browning's early poetry, especially *Paracelsus*, demonstrates that as a young man Browning was so influenced by Wordsworth—mainly by Wordsworth's attempt to fuse romantic idealism with practical realism, as demonstrated in *The Excursion*, and, in particular, in the prospectus to *The Recluse*—that he was in danger of producing pastiches of Wordsworthian doctrines.[18]

Before going further, "idealism" and "humanism" must be defined. The term "idealism" is used to describe a way of thinking almost diametrically opposed to the earlier definition of "realism"; the idealist concerns himself, not with the world as it *is*, but as it *ought* to be. He imagines other, more perfect worlds, and usually hopes to transform the "real" world into one of them. Shelley is a good example of the romantic idealist; Zola, the "realist" novelist, is his direct opposite. Idealism is humanistic, but it may not be *actively* so; the idealist may strive to create his utopia, or he may rest content with merely imagining it, and thus contribute nothing to the humanistic mission of alleviating human suffering. As will be shown, these flaws in romantic idealism troubled Browning. As for "humanism," the term is used to signify the humanitarian concern with the alleviation of human suffering that was such a strong motivating factor in the careers of many of the romantic poets; neither idealism nor realism are incompatible with this sort of humanism, but both have potentially antihumanistic flaws. For the romantics, this humanitarian belief was inextricably linked with political radicalism, in that many of the sufferings of humanity could be ascribed to oppressive governments; through fighting these rulers, the romantic humanist was helping mankind. John Woolford says that Browning's preoccupations with resistance to tyranny "mark the typical Romantic humanist," and mentions the influence of writers including Rousseau, Shelley, and Carlyle.[19] Browning's poetry, particularly that produced before 1840, is deeply imbued with this sort of "romantic humanism"; much of this influence came from Wordsworth.

Returning to the model with this in mind, Browning, if a strong poet, ought to rebel against his predecessor; this rebellion comes in *Sordello*, in which Browning performs a "creative misreading" of such magnitude that Wordsworth is brutally dismissed.[20] However, the conflict between strong poets is not to be concluded easily. In the case of Browning and Wordsworth, the embers still smoldered in 1889, when Browning wrote the prologue to *Asolando*. An examination of Browning's career after the apparent defeat or erasure of Wordsworth in *Sordello* shows how Browning's consciousness of the unfairness of his "misreading" troubled him for years.

After completing *The Ring and the Book* in 1869, Browning seems to have been forced to admit—to himself, if to no one else, at least openly—that he had been wrong about Wordsworth, and this consciousness forced him to set about making belated amends. Therefore, he set about apologizing to his predecessor in an elaborate and complex series of references to Wordsworth's work in his own poetry, primarily in *Balaustion's Adventure* (hereafter *Balaustion*) and *Fifine at the Fair* (hereafter *Fifine*), but also in his correspondence with William Knight, president of the Wordsworth Society.[21] Browning could thus assuage his conscience while gambling that his confession was so abstruse and diffuse that it would not be generally noticed—as was, in fact, the case. After 1871 (the year of the publication of *Fifine*) the conflict with Wordsworth could remain dormant; honor was satisfied. Browning had engaged in a oedipal struggle with his poetic "father" and, even if he had not emerged victorious, fought him to an honorable draw.[22] Browning, though, could not apparently resist a final trip to the old battlefield in 1889; as Bloom has written, the strongest poets "return to origins at the end, or whenever they sense the imminence of the end."[23]

This examination of Browning's relationship with Wordsworth necessitates, to some degree, a "redrawing" of the map of Browning's achievement. This study concentrates upon relatively little-read Browning poems—*Paracelsus* and *Fifine* in particular. It is in the lesser-known poems written before 1840 and after 1869 that Browning's engagement with Wordsworth is at its most profound; Browning "erased" the influence of Wordsworth from his poetry during the most successful and (for modern readers) most frequently read period of his career. Although some of the "famous" poems, like "By the Fireside" and "Childe Roland to the Dark Tower Came," do allude to Wordsworthian topoi, these allusions are of a less confrontational nature—the desire, or need, to *struggle* with Wordsworth had (temporarily) been suppressed.

Why, then, Browning and Wordsworth? The relationship between the two does not merely possess the merit of unfamiliarity.[24] Wordsworth's aesthetic influence on Browning was at least as important as that of Shelley when it came to Browning's idea of the poet's role and how s/he ought to relate to the world. In some ways, the entire course of Browning's career between 1840 and 1869 can be seen as part of a reaction against the sort of poetry Browning, in 1840, had depicted Wordsworth as writing. Browning's return to a more positive view of Wordsworth after 1869 can be seen as part of a return on his part to the poetry of his youth. Browning's relationship with his predecessor can be most profitably understood in terms of *struggle*. The relationship is a test model of a strong poet's quest for self-definition against an overbearing predecessor.

2

Wordsworth and Browning's Rejection of Romanticism

BROWNING BEGAN HIS CAREER AS A ROMANTIC POET. THE TWO SURVIVING FRAGMENTS from his lost *Incondita* volume of 1824—"The Dance of Death" and "The First Born of Egypt"—and another title, "The Death of Harold," are clearly modeled on Byron; "The Dance of Death" also demonstrates the influence of Coleridge. Browning was later to tell Elizabeth Barrett, "I always retained my first feeling for Byron in many respects . . . the interest in the places he had visited, in relics of him. I would at any time have gone to Finchley to see a curl of his hair or one of his gloves, I am sure."[1] Far more profound influences, though, were to go to work on Browning between *Incondita* and *Pauline*. These influences would initially confirm Browning in his early romanticism, before leading him, in *Sordello*, to reject the romantics as models entirely.

The most closely examined relationship between Browning and one of the romantics is that with Shelley, which began in 1826 when his cousin gave him a copy of Shelley's *Miscellaneous Poems*.[2] Browning's early admiration for Shelley, despite his rejection of him in *Pauline*, lingered on for many years (Browning's attitude toward Shelley in his "essay" on him is extremely positive) until he allowed his disgust at Shelley's treatment of his first wife to turn him entirely against the earlier poet.[3] The relationship has received more attention than those Browning had with the other romantic poets because of its open nature—Browning discussed his attitude toward Shelley on several occasions, most particularly in *Pauline* and the "Essay on Shelley" (though his reluctance to republish *Pauline* may well indicate some embarrassment at the attitude expressed in the earlier work). He did not hide what he thought of Shelley. Much less work has been done on Browning's relationship with the other romantics, and almost none on his relationship with Wordsworth. The importance of Wordsworth has not been fully appreciated; this is because Browning attempted to *conceal* the nature of this relationship as much as possible.

Browning Meets Wordsworth

Wordsworth was the only major romantic poet Browning actually met. There is a dichotomy in Browning's writings between his feelings toward Wordsworth as a man and toward Wordsworth as a poet. He seldom openly disparages the poetry, except to lament Wordsworth's failure to keep up his earlier standards, but on several occasions he attacks the old man's personality. (It was the opposite with his feelings toward Rossetti and Swinburne: he liked them as men but disliked their poetry.) This was not simply a personal dislike, though influence theory would maintain that Browning, as Wordsworth's ephebe, was troubled as much by Wordsworth *as a figure* as he was by Wordsworth as the producer of texts; Bloom compares the relationships between poets to Freudian case studies.[4] Nevertheless, Browning's problem with Wordsworth was far more aesthetic than personal.

That Browning knew Wordsworth's poetry from an early age is demonstrated in his correspondence with William Knight. In a letter of May 17, 1880, Browning told Knight, "I keep as fresh as ever the admiration for Wordsworth which filled me on becoming acquainted with his poetry in my boyhood."[5] John Maynard points out that Browning's admiration for Wordsworth's work has been obscured by his later attacks on him, most notably in "The Lost Leader" and the love letters to Elizabeth Barrett.[6] Browning was to tell Elizabeth Barrett that he preferred early works like *Lyrical Ballads* to what Wordsworth later became.[7] By 1836, when he met Wordsworth for the first time, Browning was well acquainted with Wordsworth's poetry, and impressed by at least the earlier part of it. Following the publication of *Paracelsus*, he was granted access to the leading literary figures of the age; foremost among these was Wordsworth. Not only had the Wordsworth of 1836 become a political conservative, but his personality had developed an austere and taciturn carapace. Neither his beliefs nor his manner were calculated to endear him to the young Browning.

Finding out how many times the poets met is a difficult task. The one occasion that is well documented is the famous supper in Thomas Noon Talfourd's house in Russell Square, which took place on May 26, 1836, after the triumphant first performance of Talfourd's play *Ion*, starring W. C. Macready. Browning was seated opposite Macready, who was flanked by Walter Savage Landor and Wordsworth. It is not known whether Browning conversed with Wordsworth, but there is a well-known controversy over whether Wordsworth paid the young poet the compliment of drinking his health. This is of some importance in deciding what effect meeting Wordsworth for the first time had on Browning. Browning's earliest biographers—Alexandra Orr and Griffin and Minchin—describe Wordsworth leaning across the table in response to a toast offered by Talfourd to "the youngest poet of England," declaring, "I am proud to drink your health, Mr. Browning."[8] Several later writers on Browning have repeated this story; most of them have failed to notice Betty Miller's 1953 article "'This Happy Evening': The story of *Ion*," the most detailed account of the event, in which she points out that Wordsworth could not have toasted Browning in response to Talfourd; the diary entry for May 26, 1836, by Wordsworth's friend Henry Crabb Robinson shows that Robinson had accompanied Wordsworth home before the toasting began.[9] When Talfourd proposed that the table drink to Browning, one of the seats next to Macready was already vacant. All the same, since the story appears in Orr's biography, one must assume that it came from the poet's own lips; Orr was a close friend of Browning in his later years. In fact, there is clear evidence that Browning himself repeated the story.

In February 1881, Browning, irritated by erroneous speculation about his life, allowed his friend Edmund Gosse to quiz him "for a couple of hours" once a week for a month. The accumulated notes were put into "some rough order," and vetted by Browning, who rejected much "of extreme interest."[10] The rest was worked into an article by Gosse that was approved by Browning; it appeared in the *Century Magazine* in America in December 1881, to be reprinted after Browning's death as part of Gosse's volume *Robert Browning, Personalia*. Nothing that appeared in this "Browning version" of Browning's early career was without his seal of approval. And in Gosse's volume there is the same story: "in the course of the evening Talfourd, with marked kindness, proposed the name of the youngest English poet, and Wordsworth, leaning across the table, said, with august affability, 'I am proud to drink your health, Mr. Browning!'"[11] This cannot have happened, at least not in the way Browning described it to Gosse. Nevertheless, far from being a "tradition of Browning biography," as Irvine and Honan call it, the story was told by the man himself.[12] Was Browning mistaken, or even lying? Possibly not. In 1865, the former Irish nationalist leader and current Australian politician Charles Gavan Duffy met and had a long conversation with Browning and John Forster, the substance of which he later published in his memoirs, *My Life in Two Hemispheres*, in 1898. The conversation turned to Wordsworth, and Browning described for him the *Ion* supper. Duffy recalls him as saying that "the first time he met Wordsworth was at dinner, Savage Landor was also present, and both poets invited him to take wine with them after the kindly fashion of the day; and never was a youngster so intoxicated with delight."[13]

This account is open to a slightly different, but important, interpretation. Unlike the later versions, in which Wordsworth is said to have toasted Browning formally and publicly, this account points to a private toast—or, at most, a public invitation to take a glass of wine, rather than a profession of admiration for Browning's talent. Wordsworth and Landor "invited him to take wine with them after the friendly fashion of the day"; it sounds as if they drank Browning's health out of courtesy during the meal, before Wordsworth's departure. Leaning across the table with "august affability" and complimenting Browning's poetic abilities (by implication—Wordsworth would hardly be "proud" to drink to a man whose work he disliked) in front of everybody in a formal way does not sound like the later Wordsworth at all. Considering Wordsworth's track record when it came to keeping up to date with contemporary poetry (he never bothered to read Keats's *Endymion* even after Keats sent him a copy), there is a fair chance that he had not even read the copy of *Paracelsus* that had somehow found its way into his library. One can assume that he had heard about the poem from literary acquaintances, but that is all.

If Duffy's account of Browning's conversation is to be interpreted in this way, Wordsworth did indeed drink Browning's health, but not in the public manner suggested by the later accounts. Browning seems to have implied to Gosse that the toast *was* formal; he was being slightly "economical with the truth" here. The toast, though, did take place, and the young Browning would indeed have been "intoxicated with delight" at this mark of kindness, however private.

It is not known how many times Browning met Wordsworth after the *Ion* supper in 1836. Irvine and Honan follow Orr (who may well have heard it from Browning) in stating that he saw most of "that taciturn bard" at John Kenyon's house in London; since Kenyon was a friend of Wordsworth, and sometimes accommodated him at his house on his visits, this is likely.[14] Gosse's volume says that Browning "saw much of Wordsworth during the next few years, for Talfourd invited him to his house whenever Wordsworth came up to town. He listened to his slow talk with reverence and interest, but never got over the somewhat chilling and awful personal bearing of the old man."[15] If one consults Wordsworth's movements between 1836 and 1846 (when Browning left England, never to return during Wordsworth's lifetime), one finds that Browning would have had several opportunities to listen to Wordsworth's "slow talk." Wordsworth was in London briefly twice in 1837, and again in May–June 1839, June–July 1841, May–June 1842, and April–May 1845.[16] Even if Wordsworth did not dine with Talfourd on each of these occasions, Browning was probably not exaggerating when he spoke of having seen "much" of Wordsworth during this period, whether at Talfourd's, Kenyon's, or elsewhere. Wordsworth definitely dined with

Kenyon on May 29, 1842, and with Talfourd two days later; Browning was almost certainly present on at least one of these occasions.[17] Browning's personal opinion of Wordsworth was therefore based on some familiarity. During Browning's conversation with Forster and Duffy in 1865, "[Duffy] said Carlyle considered Wordsworth the best talker in England. Browning said he was certainly not at all so in latter years; he spoke little, and only on subjects that interested himself, without respect to the taste of his audience."[18] For all his "reverence and interest," the young Browning found Wordsworth's "slow talk" uninspiring; he found Wordsworth personally disagreeable, his demeanor "chilling and awful," and his conversation a bore. This personal dislike of the older poet would be augmented both by a dislike of his political opinions and by what Browning came to see as his failure as a poet.

Browning and Wordsworth's Politics

The young Browning was a political radical.[19] Even if by 1832 he had lost the admiration for Shelley that had led to a brief period of vegetarianism and atheism, he retained many of Shelley's radical beliefs. He associated with a radical circle, including W. J. Fox and Leigh Hunt, and explicitly described *Paracelsus* to Fox as a radical poem: "[T]here are precious bold bits here & there, & the drift & scope are awfully radical,—I am 'off' for ever with the other side, but must by all means be 'on' with yours."[20] "The other side" was the Tory establishment. Wordsworth had entirely abandoned *his* radicalism by the time Browning was born in 1812; Browning could only have encountered it in Wordsworth's early poems. As he became familiar with Wordsworth's poetry, Browning would have heard how Wordsworth had changed, in a way unlikely to endear him to a man who spoke of his "republicanism" to Fanny Haworth in 1840.[21] What precisely was it about Wordsworth's political opinions that upset Browning? Browning does not *openly* disparage Wordsworth, either personally or politically, before the publication of *Sordello* in 1840. To fully understand why Browning's political difference with Wordsworth broke out into print in 1840, one must look at Browning's own early literary radicalism.

Pauline: The Problem Stated

Browning's literary radicalism is intimately associated with his early romanticism. It is clear from *Pauline* and *Paracelsus* that he continued to retain Shelley's idealistic vision of a perfectible humanity; however, these two early poems both indicate that even before *Sordello* Browning's attitude toward Wordsworth's aesthetics was ambivalent. Nevertheless, as an admirer and follower of the romantics, Browning sought out what he found congenial in Wordsworth's poetry and gestures back to it in these works.

Pauline is a confused and confusing poem; in Isobel Armstrong's words, it is "an elusive, restless and equivocal work."[22] It is not clear whether this confusion was intentional (the poem is part of a romantic tradition of "fragmentary texts") or due to inexperience; the poet was to say in his introduction to the revised edition of 1868 that "good draughtsmanship . . . and right handling, were far beyond the artist at that time."[23] The speaker of *Pauline* is tormented by a dilemma of ambition; should he dedicate himself to humanity, or merely appease his own ego? Other romantic poets faced a similar dilemma. Byron's contempt for mankind in the mass is pervasive in his poetry (and was distasteful to Browning), despite his enthusiasm for the cause of liberty; Keats's "The Fall of Hyperion" illustrates his confusion about the poet's role in the world (though it cannot have been an influence on Browning at this stage, since it would not appear in print until 1856); and Wordsworth's career was marked by his glorification of solitude and desire to separate himself from other men, becoming a "recluse." In depicting the struggles of such a character, Browning was placing himself in the romantic tradition. A "radical" poet, as Browning felt himself to be, should be a humanist as well. Browning's problem was twofold; was *he* radical enough, and were Wordsworth and the other romantic poets he admired radical enough? Isobel Armstrong argues that Browning's attitude toward the radical policies of the *Monthly Repository* group, as displayed in this poem, is similarly divided; he was "struggling both to criticize and develop *Repository* policies."[24] If the romantic poets he admired were not sufficiently "developed," then Browning had been drinking from a poisoned spring, and, as he wrote in *Pauline*, "whoso sucks a poisoned wound / Envenoms his own veins" (lines 11–12).

Thus the reason for *Pauline*'s feverish quality becomes clearer. The youthful poet was enduring a crisis produced by his need to define himself in relation to his romantic predecessors; to escape "the burden of the past." Armstrong declares that "as the creature of history . . . the speaker in *Pauline* cannot make himself anew ideologically or imaginatively until he has accomplished a traumatic break with the past."[25] This "traumatic break"—with Wordsworth, in Browning's case—would eventually take place in *Sordello*; for now, he was confronted with a number of demanding questions. Was he radical and humanistic enough? Did he live up to his predecessors' standards? Just how high *were* those standards, anyway? As one examines Browning's relationship with Wordsworth before *Sordello*, it becomes clear that Browning was not so much redefining *himself* in relation to Wordsworth, as redefining *Wordsworth* to suit his own purposes. Browning was a strong poet performing a creative misreading of Wordsworth in order to free himself from the "anxiety" of his "influence." There are, in this early period, two main "misreadings": a positive one, in which Wordsworth is seen in as humanistic a way as possible, and thus a worthy mentor for Browning, who can present himself as Wordsworth's radical successor; and a later, negative one that dismisses Wordsworth as a potential influence by demolishing his humanist credentials. The first of these "misreadings" takes place in *Paracelsus*; the second, in *Sordello*.

For all *Pauline*'s incoherence, there are indications here of the trouble that was to follow. There is a confusion over the poet's role, and over his relationship to his audience. In a rather Byronic passage, the poet depicts the poet's role as a royal one that sets him apart from his fellows:

> Nature would point at one, whose quivering lip
> Was bathed in her enchantments—whose brow burned
> Beneath the crown, to which her secrets knelt;
> Who learned the spell which can call up the dead,
> And then departed, smiling like a fiend
> Who has deceived God. If such one should seek
> Again her altars, and stand robed and crowned
> Amid the faithful!
>
> (lines 18–25)

This idea of "royal" poets, gifted with exotic powers (in this case, necromancy), and "robed and crowned," would have to go if Browning's poetry was to become truly radical. To accord this status to poets would lead to self-obsession. As the speaker declares a little later in the poem,

> I ne'er sung
> But as one entering bright halls, where all
> Will rise and shout for him.
>
> (lines 77–79)

When Browning pondered this puzzle in relation to Wordsworth, he would have had two ways of seeing him. One the one hand, the early Wordsworth had been a radical rewriter of the rules when it came to a poet and his audience. The publication of the *Lyrical Ballads*, with its openly populist manifesto, had been an attempt to democratize poetry; as Wordsworth wrote in the 1802 "Preface," "[W]hat is a poet? To whom does he address himself? And what language is expected from him? He is a man speaking to men."[26] He is at pains to emphasize the poet's humanity and the closeness he must feel to his fellows if he is to produce worthwhile poetry.

The poet ought to write "in a selection of language really used by men" and avoid the antihumanism of poets "who think they are conferring honour on themselves and their art, in proportion as they separate themselves from the sympathies of men" by using esoteric language.[27] Wordsworth sets himself up against any idea of the poet as being somehow superior to the rest of humanity when he says that "poets do not write for poets alone, but for men . . . the Poet must descend from this supposed height, and, in order to excite rational sympathy, he must express himself as other men express themselves."[28] This idea of a descent from a lofty height as a metaphor for a poet's democratizing/humanizing himself is one that Browning would use several times during his career, particularly in his later poetry.[29] Perhaps he first encountered it in Wordsworth's "Preface." It would appeal to a Browning who, as Woolford puts it in *Browning the Revisionary*, though initially propelled toward "sympathy with mankind" through his reading of the romantic poets (especially Shelley), had come to regard romantic humanism as "radically defective" in its tendencies to separate the poet from mankind and neglect religion.[30] Woolford goes on to argue that Browning's attitude toward his audience was deeply influenced by Wordsworth's.[31] In particular, he maintains that Browning's desire to write popular poetry was indebted to Wordsworth's theories, and strengthens his argument with clear verbal parallels with the "Preface," as they occur in *Sordello*, a letter to Alfred Domett, and the preface to *Paracelsus*.[32] Browning was using Wordsworth to support his radical belief that it was his political duty to seek a wide, popular audience for his work.[33] Loy D. Martin points out that in his post-1840 poetry Browning represents a vertical and hierarchical way of assigning human value as antidemocratic and conducive to a failure in human communication.[34] He argues that Browning exposes and subverts this idea through Fra Lippo Lippi's *descent* (from the window in the Medici palace) to the street and the company of "common humanity"—a "descent" that is to be applauded, as is Lippo's desire to paint "low" subjects—and through the way Cleon's hierarchical worldview traps him in self-imposed isolation at the top of his "ivory tower," an isolation that will bar him from the possibility of salvation.[35] Browning would thus be using the younger Wordsworth's democratic concept of aesthetics for his own ends while he denounced the older poet's apostasy.

However, the Browning of the 1830s could not see Wordsworth purely in this sympathetic light. The older Wordsworth had in several ways turned against his own manifesto. He had literally separated himself from his audience, retreating into rural seclusion at Rydal Mount. Was not his planned masterwork to be called *The Recluse*? His poetry had gradually become less accessible and populist, and more traditionally ornate in language and subject matter; his commitment to a democratizing vision of poetry was at least in doubt. He had also become politically conservative in his closeness to the regime, acceptance of a government post, and increasingly hysterical fear of the masses of "ordinary men" he had originally tailored his poetry toward. Eventually he would officially become the nation's "royal" poet upon his acceptance of the laureateship. (Browning's future wife referred to Wordsworth as "the king-poet of our times," thus conferring "royal" status on Wordsworth.)[36]

Browning would have seen Wordsworth's career as having moved from a "democratic" to an "elitist" aesthetic, a movement characteristic of the older generation of romantic poets. In Wordsworth's career Browning had an illustration of the conflict between democratic and elitist views of poetry. Both *Pauline* and *Paracelsus* contain evidence of this aesthetic conflict, which Browning symbolized through his references to Wordsworth in these poems. Though he appeared to have come to a conclusion by the time he wrote the visionary finale of *Paracelsus*, he would abandon this conclusion in *Sordello*. To Woolford, Browning's career was marked by an inability to decide whether he wanted to write in a popular or elitist fashion.[37] He maintains that the peculiarities of Browning's style can be attributed directly to this vacillation, and to Browning's desire simultaneously to dictate the responses of his readers to his work and allow them to participate in creating its meaning, using what Wordsworth called "the co-operating fancy."[38]

This was not the only puzzle facing Browning, and not the only one that he would use Wordsworth to help him solve. Even if Browning was to dedicate himself to humanism, how "realistic" should he force his idealistic visions to be? The problem is first addressed in *Pauline*. The speaker refers to his "wild dreams of beauty and good," which combine visions of aesthetic and political perfection, and the danger that they may lead him to seek some "strange fair world, where it might be a law" (line 35). The "wild dreams" are not to be condemned in themselves (their *intentions* are laudable), but they are actively malign if they are illusions that serve no practical purpose. Thomas J. Collins points out that Shelley's airy idealism, though admirable in its aspirations, can be seen as evading the grim realities of the human condition.[39] Addiction to these dreams is ultimately antihumanistic, and ends up serving the forces of reaction.[40] The dreamer may feel such dissatisfaction with the world that he creates an entirely imaginary "strange fair world" where his "Fancy" is the only law.

Browning recognizes this problem as early as *Pauline*. Critics who have attempted to boil the poem down to a product of Browning's personal difficulties at this time are missing the point; the real struggle that engulfed him was aesthetic and political.[41] Browning has not allowed himself to fall for the temptation to see poets as superhuman; the speaker declares that, if he could regain his innocent youth, he would

> give up all gained as willingly
> As one gives up a charm which shuts him out
> From hope, or part, or care, in humankind.
>
> (lines 128–30)

His humanizing instinct is clear. These lines echo Shelley's preface to *Alastor*, a poem Browning knew well, in which Shelley condemns those who "loving nothing on this earth, and cherishing no hopes beyond, yet keep aloof from sympathies with their kind, rejoicing neither in human joy nor mourning with human grief."[42] This, to the humanist, is the ultimate sin. The malignant "charm" Browning mentions is the self-communing arrogance that leaves one "morally dead," in Shelley's words.[43]

Shelley's preface also refers to Wordsworth. Shelley was aiming at what he saw as Wordsworth's self-serving surrender of his earlier ideals when he wrote that "those who love not their fellow-beings live unfruitful lives, and prepare for their old age a miserable grave." He follows this with an ironic (mis)quote from *The Excursion*:

> The good die first,
> And those whose hearts are dry as summer dust,
> Burn to the socket![44]

Browning seems to be referring to this attack at this point in *Pauline*. At this early stage, he may merely have been following Shelley's lead, without having given Wordsworth's literary humanism the sort of analysis that he was to give it in writing *Paracelsus*.

That Browning, at this stage, was nowhere near formulating a considered position on these matters is clear as *Pauline* proceeds; the muddled quality that many critics have noticed has a good deal of its origin in the struggle between elitist and democratic instincts.[45] The speaker, like Paracelsus in the later poem, cannot help returning to self-centered visions that exclude the suffering masses:

> I am made up of an intensest life,
> Of a most clear idea of consciousness
> Of self . . .
> linked in me, to self-supremacy,
> Existing as a centre to all things,
> Most potent to create, and rule, and call
> Upon all things to minister to it.
>
> (lines 268–76)

The speaker's "self-supremacy" is said to be "potent" to "create, and rule"; is he saying that he *creates* the worlds he then proceeds to rule like a god? Apparently so, for later he describes how Shelley's poetry encouraged millennial dreaming; the older poet's words seemed "a key to a new world; the muttering / Of angels, of some thing unguessed by man" (lines 414–15). Shelley offered the key to a *new* world, thus distracting the poet from *this* one. The speaker "was vowed to liberty, / Men were to be as gods, and earth as heaven" (lines 424–25). Though humanistic in its ambition, this scheme is flawed. Like the "wild dreams of beauty and of good" mentioned above, the overambitious nature of the scheme, its (literal) otherworldliness, can only sabotage its praiseworthy ambitions. These dreams can foster arrogance in the same way as the contempt for humanity attacked in the *Alastor* preface; the speaker bitterly recollects his ambition: "and I—ah! what a life was mine to be" (line 426). Martin argues that there is a broad tendency in Browning's poetry, as it develops toward the dramatic monologues of his maturity, to reject the excessively idealistic tendencies of romanticism described by Browning in *Pauline*.[46] His interpretation of Browning's rejection of the antihumanistic tendencies of romanticism is in accordance with the way Browning's early poems fight against and finally subdue the romantic desire to strive toward the sublime at the expense of dealing with the "real" world.

Browning's principal difficulty at this early stage was to construct some sort of synthesis of practical realism with utopian idealism. To achieve this, he would have to avoid the twin potential weaknesses of romanticism—excessive self-orientation and excessive idealism. It may seem curious to imply a connection between self-orientation and idealism, but Browning would have realized that, taken to extremes, they could be equally damaging to the humanist cause. Self-orientation could turn into a belief that one's inherent superiority to the rest of mankind freed one of any responsibility toward them, while excessive idealism could lead to such an intense focus upon the metaphysical world of "ideal" forms that mankind would suffer similar neglect. Nevertheless, romanticism would disintegrate if the poet were entirely divested of his inherent sense of his own superiority (if he was no different from his fellows, what value would his pronouncements have, and why should people listen to them?) and if he was forced to discard all of his Platonic visions of potential perfection (with nothing to aim for, why bother to struggle at all?). Romanticism needed to be "purified" of its excesses, and be molded into a movement that united the vision of the idealist with the realism of the humanist. Browning would come close to achieving this synthesis in the visionary conclusion of *Paracelsus*, cast it away in *Sordello*, and return to the task after 1869. The pursuit of this synthesis was to be one of the principal motivating forces behind Browning's career.

Browning would have to move from the sort of purely theoretical knowledge he could pick up from sources like Plato to a more practical knowledge:

> 'Twas in my plan to look on real life,
> Which was all new to me; my theories
> Were firm, so I left them, to look upon
> Men, and their cares, and hopes, and fears, and joys;
> And, as I pondered on them all, I sought
> How best life's end might be attained – an end
> Comprising every joy. I deeply mused.
>
> (lines 440–46)

Pauline is only an exposition of Browning's dilemma. He was not yet ready to build his synthesis—the dangers of both idealism and cynicism are all too apparent. The speaker presents his temporary collapse into Byronic cynicism as pernicious; in place of his "hopes of perfecting mankind" and "human love" he gained "wit, mockery, / And happiness," certainly, but this conceals a vacancy: "only God is gone, / And some dark spirit sitteth in his seat" (lines 458–72). This is Browning's first attack on the Byronic version of romanticism. Though Browning had admired Byron in his younger days, he had come to dislike what he saw as Byron's "perversion" of romanticism, as expressed, in particular, in *Childe Harold's Pilgrimage*. Though Byron had seen the dangers of idealism, he had been wrong (in Browning's opinion) to dilute his concern for the suffering and oppressed with an amused contempt for human folly. The image of the "dark spirit" must be an attack on this trait of Byron's, particularly when one recalls that Southey had attacked Byron and his imitators for founding what he called the "Satanic School" of poetry: "[T]hey are . . . characterized by a Satanic spirit of pride and audacious impiety, which still betrays the wretched sense of hopelessness wherewith it is allied."[47] Southey's attack sprang from his religious and political opinions; Browning's problem with Byron sprang from more aesthetic motives. Like Hazlitt, he would, throughout his career, be genuinely troubled by Byron's cynicism; Byron would come to symbolize how wrong romanticism could go if it weakened its commitment to humanistic ideals.[48]

This problem with Byron forces Browning to travel toward Wordsworth in his hunt for a way out of his dilemma. His reading of the romantic poets would have offered more clear illustrations of paths *not* to follow than otherwise; both Shelley's and Byron's paths led to a denial of practical humanism, and thus both poets ruled themselves out as role models. If Browning was to find a romantic he could admire and follow, he would have to turn elsewhere; as *Paracelsus* would show, it was to Wordsworth he would turn, and, in particular, to *The Excursion*. There he found evidence that Wordsworth, at least, among the romantics, had surrendered neither his humanist ideals nor his practical common sense.

Even as early as *Pauline*, though, there are hints of the reservations Browning would express about Wordsworth after 1835. He speaks of the disillusionment and despair that fill one's heart when one sees a much-loved artist in his dotage: "to see decaying wits ere the frail body / Decays" (lines 553–54). These lines cannot allude to Shelley, Keats, or Byron; their "wits" were predeceased by their "frail bodies." Browning was probably thinking of the aging Edmund Kean, whose Richard III he had seen at Richmond in October 1832; there is an allusion to Kean later in the poem (lines 669–75). However, the lines are more reminiscent of Browning's earlier implicit attack on Wordsworth in his allusion to Shelley's *Alastor* preface. Browning's later allusion to "decaying wits" may be another oblique blow at the older Wordsworth, whose later work seemed, to many, inferior to his earlier achievement; Browning's correspondence with William Knight shows that he shared this opinion.[49] There may be another allusion to Wordsworth in this vein later in the poem: "witness this belief / In poets, tho' sad change has come there too" (lines 691–92). This could refer to Shelley, but could equally refer to Wordsworth if one reads the "sad change" as having come over the *poet*, not the admirer.

Toward the end of the poem the speaker is dazzled by a plethora of "wild dreams," "knowing nor which to leave nor which to choose" (line 881). His dilemma has parallels with Aprile's confusion in *Paracelsus*; like the speaker, Aprile is unable to choose between dazzling "shapes," and instead gazes at them in awe while far away humanity remains benighted (2.520–54). The speaker's "objective" desire to "shadow out the stages of all life," like Aprile's ambition in *Paracelsus*, is broadly humanistic; nevertheless, there are dangers here that are only hinted at in *Pauline*, though they will be openly presented in *Paracelsus*. Gazing at the world serves no humanistic purpose; one must plunge boldly *into* the world. Browning needs to find a synthesis that both retains this objective "shadowing" quality and avoids a collapse into depersonalizing confusion.

Pauline is a confusing poem because Browning had barely managed to formulate his aesthetic questions, let alone decide on the answers. He needed a role model to help him escape from the blind alley of seeing poets as superhuman seers, poised calmly above the multitude, and—instead—to formulate a new type of romanticism. *Pauline* concludes with the speaker's wish that he may be "priest and lover, as of old," and in the 1888–89 edition Browning changed "lover" to the more extreme "prophet," pointing out how far his younger self would have to go in order to free himself from elitism. In *Paracelsus* Browning would announce that he had found the necessary role model he had been seeking—in Wordsworth.

3

Paracelsus: The Problem Solved?

IN 1834, A YEAR AFTER THE APPEARANCE OF *PAULINE*, HENRY TAYLOR PUBLISHED HIS dramatic poem *Philip van Artevelde*. The work's preface contains a sweeping attack on contemporary poets Taylor considered to be overly influenced by Byron and Shelley; Taylor took such poets to be deficient in "common sense" and insufficiently focused upon "real life." Woolford has suggested that this preface influenced Browning's decision to move away from Shelley and toward Wordsworth in his next poem.[1] Browning knew Taylor personally, and owned copies of a volume of his poems, another of his plays, and two copies of *Philip van Artevelde*, one, a reprint from 1872, inscribed to Browning from the author.[2] The earlier edition of the play in Browning's library was the third edition, of 1844, but it is inconceivable that Browning would not at least have been aware of the preface upon the poem's publication. Taylor attacks Byron and Shelley at precisely the time Browning was beginning to move away from these models, and implies that those who would seek something of lasting value in contemporary poetry should turn to his friend Wordsworth. He condemns Byron and Shelley on humanistic grounds, declaring that their poetry is insufficiently focused on "mankind"— "[E]ither they did not look upon mankind with observant eyes, or they did not feel it to be any part of their vocation to turn what they saw to account."[3] He declares that the works of these poets are suitable for "very young readers" (like the Browning who produced *Pauline*), but not for the mature.[4] In his words,

> [I]t did not belong to poetry, in their apprehension, to thread the mazes of life in all its classes and under all its circumstances, common as well as romantic, and, seeing all things, to infer and to instruct: on the contrary, it was to stand aloof from every thing that is plain and true; to have little concern with what is rational and wise; it was to be, like music, a moving and enchanting art, acting upon the fancy, the affections, the passions, but scarcely connected with the exercise of the intellectual faculties. . . . Spirit

> was not to be debased by any union with matter, in their effusions; dwelling, as they did, in a region of poetical sentiment which did not permit them to walk upon the common earth, or to breathe the common air.[5]

Taylor does not name a contemporary poet whose works do not neglect "the realities of nature," but it is plain that he is thinking of Wordsworth, particularly when he declares that "no man can be a very great poet who is not also a great philosopher."[6] He attacks Byron both for his failure to philosophize and for his misanthropy, which "was probably, like his tenderness, not practical, but merely matter of imagination, assumed for purposes of effect."[7] (This condemnation of Byron would be repeated in almost identical terms by Browning later in his career, suggesting that he knew the "Preface" well enough to remember this attack.)[8] Taylor then attacks Shelley, whose works are, in his opinion, utterly divorced from reality: "Mr. Shelley seems to have written under the notion that no phenomena can be perfectly poetical, until they shall be so decomposed from their natural order and coherency, as if to be brought before the reader in the likeness of a phantasma or a vision. A poet is, in his estimation (if I may venture to infer his principles from his practice), purely and pre-eminently a visionary."[9] Shelley's poetry is compared to "gorgeously coloured clouds" that disperse and leave no trace upon the memory.[10] The true poet must unite imagination and reason, unlike "a rhapsodist, a melodist, or a visionary."[11] Taylor concludes his attack with the assertion that "Mr. Shelley and his disciples . . . would transfer the domicile of poetry to regions where reason, far from having any supremacy or rule, is all but unknown, an alien and an outcast; to seats of anarchy and abstraction, where imagination exercises the shadow of an authority, over a people of phantoms, in a land of dreams."[12] The "Preface" anticipates many of the attacks Browning would go on to make on the romantic poets. In it Browning would have found an exhortation to turn away from the influence of Shelley and Byron and confront, instead, the achievement of Wordsworth, whose works clearly demonstrated that this poet, at least, walked "upon the common earth" and breathed "the common air." *Paracelsus*, which Browning began to write in September 1834 (*after* the publication of Taylor's poem), contains considerable evidence of a Wordsworthian influence; it is Browning's most "Wordsworthian" poem. Bloom has argued that in its early stages poetic influence is very similar to love, and the influence Wordsworth had on *Paracelsus* confirms this.[13] The influence is so extensive that Bloom would argue that it confirmed Browning's potential status as a strong poet; he maintains that the true ephebe's early works are distinguished precisely by their closeness to the works of the precursor.[14]

Taylor had implied that Wordsworth's strength lay in his "philosophy" as much as in his poetry; writing in 1834, he must have based this assessment largely upon *The Excursion*, since *The Prelude* was not to appear until 1850, and the "philosophical" epic *The Recluse* (of which *The Excursion* was to be a part), though promised, was never to appear at all. Contemporaries regarded *The Excursion* as Wordsworth's most important poem; echoes of it are so extensive in *Paracelsus* that it seems Browning shared his contemporaries' sense of the poem's significance. Only one other fragment of *The Recluse* would ever appear: the long passage now known as "Home at Grasmere," which was first published in 1888 and was rather hopefully entitled "The Recluse." A portion of this fragment was published by Wordsworth in 1814 as a "prospectus" to *The Excursion,* in an attempt to explain his plans for *The Recluse*; as will be demonstrated, Browning certainly knew this passage well, and used the plan of action contained within it to construct his own.

The Excursion was the most substantial poem published by Wordsworth in his lifetime. It had a poor reception on its first appearance, but, as Wordsworth grew in public estimation, it became "what contemporaries regarded as his most important poem."[15] Keats, for example, referred to the poem as one of "three things to rejoice at in this Age" in a letter to Benjamin Haydon of 1818.[16] As a reader of Wordsworth from his boyhood, Browning would have read *The Excursion* well before he wrote *Paracelsus*. His only extant reference to the poem in his correspondence suggests that he shared the general opinion of *The Excursion*'s significance; in the course of an argument with his future wife about the rationality of accepting social mores (in reference to his defense of dueling) he refers to Wordsworth's bizarre appearance at court as poet laureate: "Wordsworth decides he had better go to court—then he must buy or borrow a court-dress. He goes because of the poetry in him. What irrationality in the bag and sword—in the grey duffil gown yonder, he wrote—half through the exceeding ease and roominess of it—*The Excursion*; how proper he should go in it, therefore."[17] The fact that Browning chose to name *this* poem grants it a degree of importance, though the reference to the "exceeding ease and roominess" of Wordsworth's "duffil gown"—in contrast with the tight squeeze Wordsworth had to undergo in order to fit into the court raiment he borrowed from Samuel Rogers—suggests, at the very least, an amused glance at the work's notorious length. (The "duffil gown" may be an allusion to Wordsworth's poem "Alice Fell," in which a girl's tattered coat is replaced by one of "duffil grey," though the context suggests that Wordsworth was known to wear, and to write in, such a gown—an image entirely consistent with the "plain living" old poet.)

The Excursion and Its Influence on Browning

The Excursion's story of the Solitary—whose disillusionment with the failure of the French Revolution leads to a disgust for humanity—would have had a considerable impact on a young man who was facing a similar crisis himself. The Solitary's crisis was essentially that of the young Browning: how to overcome despair and rededicate oneself to a purified humanism. *The Excursion*, for all its conservative reputation, does not end with the triumph of either the Wanderer's natural religion or the Pastor's Anglicanism. The Solitary remains silent, having found neither of the two alternates offered him convincing. He continues to insist that both creeds fail to actively resist the tyranny of the rich over the poor, and that the Pastor's Anglicanism implicitly functions as a central buttress in the regime. Robert M. Ryan points out that the Solitary's austere refusal to accept his friends' comforting arguments demonstrates that the Wordsworth of 1814 cannot simply be seen purely as a conservative apologist.[18] That Wordsworth allowed the Solitary to retain his independence indicates that his own acceptance of Anglicanism in 1814 was by no means final: this lack of closure, says Ryan, reflects Wordsworth's uneasy mental state in 1814 and the doubts he still harbored.[19] Browning would have seen it as his mission to do what Wordsworth had (in the absence of the long-promised *Recluse*) as yet failed to do: redeem the Solitary, in the person of Paracelsus, and renew his broken contract with mankind.

Springing from humble Scottish stock, the Solitary serves as chaplain to a highland troop before settling down to marriage and fatherhood.[20] However, this scene of domestic bliss is wrecked by the deaths of his wife and children, and the grief he feels dehumanizes him; "he consumed his days, / To private interest dead, and to public care" (2.208–9). Redemption, of sorts, comes in the form of the outbreak of the French Revolution: he travels to London, and, like the young Coleridge, preaches "the cause of Christ and civil liberty, / As one, and moving to one glorious end" (2.224–25). His faith does not preach submission before the status quo; on the contrary, he sees the message of Christ as revolutionary. This would have appealed to Browning, who retained both his Christianity and his radicalism at this stage. The Solitary has managed to unite idealism with practical action in the way Browning would seek throughout his career.

The Revolution's failure is as traumatic to the Solitary as it was to Wordsworth; the dashing of his dreams destroys both his religious faith and his revolutionary idealism, and fills him with a Byronic contempt for mankind:

An infidel contempt for holy writ
Stole by degrees upon his mind; and hence
Life, like that Roman Janus, double-faced;
Vilest hypocrisy—the laughing, gay
Hypocrisy, not leagued with fear, but pride.

(2.249–53)

Humanism cannot be sustained without an idealistic basis for action. The story of the Solitary's descent into despair would have been of great significance to Browning, who had described the same process in *Pauline*. The speaker in *Pauline* has not witnessed the failure of the French Revolution, but he does experience a similar fall from grace.

The Solitary becomes antihumanistic in his desire to escape from the company of other men. In this he resembles both the speaker in *Pauline* and Paracelsus at certain stages of his life's journey.[21] The fascination of the Solitary's story, to Browning, would have been the unwritten continuation of the poem hinted at in the Solitary's promise to "share the pleasures and pursuits / Of yet another summer's day" with his new friends—his rehumanization, which Wordsworth does not show (9.776–77). Browning, like Keats, saw Wordsworth's poetry as being explorative of the "dark Passages" in which "we see not the ballance of good and evil"; like Keats, he believed that "if we live, and go on thinking, we too shall explore them," and it was a desire to penetrate further into and dissipate the darkness that led him to *Paracelsus*.[22]

Even in the depths of his despair the Solitary retains some shreds of realistic humanism; he recognizes that mankind's salvation is not to be found in imagination or metaphysics. His error is to suppose that it is not to be found on earth, either. Browning would have agreed with the Solitary's declaration that there is no hope for mankind in attempting to "quit the beaten track of life" and "soar" into metaphysical realms (3.213). The Solitary will have to learn that the way forward may not lead to "consummate good," but it will mean "progressive virtue"; heaven will have to be constructed on earth itself (3.221–22). This conclusion is echoed by the Wanderer, who says that "wisdom is ofttimes nearer when we stoop / Than when we soar" (3.231–32).

In his youth, the Solitary pantheistically embraced nature's endless cycle of death and rebirth. He dismissed fantasies of a "golden age," choosing instead to glory in the eternal process of revolution, the change "from mild to angry, and from sad to gay, / Alternate and revolving" (3.315–16). This passage is important for two reasons. First, its bold embracing of the realities of existence is fundamentally humanistic, and would thus have fitted in with Browning's aspirations. Second, the pantheistic "worship" of the decay and regeneration of nature will form part both of Paracelsus's concluding vision of a "purified" romanticism and of the visionary conclusion of *Fifine*, which marks Browning's return to such a program.[23] The narrator figure of the poem agrees with the Solitary in rejecting the utopian consolations of poetry employed "in framing models to improve the scheme / Of Man's existence, and recast the world" (3.336–37). He also attacks "grave Philosophy" (3.338) as "a Dreamer yet more spiritless and dull" (3.340), the pernicious creator of the "world-excluding groves" (3.347) of Epicureanism and the "closed . . . heart" of the Stoic (3.354–55). All-consuming metaphysical speculation does not make one self-sufficient; it *does*, though, destroy any possibility of humanistic participation in the world. "Self-sufficiency" is a delusion.

The Solitary goes on to describe how he took ship for America, hoping to find a land—and a people—pure and untainted. His desire to actively take part in social improvement has, however, been worn away, and he now reduces his role in the world to that of a neutral observer: "to observe, and not to feel / And, therefore, not to act" (3.892–93). Paracelsus feels a similar sense of isolation; initially, he longs to "trample on yet save mankind at once," declaring that he "never will be served by those I serve." Eventually, he degenerates to the stage where he wishes he had never "communicated ought to such a race."[24] This is what happens to the Solitary when he observes the "big Passions strutting on a petty stage" of the nascent America (3.900). Maintaining an amused contempt for men many miles away is easy, but when one is living with them it is soul-corroding: it may suit an "airy Demon," but not a human being (3.909). A similar idea is used by Browning at the conclusion of *Fifine* when Juan, perched upon a pinnacle, perceives the masked revelers below him as repulsively animalistic; however, when he "pitches plumb" down *among* them, their distasteful characteristics disappear. (lines 1690–1805). This is one of the central ideas Browning is expressing in *Paracelsus*: as Festus asks Paracelsus, "how can that course be safe which from the first / Produces indifference to human love?" (1.626–27). (He later calls this lack of love "an eating brand—a shame" [1.703].) He expressed it with what he saw as the tacit approval of Wordsworth.

The Solitary's disgust with the American colonists leads to him setting out into the unexplored interior of the continent, in search of Native Americans. He believes he will find examples of Rousseau's "noble savage," and imagines a rather Nietzschean figure standing upon the "top / Of some commanding eminence" (3.935–36) from which he surveys

> Regions of wood and wide savannah, vast
> Expanse of unappropriated earth,
> With mind that sheds a light on what he sees;

Free as the Sun, and lonely as the Sun,
Pouring above his head its radiance down
Upon a living and rejoicing World!

(3.938–43)

The image of the isolated figure, perched on some "height," is one to which Browning will repeatedly return. As previously demonstrated, it may well be derived from Wordsworth's preface to *Lyrical Ballads*, and its appearance here strengthens the case for its being essentially Wordsworthian. The Solitary's dream is a pernicious one—if such men existed, it would not augur well for man as a social animal—but, as he finds out, it is a delusive one as well. The "supermen" are, in fact, in the opinion of the Solitary, just a group of squalid and distasteful "savages," "remorseless, and submissive to no law / But superstitious fear, and abject sloth" (3.954–55). The Solitary's crippling antihumanism is here presented in its most naked form. In the Native Americans he perceives mankind's less pleasant characteristics without the comforting veil of civilization. The humanist must be able to look beyond mankind's meanness to perceive its *potential*; the Solitary is unable to do this.

The Solitary's "despondency" must be "corrected," and the Wanderer starts to try to do this through exhortations to commune with nature, trust in God, and love one's fellows. He also warns the Solitary against excessive reliance on metaphysical speculation (4.130–39). In particular, he points out the flimsy nature of the comforts to be derived from such speculation:

—Man is of dust: etherial Hopes are his,
Which, when they should sustain themselves aloft,
Want due consistence; like a Pillar of smoke,
That with majestic energy from earth
Rises; but, having reached the thinner air,
Melts, and dissolves, and is no longer seen.

(4.140–45)

The idea of the insubstantiality of such speculations, and of comparing them to vapor, will be repeated by Browning when he attacks those who "fume, on altitudes of self-sufficiency" (line 1882) in *Fifine*. By using this image, Browning implicitly declares his continuing debt to Wordsworth's own humanist program.

The Wanderer goes on to announce that the corporeal frame is fundamentally incapable of coping with the metaphysical world: the soul,

all the crooked paths
Of time and change disdaining, takes its course
Along the line of limitless desires

(4.183–85)

but the body is unable to keep up. It is the destiny of man to walk the "crooked paths," much as he might long to tread "the line of limitless desires"; he is inexorably bound to the wheel of "time and change." As a youth, the Solitary had taken delight in the eternal cycle of nature; here, the Wanderer maintains that he was correct to do so, and that a full-blooded immersion in life is necessary for serenity. The desire to look for *another* world is morbid, a "disorder" from which the Wanderer has managed to free himself (4.186). The Solitary, hearing this, abandons any hope of discovering some utopian state, an imaginary land inhabited by an elite (5.349–50). The solution to human suffering will only come when *all* the race, not merely a "blessed few," live in accordance with God's will.

The Pastor, who intends to persuade the Solitary to accept his sufferings as willed by God, symbolizes Wordsworth at his most reactionary; his humanism is always close to slipping into quietism. Nevertheless, the poem fails to end on a note of comfortable resolution, and there are indications later in the work that the Wordsworth of 1814 still retained some of his early radicalism. The Solitary attacks the exploitative realities of capitalist England, and the church's role as a prop of oppression; for example, he criticizes the way the church has allowed the rural population of England to remain in ignorance, destroying any potential "liberty of mind" among the rural poor (8.433). Elsewhere, the Wanderer laments the dehumanization inherent in industrial capitalism: he compares a factory to a "Temple" (8.183) where women and children are sacrificed to "Gain" (8.185). Such denunciations testify to a continued awareness of social ills in the Wordsworth of 1814 that would have impressed Browning. They do not mean that Wordsworth was still a political radical—he was writing at a period when the landed gentry had not yet become identified with capitalism, and it was perfectly possible for a man of reactionary opinions (like the later Wordsworth) to be anticapitalist—but they show that he still retained a consciousness of the sufferings imposed upon the vast majority of his fellow creatures by those who would exploit them, whether members of the old aristocratic order, or of the newly powerful manufacturing middle class.

The "Wordsworthian" Situation of Browning's Paracelsus

That Browning had assimilated *The Excursion* by the time he wrote *Paracelsus* is indisputable when it is observed how indebted Browning's poem is to its romantic predecessor—and, particularly, to its "Prospectus," published at the end of Wordsworth's preface to the poem in 1814. Wordsworth declared that the passage was "taken from the conclusion of the first book of *The Recluse*" (as if a substantial part of his masterwork were already completed). In his preface, Wordsworth described the passage as "a kind of *Prospectus* of the design and scope of the whole Poem."[25] His attempt to bring together romanticism and humanism into a purified and beneficent fusion in the "Prospectus" would have fascinated and influenced Browning.

The Paracelsus of book 1 is composed of a mixture of pity and contempt for humanity; it is out of this that a newly humanistic romanticism would have to be forged. As Herbert Tucker says, *Paracelsus* tells the story of the title character's "fortunate fall" from egoism back into integration with humanity.[26] His desire to "elevate [himself] far, far above / The gorgeous spectacle" is reminiscent of romanticism in the "perverted" Byronic form (1.467–68). (It also reminds the reader of Wordsworth, perched on mountain heights; however, Browning is more interested in co-opting Wordsworth's support in *Paracelsus* than in attacking him.) If the poet is elevated, he is capable of ignoring the suffering below him altogether; similarly, Paracelsus declares that, in a few months, Michal will remember only the pleasant times of the autumn they have spent together, "and overlook / Its bleak wind, hankering after pining leaves" (1.18–19). Tucker points out that by the end of the poem, Paracelsus will come to realize that one should not "overlook" the darker side of human experience in this fashion, but include it in a broader and more honest survey.[27] Paracelsus's situation, gazing down upon "the throng'd, / The ever-moving, concourse of mankind" has much in common with Juan's at the start of the visionary conclusion of *Fifine*, in which he is "pinnacled" and gazing down at a similar multitude: "a prodigious fair, / Concourse immense of men and women" (lines 1684–85). Browning in fact uses the same word—"concourse"—to describe both gatherings. Juan's situation is a virtual rewrite of that of the young Paracelsus; he finds the figures below "terrible," "uncouth," and "revolting," while Paracelsus finds the idea of joining the crowd insupportable (lines 1707–8). Both will have to descend from their "altitudes" if they are to humanize their imaginations. Juan "pitches plumb into the square" and finds his horror fading away as he gazes closer at the crowd (lines 1766–68). Paracelsus has to do the same if he is to inject humanism into his romantic idea of artistic superiority and isolation. At this stage, although his feelings toward mankind are benevolent, they are also contemptuous; he wishes "never to be mix'd with them" (1.477). Browning's problem in *Paracelsus* is how to purify Paracelsus's humanism and unite practicality with idealism; it is a restatement of the problem identified in *Pauline*, but tackled through a dramatically presented character. At this early stage, Paracelsus sees himself as superhuman; he compares himself to "some knight traversing a wilderness" who chances "to free a tribe / Of desert-people from their dragon-foe," but refuses their offer of kingship (1.479–91). To compare the world to a "wilderness" and humankind to a race of inferior beings shows an arrogance that Browning will repeatedly attack. One cannot help mankind if one despises them—one must bind oneself to them in a *democratic* unity, which is what the visionary conclusion of *Paracelsus* holds out as a promise for the future.

Later in *Paracelsus* Browning will use the figure of Festus to allude to Wordsworth's conservatism; in book 1, he serves as a mouthpiece for Browning's critique of Paracelsus's arrogance. Paracelsus's desire to limit his "intercourse" with mankind may "break / Into a hideous blotch," a consequence that would have distressed the radical Browning (1.624–25). The struggles of Paracelsus are intended to point the way to a *radical* future; Browning co-opts Wordsworth to support his argument. The fact that the older Wordsworth had lost his radicalism does not seem to have troubled Browning greatly at this stage. When Festus asks, "[H]ow can that course be safe which from the first / Produces indifference to human love?" there is a parallel, noted by Griffin and Minchin, with Shelley's attack on Wordsworth in the preface to *Alastor*, already cited by Browning in *Pauline*.[28] It seems unlikely that this attack is leveled primarily at Wordsworth, but more at the posturing of Byron in poems like *Childe Harold* and at the hypocrisy of a man who, for all his professed misanthropy, "cared so much about the opinions of mankind and deferred to them,"[29] as Browning put it in a letter of 1873.

In 1835 Browning was concerned to present himself as a romantic poet with his feet on the ground, but, unlike Byron, uncorrupted by cynicism. Wordsworth was a pioneer to be followed, not a presence to be exorcised. A later passage in book 1 points toward the synthesis Browning would continue to seek for many years to come, and is the first passage in which Browning's debt to Wordsworth's "Prospectus" is plain:

> No, I will learn
> How to set free the soul alike in all,
> By searching out the laws by which the flesh
> Accloys the spirit. We may not be doom'd
> To cope with seraphs, but at least the rest
> Shall cope with us. Make no more giants, God!
> But elevate the race at once! We ask
> But to put forth our strength, our human strength,
> All starting fairly, all equipp'd alike,
> Gifted alike, and eagle-eyed, true-hearted,
> See if we cannot beat thy angels yet!
>
> (1.793–803)

Paracelsus is, at a first reading, dreaming of a perfectible humanity. His vision seems a metaphysical one—he wants to discover "the laws by which the flesh / Accloys the spirit." This contempt for the flesh and, by extension, the "real" world owes much to Shelley and Plato; it symbolizes what the Browning of 1835 was attempting to cut out of romanticism. Paracelsus wishes to "set free the soul," and this seems to indicate an indifference to physical suffering. However, the passage is not entirely satirical. Paracelsus realizes that "we may not be doom'd / To cope with seraphs," but still believes that mankind can attain some sort of godlike status through "putting forth" "our strength, our *human* strength" (emphasis added). The "strength" mankind will use will be its *own*. This vision is democratic; *all* mankind will have the same opportunity—"all starting fairly, all equipped alike, / Gifted alike, and eagle-eyed, true-hearted." Paracelsus has moved beyond his earlier arrogance to a more realistic and democratic idea of his mission, one that Browning will later indicate that he took from Wordsworth. Previous utopians, according to Paracelsus, finding that their schemes were "born only to wither in this life" (1.816), foolishly refused to be realistic and moderate their desires ("to curb or moderate their longings" [1.817]); instead, they imagined another world, "and other frames meet for their vast desires, / And all a dream" (1.820–21). Browning is pointing toward the disillusionment felt by the supporters of the French Revolution, who either retreated into solipsistic indulgence or joined the forces of reaction. Wordsworth could be accused of having done both, but, at this stage, Browning is not ranking him with those who surrendered; on the contrary, these lines call on Wordsworth's support.

Wordsworth dealt with his loss of faith in the French Revolution in *The Prelude*, which was not in the public arena in 1835; however, some portions of the poem had been previously published, one of them being "The French Revolution, as it appeared to Enthusiasts at its Commencement," first published in Coleridge's journal *The Friend* in 1809, and later reprinted in Wordsworth's 1815 collection. Browning would certainly have known this poem by 1835, and *Paracelsus* makes it clear that he did, since it replicates Wordsworth's argument. In the poem Wordsworth says that the particularly thrilling thing about the Revolution was the way that it gave those "who had fed their childhood upon dreams, / The playfellows of fancy" (lines 21–22) the chance to put their schemes into practice; they

> were called upon to exercise their skill,
> Not in Utopia, subterranean fields,
> Or some secreted island, Heaven knows where!
> But in the very world, which is the world
> Of all of us, - the place where in the end
> We find our happiness, or not at all!
>
> (lines 35–40)

Paracelsus has realized the same thing. That this is not a coincidence is made clear by references to this poem that Browning inserts into later works, as will be shown.

Paracelsus's humanism is evident in his desire to "crown" life rather than "scorn" it. When he declares himself priest, he is making himself the acolyte of a faith in human life (1.821). Browning has retained the romantic trappings of "coronation" (in this case, with amaranth, a symbol of immortality), but with a twist. To the romantic poets, this sort of coronation was a serious business; Keats, for example, felt guilt when he allowed himself to be "crowned" with laurel by Leigh Hunt.[30] Browning has changed the emphasis of the coronation, and has thus achieved a more mature vision of "priesthood" than the narrator of *Pauline*, who wished to stand "robed and crowned" himself; Paracelsus wants to crown *life* with amaranth (line 24). This form of romanticism avoids solipsism and fantasy.

Wordsworth's "Prospectus" and *Paracelsus*

Since *The Recluse* was to be Wordsworth's life's work, the focus on humanity displayed in its "Prospectus" would have presented Wordsworth to Browning as a humanistic model. Wordsworth muses "on Man, and Nature, and on Human Life" (line 1). He is "intent to weigh / The good and evil of our mortal state" (lines 8–9). Yet he will sing not only of "joy in widest commonalty spread" (line 18) but also of "the Individual Mind that keeps her own / Inviolate retirement" (lines 19–20). He intends to construct a synthesis of visionary idealism (the "Individual Mind" [line 9] is subject to "conscience only, and the law supreme / Of that Intelligence which governs all" [lines 20–21]) and realism ("our mortal state" [line 22]). This was Browning's own ambition, and the debts to the "Prospectus" in *Paracelsus* prove that Browning recognized this and acknowledged Wordsworth's earlier attempt.

Paracelsus's plea to God in book 2 to let him "conclude a man" is reminiscent of Wordsworth's rejection of Miltonic visions; visions of Heaven ("Jehovah—with his thunder, and the choir / Of shouting Angels" [lines 33–34]) or of Hell ("the darkest pit of lowest Erebus" [line 36]) are put aside in favor of the awe Wordsworth feels before "the Mind of Man— / My haunt, and the main region of my Song" (lines 40–41). Wordsworth is pointing toward his ambition to gaze into the human heart—"worlds / To which the heaven of heavens is but a veil" (lines 29–30). These lines must have appealed to Browning as evidence that Wordsworth's long-promised *Meisterwerk* retained an admirable sense of where a poet ought to keep his sights.

Wordsworth's message is not purely an exhortation to cast aside utopian dreaming. He is concerned with "Beauty" as "a living Presence of the earth" (line 42), not as

> the most fair ideal Forms
> Which craft of delicate Spirits hath composed
> From earth's materials.
>
> (lines 43–45)

This is an attempt to drag "Beauty" down to earth. Those who have lost themselves in speculation have been in error, Wordsworth says, since their visions are constructed with the materials of earthly experience. He has not embraced pure empiricism; out of these "materials," the world and its inhabitants, he constructs "Beauty"—a beauty rooted in the real world. Wordsworth, through his love for what he finds around him, finds that "Beauty"

> waits upon my steps;
> Pitches her tents before me as I move,
> An hourly neighbour.
>
> (lines 45–47)

His imagination has been *humanized*. Geoffrey Hartman argues that this humanizing desire is the central impulse of Wordsworth's poetry. While discussing "Nutting," he says that Wordsworth "came under the joint imperative of English Protestantism and the Enlightenment, both of which urged him to humanize (at least in poetry) his imagination, and so to abandon the older and cosmological imaginings."[31] The "older and cosmological imaginings" are, in the "Prospectus," the Miltonic visions the poet has to "pass" in order to focus upon the world. Hartman goes on to depict the nurselike role played by nature in teaching the child to appreciate and participate in the feeling of his fellows.[32] The title of book 8 of *The Prelude* describes precisely this process, as manifested in Wordsworth's own career: "Retrospect—Love of Nature Leading to Love of Man." The visionary or "apocalyptic" imagination (as Hartman calls it), can be refocused rather than discarded.[33] Hartman argues that Wordsworth was, in fact, striving to balance the apocalyptic instinct with a concentration upon the natural world.[34] Wordsworth goes on to ask why "Paradise, and groves / Elysian, Fortunate Fields" (lines 47–48) should remain merely "A history only of departed things, / Or a mere fiction of what never was" (lines 50–51) when they can be constructed on earth through a union of "the discerning intellect of Man" (line 52) and "this goodly universe" (line 53) in "love and holy passion" (line 54). Humanity *can* be perfected, but only through working with preexistent materials. This passage also interlocks with several other Wordsworth poems, like the "Elegiac Stanzas" and "The French Revolution," also dealing with utopian dreams, that influenced Browning at later stages of his career.[35]

Wordsworth says that he will speak of "nothing more than what we are," and describes an equal partnership between "the external world" and "the individual Mind" in which neither has the upper hand (lines 62–71). Wordsworth refers to the potential for good that lies within this synthesis:

> the creation (by no lower name
> Can it be called) which they with blended might
> Accomplish.
>
> (lines 69–71)

This "creation" will be the work of mankind in league with the "external World," rather than of the work of God. Man will assume divine qualities himself, and Wordsworth grants this potential to the whole race: he speaks of the "progressive powers perhaps no less / Of the whole species" (lines 64–65). The plan is a *democratic* one, which made it even more likely to appeal to and influence the youthful Browning.

The "Prospectus" would have shown Browning that Wordsworth had recognized as early as the first years of the new century the same problem that was bedeviling him in the 1830s and had moved toward solving it in the same way—through a fusion of apparent opposites. Whether Browning was consciously modeling himself on Wordsworth in *Paracelsus*, or acknowledging that they had both arrived at the same conclusion through different routes, the influence is clear. However, by the time he wrote *Sordello* the "burden of the past" had grown intolerable, and Wordsworth's influence had to be thrown off. As Bloom says, this is a painful process, involving "savagery and misrepresentation."[36] The very weight of Wordsworth's influence at this period explains the vehemence with which Browning came to reject him.

Wordsworth uses the rest of the "Prospectus" to detail his commitment to human life as it is, in all its grimmer manifestations. The "fierce confederate storm / Of sorrow" (lines 78–79) will not be ignored, but it will not overwhelm him, either; it will be given "authentic comment" (line 81). His determination to go forth and *view* the world, before trying to change it, is paralleled by that of Paracelsus, Sordello, and Browning himself. Toward the end of the "Prospectus" Wordsworth describes his work as a "Vision" (line 98); he has not ruled out "romantic" ideas of inspiration. Like Milton, he is a "transitory Being" (line 97), granted access to this "Vision" by a power "whose gracious favor is the primal source / Of all illumination" (lines 101–2). He is creating a blend of realism and visionary idealism in an identical fashion to that of Browning at the conclusion of both *Paracelsus* and *Fifine* (itself described by its author as a "metaphysical" poem); *both* poems follow Wordsworth's lead in putting across a humanist message in visionary form.

Paracelsus: Toward Solution?

Paracelsus fails to create the synthesis detailed by Wordsworth in his lifetime because he does not realize until his last hours that a synthesis is necessary. He oscillates between realism and idealism until the poem's visionary conclusion. This structure is essential to Browning's didactic purpose; the follies of self-dedication to both pure idealism and to pure realism have to be demonstrated before Paracelsus can gesture toward the true way forward. For example, Aprile, who confronts Paracelsus in book 2 with an "objective" and humanist view of art, is reminiscent of the characters in *The Excursion*, who all serve their own didactic purpose. Aprile persuades Paracelsus to give up his quest to "know" and instead annihilate himself in all-consuming love. At first glance, his focus is laudably humanistic; he wishes to express "all passions, / All soft emotions" (lines 414–15) and presents us with a teeming vision of swarming humanity:

> Bronze labyrinths, palace, pyramid, and crypt,
> Baths, galleries, courts, temples, and terraces,
> Marts, theatres, and wharfs—all fill'd with men!
>
> (lines 406–8)[37]

Like Wordsworth in the "Prospectus," Aprile surveys humankind, but he has failed to reach the "great consummation" Wordsworth seeks; his "love" has to be blended with Paracelsus's thirst to "know." Aprile's program closely resembles that of Browning himself during the period 1840–69, during which he, like Aprile, created "sprites" aplenty and made these "offspring" of his brain "speak."[38] These lines, examined in the context of Browning's later work, demonstrate how much Browning had to change his idea of what was laudable in a poet in order to escape from romanticism in 1840. He would for a long period become what he was here describing.

Browning also uses Aprile to give Paracelsus hints of the vision he will be granted at the poem's conclusion. In an extended metaphor in which Aprile describes the artist's struggle to transport his vision from the "gentler climes" of his imagination to the "savage isle" of the mundane world, Browning is describing a Wordsworthian scheme for "bringing the divine down to the human level, and raising the human to the divine."[39] Having given his fellows some idea of "the land / Whence [he] departed" (2.504–5), the poet should not neglect the world around him for these "higher loves";

as Aprile says, "common life, its wants / And ways, would I set forth in beauteous hues" (2.484–85). This ambition wants to unite the real and the ideal: "'twould be but the selfsame spirit, clothed / In humbler guise, but still the selfsame spirit" (2.514–17). As Woolford and Karlin point out, "[T]he whole passage suggests that Browning is engaged with Wordsworth's arguments about the relation of poetry to 'common life' in, for example, the preface to *Lyrical Ballads* and the 'Ode: Intimations of Immortality'."[40] The editors are referring to the parts of the preface in which Wordsworth details his plan to eliminate "the gaudiness and inane phraseology of many modern writers" in favor of "a selection of the language really used by men."[41] He unites this determination with a desire to "chuse incidents and situations from common life" and "to throw over them a certain colouring of imagination, whereby ordinary things should be presented to the mind in an unusual way."[42] By describing such events using "simple and unelaborated expressions" Wordsworth hopes that he will forge a language "arising out of repeated experience and regular feelings" that will be a more "permanent, and a far more philosophical language, than that which is frequently substituted for it by Poets, who think that they are conferring honour upon themselves and their art, in proportion as they separate themselves from the sympathies of men."[43] Wordsworth's program centers on the "ordinary" world and its inhabitants; the world is elevated by the poet's "colouring of imagination," but not essentially changed. His quest is to bring out the beauty intrinsic to "common life," thus obviating the perverted need for "extraordinary incident" or "outrageous stimulation."[44] His focus is upon the "Mind of Man"; as he says of the poems in the volume, "[T]he feeling therein developed gives importance to the action and situation, and not the action and situation to the feeling."[45] Similarly, in the preface to *Paracelsus* Browning states that "it is an attempt, probably more novel than happy, to reverse the method normally adopted by writers whose aim it is to set forth any phenomenon of the mind or passions, by the operation of persons or events; . . . instead of having recourse to an external machinery of incidents to create and evolve the crisis I desire to produce, I have ventured to display somewhat minutely the mood itself in its rise and progress, and have suffered the agency by which it is influenced or determined, to be generally discernible in its effects alone."[46] Browning makes it clear that his venture is to be Wordsworthian by announcing that he is to make the "Mind of Man" the main region of *his* song. He has not modeled himself entirely in accordance with Wordsworth's precepts; Paracelsus is hardly a simple rustic, and Browning acknowledges toward the end of his preface that the "form" of his poem may be "difficult"; nevertheless, Aprile's speech demonstrates how much Browning owed to his predecessor. In the metaphor of the "savage isle" Browning is replicating Wordsworth's argument about the elevation of "common life"; the poet must, like God, contrive "a vesture gay" out of "a bare and skeleton framework"—like a shipwrecked mariner, he must build his palace from "Serpents' scales, / And painted birds' down, fur, and fishes' skins," not from "gems" (2.455–64). Aprile hopes to "set forth" "common life" in "beauteous hues"; in Wordsworthian phrase,

> The lowest hind should not possess a hope,
> A fear, but I'd be by him, saying better
> Than he his own heart's language.
>
> (2.506–8)

"His own heart's language" is a Wordsworthian phrase in its emphasis on both the "language really used by men" and the human "heart." Aprile wants to enter the heart of a "hind" (a peasant), in an identical fashion to that of the early Wordsworth.[47] Browning is not so much "engaged with" Wordsworth's arguments here, as replicating them. It is true that Aprile has failed to carry out his scheme; this does not, however, mean that the scheme itself is doomed to failure. It means that Aprile's humanistic focus is not fully active. He "loves" the world, but his love is that of a disengaged observer. Browning is well aware of the dangers of this "middle road"; nevertheless, his return to it in Paracelsus's final vision indicates that Aprile's Wordsworthian scheme seemed to Browning to be the way forward in 1835.

Aprile, in his description of his failure, becomes a mouthpiece for a pessimistic Browning who recognizes only too well that Wordsworth's plan has its flaws. The implicit critique of Wordsworth's "Preface" becomes more incisive. Browning sees the dangers of *too much* imagination, the flaw in romanticism that he will have to repair in order to make it into a viable program for the humanistic poet. If one is "dazzled" by "shapes" (2.524) and unable to choose between these beautiful visions, one neglects the "darkling mortals, famish'd for one ray / Of thy so-hoarded luxury of light" (2.544–45) (i.e., suffering humanity). To the radical Browning, a poet who neglected his audience in this way would be guilty of the most terrible dereliction of duty. At this stage of his career, Browning was with Shelley in seeing poets as the "unacknowledged legislators of the world."[48] Browning knows, however, that it is not enough merely to pity the sufferings of men—one has a duty to alleviate them.

Browning uses the conclusion of Aprile's long speech to attack the ideas from the preface to *Lyrical Ballads* that he appeared to be endorsing earlier:

> Didst not perceive, spoil'd by the subtle ways
> Of intricate but instantaneous thought,
> That common speech was useless to its ends—
> That language, wedded from the first to thought,

> Will strengthen as it strengthens; but, divorced,
> Will dwindle, while thought widens more and more?
>
> (2.55–63)

Browning is indicating that he sees both sides of the argument. "Common speech" cannot express the poet's visions; it is a huge obstacle for the humanistic ambitions of the poet, who is able to grasp them himself, but whose "language," "divorced" from the inner vision, will "dwindle" uselessly, thus preventing the poet from communicating his vision.[49] Aprile's previous reference to Wordsworth's argument held out the possibility of fusing the human and the divine through communication with the rest of mankind; here, the inability of human language to convey anything beyond the mundane seems to doom the poet to paralysis and silence. The lines demonstrate the degree of ambivalence with which Browning still viewed Wordsworth's aesthetic. The story of Paracelsus's career is used by Browning to dramatize his own struggles, but not in the crudely autobiographical sense that some critics have suggested; rather, he presents the story of his attempts to follow Wordsworth's scheme to humanize poetry without falling into the many pitfalls on the way. The poet has to drag himself down from his "supposed height" without descending *too* far.

Browning's struggle is reflected in the vacillations of his hero. As book 3 demonstrates, the all-too-fallible Paracelsus has failed to achieve any more than worldly success; his contempt for his audience has crippled his attempts to become humanity's redeemer. That he is still prey to the central idea of "perverted" romanticism is shown by his rapt admiration for the image of the solitary Michal singing "alone, bird-like" (3.28). "Respect all such as sing when all alone," he declares, and he is "unsettled" by the idea of her singing to an audience: "'tis a change, and I detest all change" (3.36–41). This irritated dismissal of the very idea of an audience goes against all of Browning's instincts for communication and the Wordsworthian concept of the poet as a "man speaking to men"; it is interesting, therefore, to note that the image appears to have been inspired by a Wordsworth poem, "The Solitary Reaper." The essential difference is that the "solitary Highland lass" (line 2) in Wordsworth's poem has an auditor in the poet himself, and her "plaintive numbers" (line 18), telling either of "old, unhappy, far-off things" (line 19) or "some natural sorrow, loss or pain, / That has been, and may be again" (lines 23–24) *humanize* their auditor: "the music in my heart I bore, / Long after it was heard no more" (lines 31–32). Hartman confirms the humanistic and even democratic purpose served by the girl's song; she may be singing entirely without awareness of her audience, but her song *is* heard, and spreads through her listeners, uniting them in bonds of sympathy.[50] (Browning would return to this idea in the presentation of the effects of Pippa's song in *Pippa Passes*, and it is likely that he had these lines in mind while writing that poem; Browning would find Wordsworth's influence harder to shake off after 1840 than he had supposed.) Paracelsus's vision of Michal's solitary singing differs from Wordsworth's in that Paracelsus feels guilt at having heard her at all—for him, the idea of *any* audience is distasteful. This admiration for the thoroughly antihumanistic image of an *entirely* solitary singer will have to go if his romanticism is to be purified.

Paracelsus has made some progress, though, toward devising a more realistic role for himself. Later in his conversation with Festus he makes it clear that he has abandoned some of his self-absorption. In defending his "plan, / Or plot, or whatsoe'er it was" (3.265–66), he declares that it was not the scheme of one

> Enamour'd of a lot unlike the world's,
> And thus far sure from common casualty—
> (Folly of follies!)
>
> (3.270–72)

The sort of divinely inspired visionary Browning spoke of in *Pauline* was indeed far from "common casualty"; in fact, this paragon was barely human at all. To Browning, being "enamour'd of a lot unlike the world's" would indeed be the ultimate sin. Paracelsus is crawling toward the poem's redeeming transfiguration of Wordsworthian humanism, as presented in book 5. He is himself preparing for the painful descent from his "supposed height"; the poem is the story of the gradual humanization of Paracelsus's own imagination, in accordance with Wordsworth's scheme.

Festus, in his attempts to comfort his friend, goes on to speak of the miraculous cures and alleviation of suffering he has performed. Paracelsus, like Coleridge and De Quincey, can connect both himself and others with a visionary world through the use of hallucinogens. (Browning is thinking of the historical Paracelsus's use of laudanum).[51] As Festus says,

> men in racking pain may purchase dreams
> Of what delights them most—swooning at once
> Into a sea of bliss, or rapt along
> As in a flying sphere of turbulent light.
>
> (3.345–48)

Browning is linking Paracelsus with this important visionary aspect of the romantic program in a deeply ambivalent way. On the one hand, he is condemning the way that Paracelsus gives his patients only "dreams / Of what delights them most" instead of realities; he is peddling untruths, in a similar way to the far more cynical and venal Mr. Sludge in a much later Browning poem. On the other hand, the lines demonstrate a commitment to humanistic ideals, since the visions alleviate suffering. Nevertheless, Paracelsus carries out his healing work for money; the sick "purchase" their dreams. The passage is a compressed index to Browning's troubled response to the humanism implicit in romanticism, and its visionary aspects (or the humanistic aspects of the visionary quality). How is the poet to untangle this web, in which the desire to help and the need to lie seem inextricably bound together? There is a more positive way to view the matter; the linkage of humanistic ambitions with visionary dreams will recur at the poem's conclusion. All the same, Festus ends his exhortation with a comparison of Paracelsus's power over the body with that of Martin Luther over the "fettered soul." The reader should bear this separation of soul and body in mind; Browning will recur to this division in *Sordello*, where he will cast aside his desire to save men's souls as impractical (3.685–710). Maybe the soul should be left to Luther.

As book 3 draws on, it becomes clear that Paracelsus has perceived that the essential thrust of Aprile's message is humanistic:

> 'twas a man
> Perishing in my sight, who summon'd me,
> As I would shun the ghastly fate I saw,
> To serve my race at once; to wait no longer
> That God should interfere on my behalf—
> Nor trust to time; but to distrust myself,
> And give my gains, imperfect as they were,
> To men.
>
> (3.575–82)

When he set out on his career, Paracelsus wanted to "trample on" the men he served, but no longer. A divinely inspired poet/prophet, assured of the righteousness of his cause, might well wait confidently for God's intervention (like the deranged narrator of "Porphyria's Lover," awaiting God's declaration of approval while fondling the strangled body of his beloved); Paracelsus, moved by Aprile, has abandoned this hope and moved on to a more mature "distrust" of himself based on his recognition of his own human frailty. Like Wordsworth, he will from now on focus on "nothing more than what we are." He is gradually creeping toward the revelation Browning intends for him.

Later in book 3, Browning alludes to another romantic poet—not Wordsworth, this time, but Keats. Nevertheless, the reference does lead back to Wordsworth. Paracelsus rejects aestheticism, since he is still weighed down by a consciousness of divinely ordained purpose that seems to him to forbid a mere self-immersion in love for the world; he "cannot feed on beauty, for the sake / Of beauty only" (3.705–7), nor can he take comfort in the fact that "Beauty is prodigally strewn around" (3.714). This is an allusion to the opening passage of Keats's *Endymion*, in which the poet declares that "A thing of beauty is a joy for ever" (1.1) and describes the way that "Beauty" can sustain the soul

> Spite of despondence, of the inhuman dearth
> Of noble natures, of the gloomy days,
> Of all the unhealthy and o'er-darkened ways
> Made for our searching.
>
> (1.8–11)

Keats is setting up his aesthetic creed in opposition to the "gloomy" political and social conditions that surround him in 1817—he is turning aestheticism into a *political* weapon; "some shape of beauty moves away the pall / From our dark spirits" (1.12–13). It should be apparent how relevant this is to *Paracelsus*. Keats's "beauties" are like Paracelsus's drugs, in that they alleviate the suffering of sensitive souls in a brutal world; however, they share their more negative aspects in that they do not actively oppose the malign forces, but simply relieve the symptoms.

Browning is not only using these lines to mount a critique of the dangers of Keatsian aestheticism, however; the reference leads back to Wordsworth. The editor of the Longman edition of Keats's poems points out that *Endymion*'s opening "celebration of beauty" may "owe something to Wordsworth's *Excursion* (1814), 'Prospectus' 42–7": namely, the lines in which Wordsworth declares that

> Beauty,—a living Presence of the earth,
> Surpassing the most fair ideal Forms
> Which craft of delicate Spirits hath composed
> From earth's materials—waits upon my steps;
> Pitches her tents before me as I move,
> An hourly neighbour.[52]

This is not the place to discuss Keats's debt to Wordsworth in detail; it is necessary only to recall Keats's professed admiration for *The Excursion*, and to be aware of the Wordsworthian overtones in Keats's rustic iteration of the beauty of "the sun, the moon, / Trees, old and young" (1.13–14) and "daffodils / With the green world they live in" (1.15–16), among others. The debt is even more obvious in the lines in which Keats describes the power of these memories of beauty to "haunt us until they become a cheering light / Unto our souls" (1.30–31); this idea is one of those that are considered most characteristically Wordsworthian.

Browning was an early admirer of Keats, and it is not surprising to find him referring to the little-known poet at this early stage; as Maynard has shown, he was reading, and admiring, Keats, from very early in his career.[53] Both Browning's methodology and his (apparent) intentions are of interest. First, the methodology. This technique—to mount a critique of the aesthetic ideas of a predecessor in an obscure and allusive fashion, referring through certain works to other works, creating what I shall refer to, for want of a better phrase, as a "web of reference" that requires the reader to follow these threads to their conclusions—will become characteristic of Browning in dealing with his romantic predecessors throughout his career, particularly in *Fifine*. An earlier instance of this is Browning's indirect attack on Wordsworth through his reference in *Pauline* to Shelley's *Alastor* preface. This technique extends beyond Browning's poetry into his correspondence—in particular, to his correspondence with William Knight.[54] Browning is playing a *game* with his readers, challenging them to spot his references—not out of simple intellectual one-upmanship, but out of a desire to *conceal* his changing attitude toward his predecessors. This desire to conceal his attitudes has its genesis as early as *Paracelsus*.

It is important to remember that neither Keats nor Wordsworth has divorced himself from the "real" world with his aestheticism. On the contrary, their love of "Beauty" binds them to the natural world in an almost pantheistic fashion; Wordsworth is said to have called the "Song to Pan" in *Endymion* "a very pretty piece of Paganism," ironically unaware of his own influence in pushing the youngster in this direction.[55] The beauty both Keats and Wordsworth pursue is not something otherworldly, but "prodigally strewn around," in Browning's phrase—or, as Wordsworth puts it, "a simple produce of the common day." Beauty is to be found all around us; this fits in with Wordsworth's professed desire in the "Prospectus" to humanize his idealism. If this is the case, why does Browning seem to dismiss this brand of humanistic aestheticism? Surely this type of romanticism should receive his cautious approval, always recalling the dangerous example of Aprile. Why, then, does Paracelsus seem to deny the efficacy of this type of aesthetic? There are several possible explanations. Paracelsus could merely, in his despair, be rejecting the correct path to which he will return before his death. This is initially plausible; what is Paracelsus's career but a series of vacillations? However, the path Wordsworth has set out for Browning to follow in his "Prospectus" is not one of pure aestheticism. Both Keats and Wordsworth believe that beauty serves a humanistic purpose; in Keats's case, this humanism is intimately linked with political radicalism. Even if Paracelsus has failed to realize this, Browning would certainly have done so. It is more likely that Browning is using Paracelsus's rejection of aestheticism—and, by implication, of the romantic program—as a subtle comment upon the real difficulties of creating a scheme for poetry that is both practical and visionary. It is no surprise that Paracelsus has missed the point, Browning seems to imply— it is easily done. The dividing line between the arid aestheticism of Aprile and the more nourishing variety professed by Wordsworth and Keats is a narrow one. In order to redeem himself, Paracelsus will have to retain his Wordsworthian realization that "Beauty is prodigally strewn around" while developing a visionary perception of how the world can be improved still further.

Later in the same book of the poem there is a passage spoken by Festus that does much to illuminate Browning's later attitude toward Wordsworth. Festus is attempting to counter Paracelsus's argument that "admiration blinds" and that, therefore, Festus is not fit to perceive his faults. On the contrary, Festus argues, love curses the lover with an exquisite perception of the faults of the beloved. Whether the lover's love is reciprocated, "heart answering heart" (3.834), or whether it

> spends itself
> In silent mad idolatry of some
> Pre-eminent mortal—some great soul of souls—
> Which ne'er will know how well it is adored
> . . . such love is never blind; but rather
> Alive to every the minutest spot
> That mars its object.
>
> (3.834–40)

This idea is an illuminating one when one considers Browning's changing attitude toward Wordsworth, and the extreme bitterness toward him expressed in some of his letters to his future wife.[56] Though it would be excessive to describe the young Browning as indulging in "silent mad idolatry" of his predecessor, he certainly viewed him as a "great soul of souls." By the period in which Browning wrote *Paracelsus*, Wordsworth was indeed the "pre-eminent mortal" of English poetry. Festus goes on to describe the way that the idolater tries to make excuses for the failings of the "great soul"; "is there no gallant stand / Made even for much proved weak?" (3.848–49). This is followed by a

> shrinking-back
> Lest (since all love assimilates the soul
> To what it loves) it should at length become
> Almost a rival of its idol.
>
> (3.849–52)

This is a weird foreshadowing of what Browning would do vis-à-vis Wordsworth in *Sordello*. In that poem, Browning does indeed "shrink back" lest, by continuing to write Wordsworthian poetry like *Paracelsus*, he should become a "rival" of his "idol." The subtext of this is that it is precisely as a "rival" of Wordsworth that Browning needs to redefine himself if he is to escape his influence and speak with his own voice. One should also recall that Browning's first *personal* meetings with Wordsworth took place between the publication of *Paracelsus* and that of *Sordello*, and that Wordsworth's behavior and conservatism offended Browning. Bearing these lines in mind, one can envisage just how disappointing these meetings must have been, and how the period between 1835 and 1840 must have been filled with "gallant last stands" on Wordsworth's behalf by the younger poet, until his faith finally collapsed (undermined, whether consciously or not, by Browning's need to redefine himself as a strong poet).

Most of the references to Wordsworth in this poem are approving. Later in the same book, however, comes one of Browning's first attacks upon what he would come to despise about the later Wordsworth: his conservatism. The presiding genius of *Paracelsus* is the deeply ambitious and humanistic Wordsworth of the "Prospectus," a Wordsworth who had not lost his determination to improve the world. It is not the conservative poet of the 1830s whom Browning was shortly to meet. Browning had not yet had his illusions shattered by a personal encounter with Wordsworth at the time he wrote *Paracelsus*, but he would have known that the older poet had lost his radicalism. As *Paracelsus* moves toward conclusion, it is interesting to note the way that Festus changes, as he grows older, into as near as the poem gets to a comic figure. He repeatedly questions his friend about obvious matters, and becomes more and more conventionally pious as the poem goes on. This piety is appropriate, since he is "a quiet mountain-cloistered priest" (3.875–76). This is reminiscent of the later Wordsworth, who could well be described as "quiet" and "mountain-cloistered." As for the "priest" part, Wordsworth's return to the Church of England had been so complete that he had served as chapel warden at Rydal Church between 1833 and 1834.[57] Browning was using the figure of Festus to satirize the side of Wordsworth he did not admire; his "love" for Wordsworth did not blind him to the "minutest spot / That mars its object" (3.839–40). After 1840, the "Festus" image would entirely subsume the more attractive side of Wordsworth for Browning for almost thirty years.

Browning continues to use Paracelsus as a mouthpiece for his own vision of romanticism later in book 3. He allows his vacillating hero occasional glances of the promised land that he, like Moses, is destined never to enter himself. He declares that though he has failed in his quest, his labors may have prepared the road for others to follow:

> 'Tis in the advance of individual minds
> That the slow crowd should ground their expectation

Eventually to follow—as the sea
Waits ages in its bed, till some one wave
Of all the multitudinous mass extends
The empire of the whole, some feet perhaps,
Over the strip of sand which could confine
Its fellows so long time; thenceforth the rest,
Even to the meanest, hurry in at once,
And so much is clear gain'd.

(3.883–92)

This image expresses Paracelsus's new *gradualism*. He no longer harbors the romantic dream of elevating "the race at once," but retains a humanistic idealism in his vision of gradual progression. The means, not the ends, of his ambition have changed. Paracelsus also seems to have discarded the idea that he, or the creative romantic spirit in general, is somehow superior to the mass of humanity. In its place is a far more realistic view of human progress: as a continual battering at the door of knowledge, leading eventually to its collapse. The wave that "extends / The empire of the whole" is no more effective than its predecessors; it is akin to the proverbial straw that breaks the camel's back. That it is the first to gain "the strip of sand" is due to luck, no more. Browning's Paracelsus has modified his vision of human development into a democratic one. If the lines are examined in a historicist sense, Browning may have been alluding to the reform movement of the 1830s, which used a similar form of repeated "battering" to achieve its aims—the first Reform Bill was rejected by the House of Lords three times between March 1831 and March 1832, and only became law when Lord Grey (one of the "individual minds" whose "advance" enables the "slow crowd" to follow) threatened to flood the Lords with liberal peers, forcing William IV and the Lords to pass the bill in June 1832. To a radical like Browning, the first Reform Act—which increased the electorate by 217,000, but left the lower-middle and working classes (as well, of course, as women) without the vote—would have been merely the first of what he would have hoped would be a long succession of democratic reforms, and by no means the most important; the "empire of the whole" had only been extended by "some feet perhaps." Other radicals of the time shared this view, and the People's Charter, signed by working-class radicals in May 1838, demanded far more extensive reform.

Paracelsus's later discussion of Luther with Festus casts further illumination upon Browning's attempt to remodel romanticism along radically humanistic lines. Cynical as he is, Paracelsus has not lost his humanism, or diluted it to the stage where direct action seems worthless. He praises Luther's "liberation" of the suffering, in contrast to the inactivity of more timid souls:

> the so-heavy chain which gall'd mankind
> Is shatter'd, and the noblest of us all
> Must bow to the deliverer—nay, the worker
> Of our own projects—we who long before
> Had burst its trammels, but forgot the crowd
> We would have taught still groan'd beneath the load:
> This he has done and nobly.
>
> (3.995–1001)

Luther has put the humanistic "projects" of others into practice. Indeed, his achievement is a democratic one, with radical overtones; he has dedicated himself to the struggle to free the "crowd" from the "load" imposed upon them by their rulers. Other liberal intellectuals (like Paracelsus) have been content with *private* resistance, and this is not enough.

There is no hint that Browning finds Wordsworth incompatible with a radical, if not revolutionary, program:

> And men seem made, though not as I believed,
> For something better than these times can show:
> Witness these gangs of peasants your new lights
> From Suabia have possess'd, whom Münzer leads,
> And whom the duke, the landgrave, and the elector
> Will calm in blood!
>
> (3.1004–9)

Münzer was a radical egalitarian—indeed, an anarchist—who championed the peasantry, and attempted to destroy the entire social order. His "communism" resembled that of the "Leveller" John Lilburne, greatly admired by Browning at this period. Paracelsus associates the revolting peasants with the idea that the sufferings of humanity can be alleviated, and that the race can be improved. (Historically, Browning may have been thinking of the riots which followed the House of Lords' rejection of the first Reform Bill in October 1831; Wordsworth, for example, was horrified by them, and the bourgeois Browning is unlikely to have viewed them with approval, but he would have seen them as a positive sign of the inevitability of political change.) The Peasant Wars, Paracelsus implies, are an indication that some kind of revolution *is* possible, even if Münzer and his "gangs" are doomed to defeat. With this in mind, one can see how *Paracelsus* is a radical poem, particularly when one comes to examine the "millenarian communism" of the poem's concluding vision. Irvine and Honan seem surprised that "Effingham Wilson, a friend of Fox and publisher of radical literature, was persuaded to see radical tendencies in *Paracelsus*"; when one considers passages like the one in question, his enthusiasm seems less surprising.[58] Paracelsus's tacit approval of Luther's "liberation" of "the crowd" and Münzer's openly revolutionary (and violent) action place him much closer to post-French Revolution democratic humanism than to contemporary humanists like Erasmus. Woolford maintains that "Browning's Paracelsus espouses a millenarian communism having affinities with extreme Puritan theory, and with the anarchism of Shelley and Godwin."[59] This revolutionary tendency in Paracelsus (and his creator) may seem far away from the popular image of the later Wordsworth. Nevertheless, much of Browning's radicalism as expressed in *Paracelsus* is indebted to Wordsworth's own radical vision in the "Prospectus." Paracelsus approves of Luther's "practical" efforts to help the suffering and oppressed, and holds up Münzer's uprising as an indication that progress *is* possible; in the same way, Wordsworth believes that a focus upon humanity, rather than upon abstractions, can create a kind of Paradise on earth. There is a further parallel: Paracelsus, though he foresees the bloody conclusion of the Peasant Wars, finds in them a cause for hope, while Wordsworth refuses to be downcast by similar scenes of horror (lines 72–82). Browning is indebted to Wordsworth for his decision to limit his benevolent plans for humanity to a realistic level without collapsing into cynicism.

A few lines later, Browning makes an obvious allusion to the "Prospectus." Festus has attempted to drag his friend out of his depression by alluding to the existence of "another world to mend / All error and mischance" (3.1023–24). Unsurprisingly, this infuriates Paracelsus:

> Another world!
> And why this world, this common world to be
> A make-shift, a mere foil, so fair soever,
> To some fair life to come? Man must be fed
> With angel's food, forsooth; and some few traces
> Of a diviner nature which look out
> Through his corporeal baseness warrant him
> In a supreme contempt for all provision
> For his inferior tastes—some straggling marks
> Which constitute his essence, just as truly
> As here and there a gem would constitute
> The rock, their barren bed, a diamond.
>
> (3.1024–35)

This attack will be repeated in a much cruder form as part of the attack on Wordsworth Browning uses to tear himself away from his master in *Sordello*. The irony is plain, since this sort of realistic humanism is the mainspring of the "Prospectus." In *Paracelsus*, Wordsworth is still a master to be followed, not a weight to be shrugged off, and this is particularly obvious in Paracelsus's declaration that "love, hope, fear, faith – these make humanity: / These are its sign, and note, and character" (3.1041–42). In the "Prospectus," Wordsworth says that he will sing "of Truth, of Grandeur, Beauty, Love, and Hope, / And melancholy Fear subdued by Faith" (lines 14–15). This cannot be coincidence, in the light of the fact that he speaks of "love, hope, fear, faith" in precisely the same order that they appear in the "Prospectus." To use this order clearly indicates Browning's reliance on Wordsworth's model and his determination to put Wordsworth's scheme into practice.

Browning would return to this idea many times in his work, particularly in *Sordello* and "Fra Lippo Lippi"; he had already referred to it in book 1 of *Paracelsus*.[60] His continued attachment to it will be illustrated later through his admiration for Wordsworth's "Rob Roy's Grave" and references to his "French Revolution" and *The Prelude*.[61] Browning is acknowledging that Wordsworth, a leading romantic, was a realistic humanist as well as an idealist (at least at the time he wrote the "Prospectus"), and that one could not accuse him of a lack of concern for human suffering. The "Prospectus" sets out a humanistic framework for Wordsworth's life's work, and, for all Browning knew, *The Recluse* was still to appear.

It should be pointed out that Browning may be alluding to Wordsworth's "Immortality" Ode in his attack on those who would let the perceived "traces / Of a diviner nature" outweigh the physical needs of mankind.[62] This is certainly possible, and the similarity of this glancing attack (if that is what it is) to Browning's later assault on Wordsworth suggests that even in 1835 Browning was deeply ambivalent toward Wordsworth's more metaphysical tendencies, though he had not yet felt the need to use them against him.

As the poem moves toward its conclusion, Browning uses Paracelsus to satirize the temptation to consider oneself as "above" one's fellows. The image of a poet perched upon a "height" appears in the "Preface" to the *Lyrical Ballads*, but also appears in Wordsworth's "Prospectus" in a redeemed, humanistic sense, in which the poet must hang "brooding above the fierce confederate storm / Of sorrow" (lines 77–79). The poet's elevation here is indication of an all-embracing comprehension of and sympathy for the range of human suffering. The more malign elevation will be the target of Browning's satire throughout his career; here Paracelsus is allowed a last gasp of such egotism in order to indicate what has to be cast aside:

> I am above them like a God—there's no
> Hiding the fact—and, had I been but wise,
> Had ne'er concerned myself with scruples, nor
> Communicated aught to such a race;
> But been content to own myself a man,
> And in my elevation man's would be.
>
> (4.290–95)

This is what has to be discarded: the egotism that allows Paracelsus to suppose that his own self-evident superiority would somehow raise the entirety of humanity without him bothering to get his hands dirty. There is a perverted humanism in these lines, evident in Paracelsus's determination to "own himself a man"; this is clearer in Browning's later revision of the text, in which Paracelsus speaks of "taking my natural station o'er their heads / Then owning all the glory was a man's" (as Djabal strives, unsuccessfully, to do in Browning's 1843 play *The Return of the Druses*).[63] Paracelsus still retains a vague grasp of the Wordsworthian humanism that will ultimately save him (in a manner of speaking).

Book 4 is generally a depressing read, as Paracelsus has apparently failed utterly in his self-appointed mission. Nevertheless, Browning allows him to hint at the redeeming vision that is just around the corner. One such moment comes when Paracelsus, complaining that God has failed to reward his labors, has a brief moment of insight:

> Beside, 'tis vain to talk of forwarding
> His glory otherwise; *this* is the sphere
> Alone of its increase, as far as we
> Can be concern'd, or I am much deceived:
> *We* are his glory; and if *we* be glorious,
> Is not the thing achieved?
>
> (4.571–76)

This is a humanistic belief; it is fruitless to seek to increase God's glory in metaphysical worlds—he has placed us here, and must therefore have intended us to concern ourselves with the quotidian world around us. If the idea that humanity is God's glory is not a humanistic one, it is difficult to know what is. However, these lines are not purely humanistic—they hint at a *fusion* of the metaphysical (the desire to increase "God's glory" points *beyond* the merely physical) and the realistically humanistic (this apparently metaphysical ambition can only be realized *here*). It is this very synthesis that Browning will seek throughout his career, briefly embracing it in book 5, and to which he will try to return after 1869. The synthesis is a Wordsworthian one; try as he might, Browning could never escape from Wordsworth's influence.

Browning uses the conclusion of *Paracelsus* to outline his own vision of a fusion of idealism and practical realism into a radical synthesis: a vision of humanity progressing toward perfection in a gradualist way. Paracelsus's career has not been in vain, and its final outcome is profoundly humanistic; as Tucker puts it, "Paracelsus has affirmed his deepest humanity."[64] The race cannot be perfected "at once," but, like the waves crashing on the beach in a previous image, will gradually ascend toward godhood. Woolford points out that despite the fact that Paracelsus will never see his ideas come to fruition, he is symbolic of the democratic possibilities of the future.[65] The whole poem has been an exposition of the dangers of both excessive idealism and pure cynicism, and Browning cannot resist using Paracelsus to utter a final condemnation (through the imagined voice of the dead, and now chastened, poet) of the metaphysical indulgence that destroyed Aprile:

> "How couldst thou still remain on earth, should God
> Grant thee the great approval thou dost seek?
> But men would murmur, and with cause enough;
> For when they saw thee, stainless of all sin,
> Preserved and sanctified by inward light,
> They would complain—'a comfort shut from us,
> He drinketh unespied; for we live on,
> Nor taste the quiet of a constant joy,
> For ache, and care, and doubt, and weariness,
> While he is calm! Help is vouchsafed to him,
> And hid from us!'"
>
> (5.225–36)

The poet here has moved *beyond* the earth, and his communion with God robs him of communion with his fellow men. In the eyes of Paracelsus, such a relationship with the divine is pernicious, since it dooms the gifted one to isolation and "self-sufficiency." "Ache, and care, and doubt, and weariness" have to be fought, not ignored. This does not mean that any relationship with the divine has to be put aside; God's glory must be forwarded *on earth*. Browning would have realized that a humanism entirely drained of idealism is a flimsy thing indeed; surely, in that case, cynicism would be the logical option. In any case, these lines are part of Browning's extensive debt to Wordsworth's scheme for making Paradise "a simple produce of the common day" ("Prospectus," line 55). "*We* are His glory" (*Paracelsus*, 4.575).

Nevertheless, there is a degree of ambivalence on the poet's part toward Wordsworth, or, at least, toward the older Wordsworth. Festus has become, by this stage, a mouthpiece for the sort of conservative Christianity characteristic of the later Wordsworth. To pervert his gifts and serve the forces of reaction would have been Wordsworth's greatest sin, in Browning's eyes. At this stage, Browning's qualms are implicit—he had not even met Wordsworth by this stage—but they are undeniably present in the "quiet mountain-cloistered priest," Festus. Particularly culpable, in Browning's eyes, would have been Festus's quietist use of Christian metaphysics:

And can it be,
Dear Aureole, you have then found out at last
The utter vanity of worldly things?
That man is made for weakness, and should wait
In patient ignorance?

(5.518–20)

The idea that "worldly things" are "vain" is anathema to a devotee of practical humanism, and the belief that man is "made for weakness" leaves the door open for the forces of oppression. Metaphysics can easily be used to reduce mankind to servitude; Festus ranges himself with the forces of reaction when he says,

'Tis fruitless for mankind
To fret themselves with what concerns them not;
They are no use that way: they should lie down
Content as God has made them, nor go mad
In thriveless cares to better their condition.

(5.559–63)

Browning is plainly using Festus's querulous conservatism to satirize the later Wordsworth. Browning's debt to Wordsworth in *Paracelsus* is so strong that one can understand the disappointment Wordsworth's conservatism must have created, and how, coupled with a desire to establish his own identity as a strong poet with no need of mentors, it led to a vicious reaction. After 1840 Wordsworth would *become* Festus in Browning's eyes.

Festus is also presented as being slow on the uptake, as well as reactionary, as is shown amusingly (for this poem, anyway) in the following exchange:

Paracelsus. I am not all so valueless;
I have been something, though too soon I left
Following the instincts of that happy time . . .
Festus. What happy time? For God's sake, for man's sake
What time was happy? All I hope to know
That answer will decide. What happy time?
Paracelsus. When, but the time I vow'd myself to Man?

(5.574–80)

These lines are not solely of interest for light relief. Browning's French friend, Monclar, sent him a general concept of what he believed to be Browning's overall plan of the poem, to which Browning added notes that elucidate his intentions. Monclar's note to this passage (in French) ran as follows: "[H]e realizes that his first aim was the true one. He repents of his despair." Browning underlined "his first aim," adding "i.e. the good of mankind." He also added the following to the last sentence: "—but he also sees that his path was not the true one—'One should unite in oneself etc.'"[66]

Browning's mission in book 5 was to present the reader with a synthesis that would make clear the path for Paracelsus's heirs (all mankind) to follow. Paracelsus's "first aim" was "the true one," and that "aim" was "the good of mankind"; the fundamental drive behind both Paracelsus and his creator is practical humanism. Nevertheless, his "path" was a false one, since he failed to produce a synthesis of love for mankind with a clear-headed vision of what could be done for them. Paracelsus was right to "vow himself to man," but failed to follow Wordsworth's lead and turn this vow into an active commitment. Browning would go on to draw extensively on Wordsworth's program in creating his concluding vision.

The Vision

The bulk of *Paracelsus* is, in many ways, simply a prologue to Browning's depiction of a possible unification of the idealist and realist strands he had found such difficulty in reconciling. To do this would be to create a purified brand of romanticism, following Wordsworth's lead, that also managed to fit in with Browning's own radical and democratic sympathies. The vision is a revolutionary one, and it is no surprise that Effingham Wilson was persuaded to publish the work "more, we understand, on the ground of radical sympathies in Mr. Fox and the author than on that of its intrinsic worth."[67] It should be noted that the use of a vision to present a unifying design to the viewer (and the reader) will be repeated in *Fifine*; the later poem returns to the very questions debated in *Paracelsus*. In using a vision, Browning is utilizing a romantic technique (as used by Coleridge, De Quincey, and Shelley, among others) to serve his quasi- or postromantic ends. The vision shows several explicit debts to Wordsworth; as Woolford and Karlin have noted, the pantheistic aspects of the vision, in particular, are Wordsworthian.[68]

Paracelsus follows a lyrical depiction of God's pantheistic presence, and a declaration of man's status as both the summit of creation and a microcosm of the world (thus dragging together pantheism and evolution) with an attempt to reconcile pantheism with polytheism that is indebted to Wordsworth. Polytheism is outwardly impossible to reconcile with pantheism; here Paracelsus suggests that man (who is, after all, a microcosm of creation) used polytheism as a method of projecting his *own* qualities onto the natural world:

> Man, once descried, imprints for ever
> His presence on all lifeless things—the winds
> Are henceforth voices, wailing, or a shout,
> A querulous mutter, or a quick gay laugh—
> Never a senseless gust now man is born.
>
> (5.706–10)

Browning's motives here are humanistic; he would later attack Byron for his depiction of man as inferior to "symbols of immensity" like the ocean, and polytheism would have been anathema to him. However, if polytheism has its origins in man's desire to impose his *own* identity and qualities on the world, it is a sign of strength. It can therefore be made to fit in with Browning's depiction of man as the summit/microcosm of creation, and serve his humanistic purposes: "and this to fill us with regard for man, / Deep apprehension of his passing worth" (5.725–26). This attempt to turn pantheism into a manifestation of humanistic power is Wordsworthian; specifically, its forerunner is to be found in book 4 of *The Excursion*:

> Upon the breast of new-created Earth
> Man walked; and when and whereso'er he moved,
> Alone or mated, Solitude was not.
> He heard, borne on the wind, the articulate Voice
> Of God; and Angels to his sight appeared
> Crowning the glorious hills of Paradise;
> Or through the groves gliding like morning mist
> Rekindled by the sun.
>
> (4.631–38)

When Browning says that "the winds / Are henceforth voices" he is recalling the "articulate voice / Of God" "borne on the wind" in Wordsworth's poem. He is using Wordsworth to back up his argument—a method entirely consistent with the way he has been indebted to Wordsworth throughout the poem.

Browning follows this with a vision of human progression toward equality and quasi divinity. This is as close as Browning, following Wordsworth's lead, would get to the fusion of realism and idealism that he would still be hunting over thirty years later. It is fascinating to see how radical this argument, with its Wordsworthian debts, actually is; how Browning had managed to find a democratic radicalism in his predecessor. It is a vision of perfectible humanity, like that of the wilder romantic visionaries (Shelley, for example), that differs from theirs in that, *unlike* the dreams Browning had earlier condemned in his work, it retains a grasp of the actual: "all the race is perfected alike / As *man*, that is" (5.756–57). It aims to make man as perfect as possible without losing sight of the essential qualities that make him human. Only when the race is perfected "As *man*" will the stage have been reached in which "in completed man begins again / A tendency to God" (5.759–60). In fact, the *process* of change in which man struggles to transcend his humanity is, paradoxically, the essential fact about the human race that separates mankind from the beasts; as Tucker puts it, "[T]he poem celebrates a humanizing energy that leaps into the future to overcome the sterilities of a mistaken dualism."[69] One must not try to run before one can walk, and try to attain divine status before one has eradicated human weakness. It is not fruitless idealism to hope to make men like gods; but one must follow the correct path, and the road will be a long one. One condition is particularly emphasized by the radical Browning: *equality* must be attained before humanity can be perfected. Tyranny progresses toward democracy, slowly but surely; "progress is / The law of life" (5.729–30). At present, the majority of mankind is trapped in servitude, but "here and there a towering mind / O'erlooks its crawling fellows" (5.734–35). Browning thus holds on to the romantic idea of "great men" while looking forward to the day when "great men" as such will no longer exist, since *all* will be great. As Paracelsus said in book 3, the idea that "great men" exist can be fitted into a vision of human progress if one sees them as dragging their fellow men along behind them—eventually, after generations of failure, one will succeed in pushing the race a little further down the road to democratic equality. "One wave" out of the "multitudinous mass" will triumph. Paracelsus may have failed in his mission, but others will follow him. This has its parallel in Browning's own relationship to Wordsworth, himself a "great man"; Wordsworth, in the "Prospectus," had pointed out the path for others (in this case, Browning) to follow.

Browning has thus managed to turn to his own humanistic ends a romantic concept that could be seen as antihumanistic. He has "purified" the idea, and shown how it can fall away once it has been useful in a humanistic sense. The existence of such superior men is an augury of the potential inherent in all mankind:

> Prognostics told
> Man's near approach; so in man's self arise
> August anticipations, symbols, types
> Of a dim splendour ever on before,
> In the eternal circle life pursues:
> For men begin to pass their nature's bound,
> To have new hopes and cares which fast supplant
> Their proper joys and griefs; they grow too great
> For narrow creeds of right and wrong, which fade
> Before unmeasur'd thirst for good; while peace

Rises within them more and more.
Such men are even now upon the earth –
Serene among the half-form'd creatures round,
Whom they should save and join with them at last.

(5.760–73)

The idea of men passing "beyond their nature's bound" is one Browning had previously considered in *Paracelsus*; here it is a positive idea, since the "bounds" that are being passed are restricting. In passing them, man is becoming *more* human, since the potentiality of godhood is inherent in mankind. Paracelsus had previously pointed toward Münzer's peasant uprising as a sign of mankind's potential: "men seem made . . . for something better than these times can show" (3.1004–5). Revolutionary activity is a sign of hope; bearing this in mind, it seems likely that in these lines Browning is alluding to recent political events that seemed to point toward the eventual triumph of the radical cause (in particular, to the passing of the Reform Bill). *Paracelsus* is, indeed, a radical text, and Browning a radical poet. His radicalism is at its clearest in the following lines:

For wherefore make account of feverish starts
Of restless members of a dormant whole—
Impatient nerves which quiver while the body
Slumbers as in a grave? O long ago
The brow was twitch'd, the tremulous lids astir,
The peaceful mouth disturb'd—half-utter'd speech
Ruffled the lip; sometimes the teeth were set,
The breath drawn sharp, the strong right-hand clench'd stronger—
As it would pluck a lion by the maw:
The glorious creature laugh'd out even in sleep!

(5.740–49)

The lines hint at a future democratic uprising by "the glorious creature"—the mass of mankind. Browning reduces the aspirations of "great men" to "feverish starts / Of restless members of a dormant whole"—only significant in that they hint at the great awakening to come. (Perhaps these lines also hint at the glorious failure of the French Revolution, or some other abortive popular uprising.) Milton, Burns, and the rest (including Paracelsus, and, by implication, Browning himself) are but spasmodic twitches; the *real* cause for celebration is still to come:

But when arous'd—each giant-limb awake,
Each sinew strung, the great heart pulsing fast—
He shall start up, and stand on his own earth—
Then shall his long triumphant march begin—

Thence shall his being date; what thus collected
He shall achieve, shall be set down to him!

(5.750–55)

This revolution is not led by "great men," and will not collapse into murderous tyranny like the French Revolution; mankind will take possession of "his own earth" in democratic equality, and all he will achieve "shall be set down to him," not to "heroes" who aim only at self-aggrandizement.

Browning's scheme is overtly Wordsworthian. What appears baffling, at first glance, to the reader is the contrast between this revolutionary scheme and the reactionary Wordsworth had become by 1835. The Wordsworth Browning was acknowledging as his mentor in 1835 was not the man he would meet the next year, and this is almost certainly the reason for Browning's *personal* dislike of Wordsworth. As *Paracelsus* demonstrates, though, the reality of what Wordsworth had turned into did not invalidate what he had written earlier in his career; to devalue the earlier poems in the light of a later tailing off would be illogical.

As *Paracelsus* moves toward its conclusion, Browning is at such pains to leave the reader with a clear idea of his message that he hammers home his conclusions repeatedly: "God is glorified in man, / And to man's glory vow'd I soul and limb" (5.791–92). Religious faith is not incompatible with revolutionary fervor; they are united in a focus on man, God's supreme creation. Through man, one can reach out to God; the "Mind of Man" will be *Browning's* "main haunt," and the "main region" of his song. Nevertheless, such an intensive focus upon the present situation of humanity must not lead the aspiring practical humanist to a rejection of history: "I saw no cause why man / Should not be all-sufficient even now" (5.804–5). The humanist future must be built on secure foundations, and the desire to ruthlessly erase the lessons of history and build the world afresh must be avoided. In his dying moments, Paracelsus foresees a race that will retain its essential humanity and remember its earlier errors—"deep warnings of the proper tenure / By which thou hast the earth" (5.816–17). Man is *not* "some spirit / Flying secure and glad from heaven to heaven," and cannot be treated as if he were; like Wordsworth, Browning believes that the "heaven of heavens" is "but a veil" to the "Mind of Man" (5.822–23). He follows his mentor in passing "the choir / Of shouting Angels, and the empyreal throne" "unalarmed," exhorting his fellows to retain their consciousness of their own humanity: "but hope, and fear, and love, shall keep thee man."[70] This blatant repetition of his earlier reference to Wordsworth's humanistic list in the "Prospectus" confirms the hypothesis that Browning was following Wordsworth's lead in creating his concluding synthesis, and acknowledging his debt.

It is not enough to "love" mankind; one must have the "power" (i.e., the practical ability) to turn one's "love" into active assistance: "love still too straiten'd in its present means, / And earnest for new power to set it free" (5.846–47). If these two can be united, then progress can be made. The vision concludes with a declaration, in the optimistic spirit of radicalism, that mankind has an instinctive hankering after self-improvement. This proves that the humanistic mission Paracelsus has outlined will ultimately find success:

> All with a touch of nobleness, for all
> Their error, all ambitious, upward tending,
> Like plants in mines which never saw the sun,
> But dream of him, and guess where he may be.
>
> (5.867–70)

With these sparks of godliness in mind, future followers of Paracelsus will be able to unite Aprile's disinterested "love" for mankind and Paracelsus's practical focus on "power" to form "a temperate and equidistant world" in which humanity may be nursed toward fulfillment of its potential. With these hints, Paracelsus ends his sermon, and Browning concludes his poem, having used it to outline his vision of the potential inherent in Wordsworthian humanism. Things would change, however, and with surprising swiftness.

4
Wordsworth Rejected

IN 1835, BROWNING WAS HAPPY TO USE WORDSWORTH AS A MODEL. IN *SORDELLO*, published in 1840, there is a complete rejection of Wordsworth; he is condemned for ignoring the suffering around him. After 1840, Browning's poetry largely eschews Wordsworthian models, and he even explicitly attacks him in "The Lost Leader." His work concentrates on an "objective" study of "men and women," retaining the humanistic focus he had found in the work of Wordsworth and Shelley, but rejecting any "romantic" ideas of the poet as inspired visionary. Tucker points out that Browning's often "grotesque" and vigorous language implies a concern for the rough lives of ordinary people.[1] Loy D. Martin goes further, arguing that the peculiar merging of formality and colloquialism one finds in the dramatic monologue obviates altogether the romantic idea that one must choose between these two modes of poetry.[2] He goes on to argue that this blending of the conventional with the "rough" and "colloquial" could have been the product of a conflict on Browning's part with Wordsworth's superficially "radical"—but in fact overly idealistic—decision to introduce the language of "ordinary" people into poetry.[3] According to Martin, Browning refused to adopt the "extreme idealist solution" proposed by Wordsworth, which propounded an ahistorical language, choosing instead, after completing *Sordello*, to attempt to write a poetry more fully connected with "a particular time and place"—i.e., his own. Martin also argues that the synthesis Browning was struggling towards attempted to reconcile man with his own history, thereby avoiding the ahistoricizing instinct prevalent in Wordsworth's "idealist" language.[4] This perception of Browning's desire to rehistoricize poetry is shared by Tucker.[5] According to Martin, one of Browning's main arguments against Wordsworth after 1840 was that his excessive idealism distances man from the realities of his present as well as his past. He argues that Browning's post-1840 poetry demands the participation of the reader in a "democratic" sense, eschewing what Browning must have seen as the romantic tendency to preach.[6] As will be shown, Browning depicted Wordsworth in *Sordello* as a self-absorbed figure whose pronouncements neither encourage nor allow any sort of audience participation. What Martin calls the "autonomous poetic reality" is, after 1840, dismissed in favor of a poetry that is "an occasion for both poet and reader to express their independence."[7] Bloom has written how this "reductive" tendency to condemn one's predecessors for excessive idealism is a common one, and says that it characterizes Browning's relationship with Shelley: "[A]s the poets swerve downward in time, they deceive themselves into believing they are tougher-minded than their precursors."[8] This tendency is also manifested in Browning's misreading of Wordsworth in *Sordello*.

The movement from the inspired Wordsworthian synthesis of idealism and realism Browning presents to us in *Paracelsus* to a starker and more "grotesque" humanism (as Tucker puts it) is puzzling, particularly in conjunction with the misrepresentation of Wordsworth in *Sordello*. Browning knew perfectly well that Wordsworth was no deluded visionary. He had adopted Wordsworth as his poetic "father" by explicitly attempting to follow in his footsteps; what takes place in *Sordello* is, in fact, a form of poetic parricide. Why did Browning feel it necessary to "kill" his "father"?

What could have happened between 1835 and 1840 to turn Browning against Wordsworth? Browning met Wordsworth for the first time in 1836, and could have met him again on two brief occasions in 1837, and in May–June 1839. He would go on to meet him several times more, but only *after* the publication of *Sordello*. He told Gosse that he found Wordsworth's bearing "chilling and awful," and Gavan Duffy and Forster that his conversation was uninspiring. Thus, by 1840, Browning had met the old poet enough times to develop a personal dislike of him. Whether he heard Wordsworth discuss his conservative political opinions at any of these personal encounters is unclear, but Wordsworth's sole reference to Browning in a letter to Moxon (in reference to his marriage) is quietly sarcastic enough to indicate that the dislike was mutual.[9] Wordsworth certainly does not seem to have thought much of Browning's work, in the light of his reference to his "unintelligibility" (all the same, this reference does not mean that Wordsworth had actually read any Browning; he was probably parroting the fashionable cry about the "unreadable" *Sordello*). The only other reference to a comment of any kind by Wordsworth about Browning comes in a letter of 16 April 1846 from Browning to his future wife, and is similarly uncomplimentary (although rather more amusing, by Wordsworth's standards): "[T]here is a vast view from our greatest hill—did I ever tell you that Wordsworth was shown that hill or its neighbour; someone saying 'R.B. lives over *there* by that hill'—'Hill'? interposed Wordsworth—'*we* call that, such as that, a *rise*!'"[10] This dry comment links Browning with the insignificance of the miniature Parnassus on which he dwelt. The hills of Camberwell must have indeed appeared of little account to a man used to roaming the rugged fells of Cumberland, but one cannot help supposing Wordsworth was using the unimpressive London "rise" as an implicit analogy for the unimpressive London poet who dwelt by it. Real poets like himself, Wordsworth implies, live surrounded by *real* mountains. Cockney scribblers like Browning do not.

Browning would have found that the Wordsworth he met had little in common with the respected figure whose lead he followed in *Paracelsus*. Could this disappointment have disillusioned Browning to the extent that he was prepared to deny all that Wordsworth *had* symbolized to him? This seems improbable, particularly since Browning has little record of allowing personal feelings to influence his opinions of the work of fellow artists. Indeed, he was shocked when an attack on some of Rossetti's work in *Fifine* helped to drive the deeply disturbed poet and painter, a personal friend, to a suicide attempt.[11] Browning had the ability to avoid judging the man by the work, and vice versa; it is unlikely that he would have been so horrified by what Wordsworth had become that he felt compelled to deny the importance of everything he had ever written.

Could Browning have *heard*, or *read*, anything about Wordsworth during the period 1835–40 that would have influenced his opinion of him to such a radical extent? There is one obvious candidate for producing such material—Thomas De Quincey. As far as is known, Browning and De Quincey never met; during Browning's early London years, De Quincey was living (and usually hiding from his creditors) in Edinburgh. However, in January, February, and April 1839, *Tait's Edinburgh Magazine* published the first three parts of De Quincey's "Lake Reminiscences, from 1807 to 1830," and these articles dealt with De Quincey's unhappy relationship with Wordsworth in some detail.[12] By 1839, De Quincey's feelings towards Wordsworth had mutated from unquestioning admiration into something not far from hatred. Wordsworth's failure to assist him during his financial difficulties, coupled with the way the Wordsworths sneered at his lowborn wife, created a tremendous bitterness; following his wife's death in 1837 De Quincey's penury, coupled with his desire for revenge, led him to write three articles about Wordsworth for *Tait's*. It is strange that De Quincey should have chosen this magazine to publish these articles (and, indeed, the entire series of twenty-five articles he published there between 1834 and 1841 under the heading of "Sketches of Life and Manners: From the Autobiography of an English Opium-Eater"), since his own political opinions were of a Tory cast, and *Tait's* was a cheap radical magazine. Its publisher, William Tait, was Benthamite, and its contributors had included J. S. Mill, John Bright, Ebenezer Elliott, and Cobden.[13] De Quincey's parlous financial situation evidently meant that he could not afford to be too choosy about where his work appeared.

The articles on Wordsworth both filled De Quincey's purse and enabled him to publicly humiliate his former friend. Edmund Baxter has argued that the articles must also be seen as part of De Quincey's continuing attempt to *define* himself against his overwhelming contemporary.[14] He goes on to maintain that De Quincey is unable to free himself from Wordsworth's influence, since the poet is essentially unreachable. Faced with the impossibility of coming to grips with Wordsworth himself, De Quincey attempts to assert control over the poet's *works*, and in this he is more successful: "[B]y becoming, as it were, the original quoter of Wordsworth, De Quincey finishes Wordsworth's work."[15] Browning may therefore have been drawn to the articles by more than their subject matter. The evidence they contained of a struggle on De Quincey's part with Wordsworth, described by Baxter as "a figure of destructive energy" and "the prototype oppressor," and the way they depict De Quincey *misreading* Wordsworth's poetry in order to exercise control over him, would have reminded Browning of his own relationship with Wordsworth.[16] Unfortunately for Browning, the contents of the articles would not have made this relationship any easier.

The articles are particularly vicious in their subtlety—for example, De Quincey protests that while Wordsworth did indeed have ugly legs, "there was no absolute deformity about them."[17] More seriously, he declares the egocentric Wordsworth incapable of love: "that self-surrender . . . it seemed a mere impossibility that Wordsworth should be brought to feel for a single instant; and what he did not sincerely feel, assuredly he was not the person to profess."[18] De Quincey characteristically leavens his criticism with an implied compliment to Wordsworth's sincerity; even at this late stage, his attitude towards Wordsworth was a confused mixture of hatred, jealousy, and love. He goes on to portray Wordsworth as a man with a tendency to "admonish and lecture" his intellectual inferiors; he is said to be "looking down on the lady of his heart, as upon the rest of the world, from the eminence of his own intellectual superiority" (rather like the poets Wordsworth condemned in his "Preface").[19] Donald G. Marshall, in his foreword to Hartman's *The Unremarkable Wordsworth*, points out how Wordsworth was himself aware of the dangers of this way of seeing the world, and expresses this awareness in his poetry.[20] Browning would come to perceive Wordsworth's own consciousness of the dangers of this temptation later in his career, but at this stage he was coming, like De Quincey, to regard Wordsworth as simply a living exemplar of this sort of arrogance.

Spurred by resentment of his own poverty, De Quincey expresses bitter amusement at the singular fact that Wordsworth had experienced the greatest good fortune in financial matters: "[A]t measured intervals throughout the long sequel of his life since then, a regular succession of similar but superior God-sends have fallen in, to sustain his expenditure, duly as it grew with the growing claims upon his purse."[21] Indeed, De Quincey sneers, people dropped dead with such obliging promptitude as soon as their demise could be of any possible benefit to the poet that "had I happened to know of any peculiar adaption in any estate or office of mine, to any existing need of Wordsworth's—forthwith, and with the speed of a man running for his life, I would have laid it down at his feet. 'Take it', I would have said—'take it—or in three weeks I shall be a dead man.'"[22] Thus, declares De Quincey, "at all times he has been blessed with leisure, the very amplest that ever man enjoyed, for intellectual pursuits the most delightful; yes, that even for these delicate and coy pursuits, he had possessed, in combination, all the conditions for their most perfect culture—the leisure, the ease, the solitude, the society, the domestic peace, the local scenery—Paradise for his eye, in Miltonic beauty, lying outside his windows, Paradise for his heart, in the perpetual happiness of his own fire-side."[23] De Quincey is emphasizing Wordsworth's amazing good luck out of sheer resentment as he looks back at the sorry saga of his own life. At no time does he say that Wordsworth failed to make the proper *aesthetic* use of this lifetime of bliss, and failed to produce the work he owed the world for such an easy passage. On the contrary, he retained his admiration for Wordsworth the poet even as he lost faith in Wordsworth the man. What is interesting for the purpose of this study is the way De Quincey's emphasis on the ease of Wordsworth's life is repeated, as will be shown, by Browning in an angry letter to his future wife, in which he berates the older poet for producing nothing but *pulvis et cinis* (i.e., dust and ashes) after a lifetime living "the way of his own heart."[24] The letter was written in response to Elizabeth Barrett's description of a letter from Harriet Martineau that detailed the Wordsworths' domestic bliss; nonetheless, perhaps it was in De Quincey's article that Browning first encountered the idea.

All in all, the article is brutally offensive, particularly in the way it cruelly swipes at Dorothy Wordsworth, who is portrayed as a twitching, stuttering, "sexless" neurotic.[25] De Quincey even makes fun of Mary Wordsworth's eyes.[26] Unsurprisingly, Wordsworth was furious, though he claimed (unconvincingly) never to have read the "infamous production." "A man who can set such an example, I hold to be a pest in society, and one of the most worthless of mankind," he snarled.[27]

Could Browning have read De Quincey's articles, and could such a reading, coupled with his depressing encounters with the elderly poet at various social occasions, have turned Browning against Wordsworth to the dramatic extent that is found in *Sordello*? *Tait's*, a radical journal, would have been an obvious read for the Browning of the late 1830s. There is no direct evidence that Browning read it regularly, but there is, in the Armstrong Browning Library, a single copy of the September 1847 edition, containing an article on Elizabeth Barrett Browning by George Gilfillan, and inscribed with the poet's name "in an unidentified hand."[28] Browning would have obtained this copy simply to read the article about his wife, but this is at least an indication that he did not object to reading or purchasing *Tait's* on principle. De Quincey's articles created considerable controversy, and Browning could hardly have failed to be aware of them; it is extremely likely that he would have read them. Nevertheless, it seems unlikely that they did much more than confirm Browning in his *personal* dislike of Wordsworth. Reading about the way Wordsworth treated his wife would hardly have filled Browning with the desire to pop up to Rydal Mount for a quick visit, but it could not have inspired him to the heights of disparagement of Wordsworth's *poetry* he displays in *Sordello*. To discover the roots of Browning's savage attack on Wordsworth in *Sordello* one must look at the poem itself for clues.

Sordello, like Paracelsus, is a man on a mission: essentially, the same mission as his predecessor. Browning uses his career to present a man's struggle between the desire to separate oneself from one's fellows, and the contrasting desire to render assistance to mankind. All of this is very familiar, since both the narrator of *Pauline* and Paracelsus were equally torn. What is odd is that Browning should have felt it necessary to go over this ground *again*. Did not *Paracelsus* conclude with a vision of the solution of the problem? Why did Browning use *Sordello* to open old wounds? One has to put oneself in Browning's position when he completed *Paracelsus*. That poem's conclusion seemed to leave him with few options if he wished to continue writing poetry. Having set out his Wordsworthian vision, any future poems he would write would have to follow a set pattern and continue to describe the future awaiting mankind when it succeeded in creating for itself the synthesis glimpsed by the dying Paracelsus. It is hard to see how they could have been anything but rewritings of the earlier poem. In allowing himself to become so indebted to the earlier poet in writing *Paracelsus* as the conscious continuation of Wordsworth's scheme, Browning had simply followed in the direction in which Wordsworth was pointing. He had not attempted to define his own aesthetic identity apart from that of an astute and dedicated follower of Wordsworth.

It is an *aesthetic* motivation that must be sought for what happens in *Sordello*. If influence theory is used as a model, all becomes a good deal clearer. If Browning was a strong poet, he would have found the self-imposed burden of Wordsworth's inheritance intolerable. To break away, Browning would have had to find a way of dismissing Wordsworth as an appropriate model. His essential ambition—to write poetry that combined visionary and practical qualities—would remain unchanged; what he needed to do was to *misread* Wordsworth in such a way that he would be destroyed as a role model. Wordsworth would have to be misrepresented as antihumanistic. Browning would therefore have to go against everything he wrote in *Paracelsus*, and write as if that earlier Wordsworthian poem had never been written; such is the price demanded by the Cerberus who guards the path to strong poethood. The misreading performed in *Sordello* would combine clinamen and tessera. In fact, Browning represents *himself* as having picked up the torch Wordsworth has culpably dropped (or sold). The sheer unfairness of this misreading, in the light of *Paracelsus*, should be clear. Wordsworth *had* gone "far enough," and Browning knew it.

Using such a model, the rejection of Wordsworth in *Sordello* becomes much easier to understand; it is an act of aesthetic parricide performed by a son previously characterized by his obedience to the paternal will and conformity with the paternal life plan. Though Bloom has written how this process is usually neither "perverse" nor "ill-willed," Browning's misreading is *both*—the way he "forgets" *Paracelsus* is indeed "perverse," while his attack on Wordsworth in *Sordello* is actively aggressive.[29] The son must step over his father's corpse to achieve selfhood. Ironically enough, Sordello's *own* failure to achieve self-definition in this way is so total that the poem concludes with precisely the opposite image: the corpse of Sordello crumpled at the feet of his father, Salinguerra. Even more ironic is the realization that Sordello's demise can also be seen as a weird sort of "triumph" over his father, in that through his death he rejects Salinguerra's attempt to anoint him leader of the Ghibelline cause. In these ways the story Browning tells in the poem can be seen as a distorted reflection of his own battle against Wordsworth's "oppressive" influence.

The Father Slain: *Sordello*

Sordello's career has its parallels in Browning's two previous major poems, particularly in his vacillations between his idealist tendencies and his humanistic desire to focus on this world and his fellow men. He spends six books attempting to decide which path to take, and although he dies without any real earthly achievement the poem ends with a pointer towards the path of practical humanism espoused at the conclusion of *Paracelsus*, though it is stripped of many of the more visionary trappings of Paracelsus's vision. Nevertheless, in this poem Wordsworth is clearly linked by Browning to the visionary/idealist strand, to such a degree that his work is dismissed as antihumanistic. By the end of *Sordello*, it is clear that, for Browning, Wordsworth is not an acceptable model.

From the start of the poem it is clear that the conflict between the lyrical and idealistic self-expression of poets like Shelley and the more down-to-earth humanism Browning felt such poets to lack has broken out afresh. Browning imagines Shelley rebuking his attempt to address a wider audience, his "pure face" expressing distaste for the way his erstwhile admirer is behaving; indeed, Shelley's idealism is *so* pure that even Aeschylus and Sidney sound grating in comparison (1.59–73). This "purity" is attractive but dangerous. Later in book 1, Browning describes the two main classes of poetic temperament. The first class "use their senses introjectively: that is, their primary concern is with their own mind, considered as a repository for Platonic 'forms,' and they value experience only in so far as it prompts an inner manifestation of those forms."[30] The other class "worship the world rather than themselves" and "work towards the knowledge of God" in a gradualist fashion, running the risk, like Aprile, of becoming so lost in love for each successive object that the final vision is delayed or never attained:

> they would belong
> To what they worship—stronger and more strong
> Thus prodigally fed—that gathers shape
> And feature, soon imprisons past escape
> The votary framed to love and to submit
> Nor ask, as passionate he kneels to it,
> Whence grew the idol's empery.[31]

The real problem is with the first type of poet; although its introspective tendencies enable this class to avoid the perils of falling into thrall to the beauties of the world, such self-centeredness is corrupting. Browning sarcastically inquires of Sordello (who is at this stage categorized with the first class of poet) whether his own transcendence of earthly mundanity will help his less-privileged fellows:

> In truth? thou hast
> Life, then—wilt challenge life for us: thy race
> Is vindicated so, obtains its place
> In thy ascent, the first of us; whom we
> May follow, to the meanest, finally,
> With our more bounded wills?
>
> (1.548–53)

The implicit answer is no; Sordello's inner raptures will help the rest of mankind not a jot. In *Paracelsus* it was stated that progress was only possible through the "advance of individual minds"; here that gradualist vision is viewed in a more skeptical light. In fact, Browning makes it clear that this is not the path to follow:

> Ah, but to find
> A certain mood enervate such a mind,
> Counsel it slumber in the solitude
> Thus reached nor, stooping, task for mankind's good
> Its nature just as life and time accord
> (Too narrow an arena to reward
> Emprize—the world's occasion worthless since
> Not absolutely fitted to evince
> Its mastery).
>
> (1.553–61)

This "mood" is "enervating" because it corrodes any humanistic impulses in the poet. It will be recalled that in his "Prospectus" to *The Recluse* Wordsworth wrote of his ambition to describe

> How exquisitely the individual Mind
> (And the progressive powers perhaps no less
> Of the whole species) to the external World
> Is fitted: —and how exquisitely, too—
> Theme this but little heard of among Men—
> The external world is fitted to the Mind.
>
> (lines 63–68)

This is the *healthy* balance. Similarly, Wordsworth used the "Prospectus" to dismiss any ambitions to write of *other* worlds—his focus was to be "the Mind of Man." That Browning realized this was clearly demonstrated in *Paracelsus*. It is intriguing, then, to find Wordsworth ranked with this group of perniciously egocentric poets in *Sordello*. At first, there are only hints that Wordsworth is being associated with the traits Browning is condemning. Sordello is described as being in the "regal" class of men whom "Nature has broadly severed from her mass / Of men and framed for pleasure," which reminds the reader of Wordsworth's preface to *Lyrical Ballads* (1802): "[W]e have no sympathy but what is propagated by pleasure."[32] As Woolford and Karlin remark, this is "an important Romantic idea, usually with positive connotations."[33] Here, the connotations are rather less than positive, since Sordello, as a representative of the first class of poet, is soon to be associated with the dangerous traits previously described. For the first time, Wordsworth's *aesthetics* are being called into question. His "pleasure principle" is being linked with the egocentricity that will drag Sordello away into the arid tracts of introspection.

As book 1 continues, Browning describes his childhood at Goito, commencing with his apprehension of the natural world. The idea that the child has an awareness of the significance of the natural world that is unavailable to the adult is one that Browning would have found in many of Wordsworth's poems, including, most obviously, the "Immortality" Ode. This is where Browning really begins to attack Wordsworth's aesthetics; when he says that "amid his wild-wood sights [Sordello] lived alone: / As if the poppy felt with him" (1.704–5), he is taking the first of what will be several savage kicks at "nature" poetry like Wordsworth's. He had never before attacked Wordsworth's *poetry* in this way. The idea of "living alone" is a deeply suspicious one, humanistically considered; here Wordsworth is denigrated for his supposed obsession with rustic solitude. This attack was paralleled in several later Victorian critiques of Wordsworth; Matthew Arnold, for example, comparing Wordsworth (to his disadvantage) with Byron and Shelley, declared that he had "retired (in Middle-Age phrase) into a monastery. I mean, he plunged himself in the inward life, he voluntarily cut himself off from the modern spirit."[34] In the context of this passage, the attack is a fair one; but in the light of *Paracelsus*, it seems to be a calumny. When Browning concludes the first book of *Sordello* with the hero's plunge into "the veritable business of mankind" there is an implicit contrast with the concentration upon nature, which Browning will from now on associate, in this poem, with Wordsworth. Wordsworth has been firmly pushed into the camp of the enemies of humanism.

Sordello, in his continual introspection and arrogance, runs Paracelsus's risk of becoming antihumanistic almost by default. During a particularly excessive bit of self-adoration in book 2, during which Sordello has declared that he deserves "unexampled worship" since he idolizes only himself, Browning breaks into his reverie:

> (Dear monarch, I beseech,
> Notice how lamentably wide a breach
> Is here! discovering this, discover too
> What our poor world has possibly to do
> With it! As pigmy natures as you please—
> So much the better for you; take your ease;
> Look on, and laugh; style yourself God alone;
> Strangle some day with a cross olive-stone;
> All that is right enough: but why want us
> To know that you yourself know thus and thus?
> Nay finish—).
>
> (2.415–25)

This denunciation is one that Browning will repeat later in his career, aimed at Byron's scorn for his readers. Here, for the first time, Browning begins launching attacks on the very quality of Wordsworth's poetry that he saw as admirable in *Paracelsus*—his determination to focus on the workings of the "human heart." He uses Sordello's friend Naddo to utter a distorted and philistine reflection of Wordsworth's argument in the *Lyrical Ballads* preface that the poet is endowed with "nothing differing in kind from other men, but only in degree" since his "passions and thoughts and feelings are the general passions and thoughts and feelings of men":

> "The man, said we, tells his own joys and woes—
> We'll trust him. Would you have your songs endure?
> Build on the human heart! —Why to be sure
> Yours is one sort of heart—but I mean theirs,
> Ours, every one's, the healthy heart one cares
> To build on!"
>
> (2.796–801)

Naddo is clearly meant to be seen as an object of derision. What is bizarre is the fact that the desire to "build on the human heart" is surely the most humanistic of ideals, and a central ambition of the humanistic Browning. What reason could Browning have had to hold one of his most cherished desires up for mockery? The answer lies in the fact that it was not the *idea* that was being mocked, but the man who had expressed it. The reference to the "human heart" may be a covert allusion to Hazlitt's praise for Wordsworth in *The Spirit of the Age*, and thus a sneering allusion to this supposed ability of Wordsworth.[35] By 1840, Browning's desire to cast off Wordsworth's influence had become so intense that he was willing to resort not only to selective amnesia when it came to Wordsworth's humanistic track record, but also to attacks on aspects of Wordsworth's poetry he had always admired. In *Sordello* any aspect of Wordsworth's work is a fair target—his nature poetry, his theories of poetic composition, and even his humanism itself. Browning was determined to rid himself of Wordsworth and redefine himself as a strong poet, and was willing to do almost anything to discredit Wordsworth's achievement.

Browning may well be continuing to satirize Wordsworth through Naddo (as he did through Festus in *Paracelsus*) when Naddo ironically asks Sordello

> what avails a poet's heart
> Verona and her gauds? five blades of grass
> Suffice him. News? Why, where your marish was,
> On its mud-banks smoke rises after smoke
> I' the valley like a spout of hell new-broke.
>
> (3.226–30)

Naddo is making fun of Sordello's absorption by pretending to believe that poets should focus only on the natural world—the "five blades of grass"—and ignore the wider world of human activity. This seems, in the light of the earlier swipes at Wordsworth, to be another rather unfair attack upon him.[36] A few lines later, Naddo sneeringly asks Sordello whether he has "groped / Out wisdom in the wilds here?" (3.242–43). As Woolford and Karlin point out, in the Syracuse copy of the poem Browning penciled in "the new wisdom says custom" in the margin next to these lines—apparently indicating that the philistine Naddo ("Custom") is satirizing the "new wisdom" of nature, as employed by Wordsworth and the romantic poets in general.[37] There is a concern throughout the poem to trivialize Wordsworth's achievement, and—more importantly—to make it sound as antihumanistic as possible, in order to render Wordsworth unworthy of emulation.

Browning's Rededication to Humanity—and His Dismissal of Wordsworth

Browning uses the conclusion of book 3 of *Sordello* to remind himself of his duty to humanity. Sitting on "an empty palace-step / At Venice" he gazes upon the figure of a pathetic beggar-woman (or prostitute) and uses her suffering to remind himself of his responsibility (3.656ff.). It has not hitherto been pointed out that this situation has its parallel in *The Prelude*, in which Wordsworth's republican friend Beaupuis is inspired by the sight of a starving girl and her horse by the side of a road near Orleans to a fresh determination to fight against tyranny (9.509–32). Browning could not have read the lines in *The Prelude* at this stage, but he could have known of the story through De Quincey's retelling of it in one of his Wordsworth articles.[38] If the story was indeed in Browning's mind as he wrote book 3 of *Sordello*, it is interesting to speculate on his motives in re-creating the situation in his poem. Perhaps he was attempting to prove to the reader that the scene before him would lead *him* to a lasting self-consecration to humanity, rather than having little long-term effect, as it served his purposes to imply of Wordsworth. Browning admired Beaupuis, as described in *The Prelude*, and came to view him as a suitable model for those who would combine a "passion for reforming the world" (in Shelley's phrase) with practical action.

The "sad dishevelled ghost" who begs Browning for alms becomes a symbolic figure: in the running heads to the revised 1863 edition of *Sordello* she is referred to as "suffering humanity."[39] Her misery reminds Browning of his commitment to radical humanism. He imagines a young queen—perhaps Victoria (crowned a little over three weeks after Browning seems to have had this encounter)—casting aside the "crownet" that symbolizes her separation from her subjects and joining them:

> (e'en her disguised
> —Jewels in the locks that love no crownet like

Their native field-buds and the green wheat-spike,
So fair! —who left this end of June's turmoil,
Shook off, as might a lily its gold soil,
Pomp, save a foolish gem or two, and free
Came join the peasants o'er the kissing sea).

(3.678–84)

This is a republican vision of a new social order—for the queen to join the "peasants" is truly revolutionary in its implications.

Browning explained in a letter of May 1840 to his friend Fanny Haworth that the ragged figure who "plucks" at him was one "in which I put, comprize, typify and figure to myself Mankind, the whole poor-devildom one sees cuffed and huffed from morn to midnight, that, so typified, she may come at times and keep my pact in mind, prick up my republicanism and remind me of certain engagements I have entered into with myself about that same."[40] The "ghost" prods Browning firmly back onto the path of practical humanism and a revolutionary radicalism. The "engagements" are those Browning has "entered into" in order to use his poetry for humanistic purposes.

Browning goes on to emphasize the *realism* of his commitment in implied contrast to the dreams of utopians. He recognizes that to make the whole human race equally happy and prosperous is impossible; addressing the "vision," he admits that there is not even enough happiness to be shared between mother and child:

Confess
You have so niggard stock of happiness
To share that, do one's uttermost, dear wretch,
One labours ineffectually stretch
It o'er you so that mother, children, both
May equitably flaunt the sumter-cloth!

(3.685–90)

All one can do is try to make the best of what little happiness there is to spare:

No: tear the robe yet farther: be content
With seeing some few score pre eminent
Through shreds of it, acknowledged happy wights,
Engrossing what should furnish all, by rights—

(3.691–94)

This is cold comfort—that one should parade the happier members of society, "be they Peasants, be they Queens" "for the common credit," and shrug that the "luckless residue" who "we send to crouch / In corners out of sight" had an equal chance of happiness, thwarted only by bad luck (3.705–12). All art should do is present the world as it is, rather than create unrealistic pictures of "scholars, chiefs and kings" (3.695). In the 1863 edition of the poem, this passage has been rewritten in order to make Browning's criticism of idealism more evident:

> I ask youth and strength
> And health for each of you, not more—at length
> Grown wise, who asked at home that the whole race
> Might add the spirit's to the body's grace,
> And all be dizened out as chiefs and bards.[41]

"[A]t home"—i.e., in England—Browning pursued unrealistic dreams of a perfectible humanity, all of whom could be helped in a spiritual rather than merely physical way. Browning is condemning the democratic vision of Paracelsus as delusory. All the humanist can realistically hope to achieve, he seems to be saying, is to alleviate *bodily* suffering—grant as many people as possible "youth and strength / And health"—no more. They can never become "chiefs and bards." Browning has lowered his aims. He seems to find a strange joy in this abandonment of so much of what he had believed possible. Indeed, he sees something positive in human suffering, a necessary sacrifice, part of the divine plan: "warped men, souls, bodies! yet God spoke / Of right-hand foot and eye – selects our yoke" (3.755–56). The "warped men" fill him with horror, but also with hope. This is all very well, but it does not alter the fact that Browning has detached himself from the scheme delineated at the conclusion of *Paracelsus*. Where does this leave Wordsworth?

If the rejection of the Wordsworthian aesthetic embraced in *Paracelsus* is part of Browning's attempt to escape from Wordsworth's influence, then it would be logical for him to disparage Wordsworth's influence even on his new, more realistic brand of humanism. Browning is distorting the angle from which he sees Wordsworth, in order to make him appear as ridiculous as possible. He is plainly talking of Wordsworth when he attacks poets who hint that they have profound insights to communicate while producing trivial verse:

> A slight advance
> Merely to find the sickness you die through
> And nought beside: but if one can't eschew
> One's portion in the common lot, at least
> One can avoid an ignorance increased
> Tenfold by dealing out hint after hint
> How nought is like dispensing without stint

The water of life—so easy to dispense
Beside, when one has probed the centre whence
Commotion's born—could tell you of it all.

(3.778–87)

Browning is satirizing the claim of Wordsworth's admirers that he was privileged with the ability to gaze "into the human heart" and dispense the "water of life." It is unlikely that Browning had read Keats's letters at this stage—they would not be published until 1848—but he was acquainted with Richard Monckton Milnes, and *may* have been able to read those in his collection. If so, his dismissal of Wordsworth's ability to probe "the centre whence / Commotion's born" (i.e., the human heart) may have been influenced by Keats's declaration that Wordsworth's poetry was explorative of the "dark passages" of human existence.[42] Here this claim is said to be fraudulent. If Keats may be alluded to here, Hazlitt definitely is: in *The Spirit of the Age* he had given Wordsworth the very high humanist praise that he sees "nothing loftier than human hopes, nothing deeper than the human heart."[43] Later in the passage is a more explicit allusion to Hazlitt. This praise is negated entirely in the lines that follow. The "Wordsworth" figure cannot offer his listeners "the water of life"; instead, he expects them to draw sustenance from his trivial nature poetry: "meantime, just meditate my madrigal / O' the mugwort that conceals a dewdrop safe" (3.788–89). Browning goes on to make it clear that he despises this sort of poet in an allusion to the Exodus story of the thirsty Israelites traveling through the wilderness of Zin:

What, dullard? we and you in smothery chafe,
Babes, baldheads, stumbled thus far into Zin
The Horrid, getting neither out nor in,
A hungry sun above us, sands among
Our throats, each dromedary lolls a tongue,
Each camel churns a sick and frothy chap,
And you, 'twixt tales of Potiphar's mishap
And sonnets on the earliest ass that spoke,
Remark you wonder any one needs choak
With founts about!

(3.790–99)

All of the human race are in the same predicament, and Browning is angry at the way the poet produces indulgent, irrelevant poetry rather than work that recognizes human suffering. All this distorted Wordsworth can offer his listeners are pointless stories and, worse still, "founts" of "the water of life" that exist only in his reveries. He has completely neglected the "engagements" Browning had entered into. Browning is so furious at this dereliction of duty that he recommends that the "dullard" be thrown aside, to be replaced with a poet who has a better idea of his duties:

> Potsherd him, Gibeonites,
> While awkwardly enough your Moses smites
> The rock, though he forego his Promised Land
> Thereby, have Satan claim his carcass, and
> Dance, forsooth, Metaphysic Poet . . . ah
> Mark ye the first dim oozings? Meribah!
>
> (3.799–803)

Who is the "Moses" who, "awkwardly" enough, strikes the rock and brings his people sustenance? It is Browning himself, who, despite his unpolished style, has retained his humanistic instincts and can thus actually provide the "founts" the other poet saw only in visions. Browning knows that he will be calumniated as a "Metaphysic Poet" whose knotty complexity alienates his audience, but is confident that his ambitions will eventually lead to the waters of Meribah. It is the other poet who is the true "Metaphysic Poet" (in a pejorative sense).

That Browning is speaking about Wordsworth is confirmed by another Hazlitt reference. In *The Spirit of the Age* Hazlitt says of Wordsworth that "he gathers manna in the wilderness; he strikes the barren rock for the gushing moisture."[44] Thus he grants Wordsworth the very ability that Browning denies him in *Sordello*. Browning dethrones Wordsworth from the humanistic position in which Hazlitt had placed him, and assumes that throne for himself. The lines are the clearest illustration in *Sordello* of the "creative misreading" Browning is performing; the dismissal of Wordsworth's humanism allows Browning to present him as a "dullard" who must be thrown aside. It is interesting that it is the Gibeonites whose duty it is to destroy the useless poet, since they were a tribe condemned to be "hewers of wood and drawers of water" for the Israelite temple: "[T]hey traditionally symbolize the common labouring people."[45] The poet has principally failed to help these people; it is entirely appropriate that they should punish him. By misrepresenting Wordsworth in this fashion Browning could then step forward himself to assume the crown Wordsworth had worn unworthily. He could thus stand self-defined as a strong poet, free of the "burden of the past," and ready, "awkwardly enough," to continue his humanistic work, while Wordsworth groveled in the dust.

With Wordsworth out of the way, Browning is free to use the rest of Sordello's career to illustrate the program he wants to pursue—in much the same way as he used Paracelsus. Sordello follows his creator in dedicating himself to the masses, deciding to serve, not rule, mankind, and hoping to achieve some sort of union with them. "How render then these people happy?" he asks himself; his mission is to first drag them all "up to the (average) mark—& thence proceed to the further development," as Browning wrote in a marginal note in the Syracuse copy of the poem.[46] Later in book 4 Sordello uses the story of the republican hero Crescentius to spur himself on, and decides to espouse the Guelf cause as the closest approximation to his ideal (4.927–75). He has to embrace a gradualist vision of human progress, as Paracelsus did in his concluding vision (5.1–73). In all this there is little change from the scheme propounded at the conclusion of *Paracelsus*; the real difference is the way that Wordsworth has been removed from the equation so utterly.

Sordello is haunted by the idea that he may abandon his mission and devote the rest of his life to bland, conformist poetry:

> —One way or other idle life out, drop
> No few smooth verses by the way – for prop
> A thyrsus these sad people should, the same,
> Pick up, set store by, and, so far from blame,
> Plant o'er his hearse convinced the better part
> Survived him. Rather tear men out the heart
> Of the truth! Sordello muttered.
>
> (5.365–71)

This may be an attack on the way Wordsworth devoted his later life to producing "no few smooth verses," either apolitical or reactionary in content. The reference to the way the deluded people set the poet's inferior work up as his most appropriate monument, or greatest work, may be an indication of how much Browning's attitude had changed towards *The Excursion*. In 1835, Browning admired the poem. Come 1840, there is what seems to be a declaration that those who believed *The Excursion* to be Wordsworth's "better part" were mistaken. Wordsworth is no longer accorded the ability to "tear men out the heart / Of the truth."

Nevertheless, Browning is not entirely successful in his attempts to free himself from Wordsworth. Several times in the later books of *Sordello* he uses Wordsworthian ideas to clarify Sordello's mission—as when Sordello tells the yawning Salinguerra that "Song" is the product of gradualist progression (an idea first mooted in *Paracelsus*):

> The fullest effluence of the finest mind
> All in degree, no way diverse in kind
> From those about us, minds which, more or less,
> Lofty or low, in moving seek impress
> Themselves on somewhat; but one mind has climbed
> Step after step, by just ascent sublimed.
>
> (5.541–46)

This seems to have its source in the preface to *Lyrical Ballads*, in which Wordsworth declares that "among the qualities which I have enumerated as principally conducting to form a Poet, is implied nothing differing in kind from other men, but only in degree."[47] Similarly, later in the same book, Browning's description of Sordello's insistence on the active participation of the reader reminds one of Wordsworth's description of the "co-operating *power* in the mind of the Reader" in the "Essay, Supplementary to the Preface" of 1815.[48] Again, Wordsworth is cited (only to be superseded) when Browning speaks of the poet's need to communicate intelligibly with his fellows:

> leave the mere rude
> Explicit details, 'tis but brother's speech
> We need, speech where an accent's change gives each
> The other's soul—no speech to understand
> By former audiences—need was then expand,
> Expatiate—hardly were they brothers! true—
> Nor I lament my less remove from you,
> Nor reconstruct what stands already.
>
> (5.614–21)

This updates Wordsworth's insistence that the poet must "express himself as other men express themselves." Woolford and Karlin point out that in this passage Browning "shares Wordsworth's concern with breaking down artificial stylistic barriers," with the qualification that he sees the earlier poetic style as having been useful, and this is certainly the case; Browning would also use the idea of the poet perched on a "supposed height" (also in this passage) several times later in his work, to symbolize the dangers of introspection.[49] What is puzzling here is the way that Browning, having dismissed Wordsworth so brutally, should then return in the same poem to Wordsworthian passages that support his arguments. The solution probably lies in the sheer totality of Wordsworth's dismissal; the clothes of the vanquished can be rifled for the spoils of war without any chance of resistance. Having been "potsherded" (a Browning neologism that seems to mean that Wordsworth has been smashed into small pieces, like a broken pot), Wordsworth is in no condition to resist if his ideas are brazenly flaunted by his conqueror. (Interestingly, Bloom has taken the name of one of the revisionary ratios he discusses—tessera—from the "ancient mystery cults"; Browning is, in the present case, using the "fragments" of the shattered Wordsworth for his own purposes.)[50] He has been reduced to a simple store of potentially useful aesthetic ideas, like any other previous writer with whom Browning had no power struggle, no anxieties of influence.

With Wordsworth thus emasculated, Browning is rendered free to continue his self-definition as a strong poet. Sordello experiences a similar epiphany to that of his creator when he is confronted by a visionary apparition of "the People," who mock the lifeless indulgence of his so-called "self-sufficiency":

> And now content thy stronger vision, brood
> On thy bare want; the grave stript turf by turf,
> Study the corpse-face thro' the taint-worm's scurf!
>
> (5.154–56)

He determines to deal with the present existence of the common people: "down sank the People's Then; uprose their Now" (5.159). As he later says, "'twere too absurd to slight / For the hereafter the to-day's delight" (5.381–82). Sordello is unable to put his plans into practice; nevertheless, he dies focused on the path of practical humanism, having rejected the idle vision of "self-sufficiency" that tempted him (as it had tempted the *Pauline* narrator and Paracelsus before him). The ultimate conclusion of Sordello—that one must focus on the quotidian world—is little changed from that of *Paracelsus*.

The Browning who published *Sordello* felt himself to be a free man. The situation of power that had been in place in 1835 had been completely reversed, and Browning, the strong poet, was now the master, free to pursue his own path (leading ultimately to the humanist epic *The Ring and the Book*) without fearing that he was merely regurgitating romantic, and specifically Wordsworthian, ideas. For almost thirty years, he would limit his references to Wordsworth to the dismissive, or openly abusive, as he strove to write his own unique kind of poetry. However, Wordsworth's ghost, "chilling and awful," could not be dismissed so easily. The struggle would be renewed, and would never be resolved.

5

Wordsworth Erased

The "Essay on Chatterton"

It is unclear how much of Browning's misreading was the result of a conscious decision. That Browning had a pretty clear idea of the way poets struggle to throw off the influence of their predecessors is, however, apparent from a reading of his "Essay on Chatterton," which appeared anonymously in the *Foreign Quarterly Review* in July 1842, about two years after the completion of *Sordello*. The essay contains an open attack on Wordsworth when Browning declares that "in a word, Chatterton's life was not the Lie it is so universally supposed to have been; nor did he 'perish in the pride' of refusing to surrender Falsehood and enter on the ways of Truth."[1] Browning is here misquoting "Resolution and Independence" and using Wordsworth as an exemplar of those who have, in his opinion, misinterpreted Chatterton's career. Of more interest with regards to *Sordello* is Browning's attempt to explain Chatterton's career, which sheds considerable light on his own interpretation of his pre-*Sordello* career. He interprets Chatterton's first forgeries as having sprung out of aesthetic, not merely mercenary, motives:

> Genius almost invariably begins to develop itself by imitation. It has, in the short-sightedness of infancy, faith in the world: and its object is to compete with or prove superior to, the world's already recognized idols, at their own performance and by their own methods. This done, there grows up a faith in itself: and, no longer taking the performance or method of another for granted, it supersedes these by a process of its own. It creates, and imitates no longer. Seeing cause for faith in something external and better, and having attained to a moral end and aim, it next discovers in itself the only remaining antagonist worthy of its ambition, and in the subduing what at first had seemed its most enviable powers, arrives at the more or less complete fulfillment of its earthly mission. The first instinct of Imitation, which with the mediocre takes the corresponding mediocre form of an implied rather than expressed appropriation of some other man's products, assumed

> perforce with Chatterton, whose capabilities were of the highest class, a proportionably bolder and broader shape in the direction his genius had chosen to take.[2]

If this theory is applied to Browning's own career, an almost perfect match will be found. As Maynard points out, he began his own poetic career "by imitation": first of "Ossian," then of Byron, in the lost *Incondita* volume.[3] He was trying "to compete with, or prove superior to, the world's already recognized idols"—mainly Byron in these very early works—"at their own performances and by their own methods." By *Pauline* tension had already began to arise between his romantic models and his own desire for self-definition outside the romantic pattern. These tensions give *Pauline* its tortured quality, as Browning's instinctive desire to create a more humanistic form of romanticism began to push him away from his models. Donald Smalley points out how closely Browning's aesthetic scheme fits the career of the poet-narrator of *Pauline*—and thus that of Browning himself.[4] Browning's humanistic and radical instincts served as the "moral end and aim" that propelled him, after *Pauline*, along the path to self-definition. *Paracelsus* was Browning's last effort to force his own ambitions to run along the lines established by his predecessors—in this case, Wordsworth. In *Paracelsus* Browning was attempting to "compete with, or prove superior to" Wordsworth by writing the sort of poetry Wordsworth had perceived as possible, but found it impossible to write. Nevertheless, the very Wordsworthian premise and nature of the poem marked him out as an imitator rather than an innovator. Browning knew that his abilities were "of the highest class"; unfortunately, in *Paracelsus* they had merely produced an imitation of "a proportionably bolder and broader shape" than other followers of Wordsworth were capable of writing, rather than an original work that would serve as the "complete fulfillment of [Browning's] earthly mission." Browning would have realized that he would have to subdue his desire to follow the romantics (and Wordsworth in particular)—"what had at first seemed [his] own most enviable powers"—in order to stand on his own two feet as a strong poet.

Browning's task was easier than Chatterton's. Unlike Chatterton, he had not foisted his early imitative works on the world under assumed identities (though his famous note to Forster on the copy of *Pauline* he presented to him implies that the younger Browning had, for a period, dreamed of such a Chattertonian enterprise).[5] He had not built up a "worse than St Anna dungeon" for himself through his own deceptions, and was able to proceed on his task of self-definition with fewer hindrances. The passage does not deal with the misreading Browning had to perform to give himself the freedom to set about the "complete fulfillment" of his aesthetic mission; nevertheless, the parallels indicate that Browning had a pretty shrewd idea of the nature of his difficulties with Wordsworth, and was robust in his belief that imitative works had to be abandoned, however unfairly, if he was to progress.

Another part of the "Essay" seems, weirdly, to point forward to Browning's later reexamination of romanticism. In describing Tasso's "madness," Browning says that his imprisonment at St. Anna "was but an unremitting attempt to free himself from the effect of this false step without being compelled to reveal the truth, and disavow his whole proceedings since the time of that sad starting-aside from the right way."[6] As will become apparent, this is an amazingly accurate description of the quandary Browning was to find himself in once he had admitted to himself that the dismissal of Wordsworth (and romanticism) in *Sordello*—his own "sad starting-aside from the right way"— had led to a protracted barking up the wrong tree that encompassed all his most famous work. The baffling *Fifine* would be—in part—Browning's attempt to "free himself" from his "false step" (i.e., his misreading of Wordsworth) without "being compelled to reveal the truth."

"The Lost Leader"

The misreading of Wordsworth left Browning free to attack his predecessor more openly than in that poem. *Sordello* met almost universal derision and incomprehension upon its appearance, and there is no indication that any critic read the poem carefully enough to uncover the attack on Wordsworth within it. It became a byword for incomprehensibility, and that is all. Indeed, there is an indication that Wordsworth himself had heard of its reputation in his cutting remark upon Browning's marriage; he wrote to Edward Moxon on October 12, 1846, "Miss Barrett, I am pleased to learn, is so much recovered as to have taken to herself a Husband. Her choice is a very able man, and I trust that it will be a happy union, not doubting that they will speak more intelligibly to each other than, notwithstanding their abilities, they have yet done to the public."[7] This is Wordsworth's only extant reference to Browning's work. Despite the description of Browning as a "very able man," it hardly exudes warmth—more the "chilling and awful" quality Browning spoke of to Gosse. One wonders, all the same, why Wordsworth bothered to call Browning "very able"; perhaps he had, after all, glanced at *Paracelsus*, which would certainly have been more to his taste than *Sordello*.

After *Sordello* Browning could afford to return the "compliment," and he did so, most famously in "The Lost Leader" and in his courtship correspondence. Wordsworth accepted the position of poet laureate on April 4, 1843; Browning saw this as his final surrender to the forces of conservatism. In fact, Wordsworth's acceptance of the post could not have come at a better time. After *Sordello*, any aspect of Wordsworth's behavior that discredited him could be eagerly seized upon by Browning and used to confirm the negative picture of Wordsworth he had to maintain. Seen in this light, the image of Wordsworth on his knees in front of the queen was a positive boon.

This combination of hatred and indignation emerged into the public domain in "The Lost Leader." It would be published in November 1845, in *Dramatic Romances and Lyrics*, and it stands as Browning's most explicit *public* attack on Wordsworth. Several times later in his career, Browning himself admitted that the "Lost Leader" was modeled on Wordsworth.[8] In response to an inquiry by Alexander Grosart in 1875 he confessed,

> [I] *did* in my hasty youth presume to use the great and venerable personality of Wordsworth as a sort of painter's model; one from which this or the other particular feature may be selected and turned to account: had I intended more, above all, such a boldness as portraying the entire man, I should not have talked about "handfuls of silver and bits of ribbon." These never influenced the change of politics in the great poet; whose defection, nevertheless, accompanied as it was by a regular about-face of his special party, was to my juvenile apprehension, and even mature consideration, an event to deplore . . . so, though I dare not deny the original of my little poem, I altogether refuse to have it considered as the "very effigies" of such a moral and intellectual superiority.[9]

One should note the reluctance Browning displays in confessing to his use of Wordsworth, and the qualifications he hedges around this confession; this reluctance has its parallel in Browning's correspondence with William Knight about Wordsworth, and stems from a reluctance to openly discuss a later change of opinion that led Browning to see Wordsworth once again in a positive light.

Browning used "The Lost Leader" to attack Wordsworth's conservatism, having destroyed his *aesthetic* worth in *Sordello*. The poem does not merely make a vague accusation of complicity on Wordsworth's behalf, but mounts a more specific attack that alleges that Wordsworth used his poetic abilities to assist in the state's suppression of protest; this attack has a source in a particular Wordsworth poem. Wordsworth published "The Warning" in his *Yarrow Revisited* volume of 1835. It is an openly political work, "composed during the fever spread through the Nation by the Reform Bill," as Wordsworth tells us in a short preface to the poem. The poem is a rather hysterical "warning" to the people of Britain to avoid being ensnared by the traps of wicked leaders motivated by personal ambition. The people may, Wordsworth alleges, be

> to the giddy top of self-esteem
> By Flatterers carried, mount into a dream
> Of boundless suffrage, at whose sage behest
> Justice shall rule, disorder be supprest,
> And every man sit down as Plenty's Guest!
>
> (lines 124–28)

The poem reflects an accusation of Browning's. One of the worst crimes of the Lost Leader is that he instructed the oppressed masses to *bear* their burden rather than rise up against their rulers: "deeds will be done, while he boasts his quiescence, / Still bidding crouch whom the rest bade aspire" (lines 19–20). The Lost Leader "boasts" of his own patient acquiescence in tyranny and tells the victims of oppression to meekly do the same. In "The Warning" Wordsworth asks,

> Thus ungrateful Nation!
> If thou persist, and, scorning moderation,
> Spread for thyself the snares of tribulation,
> Whom, then, shall meekness guard? What saving skill
> Lies in forbearance, strength in standing still?
>
> (lines 146–50)

Wordsworth is suggesting that "meekness," "forbearance," and "standing still" are the true ways forward. He is "bidding" the masses "crouch" and "bear" their yoke; "aspiration" is, for him, an illusion. He concludes the poem on a similar note, instructing his soul to "seek for the good and cherish it—the ill / Oppose, or bear with a submissive will" (lines 161–62).

Here Wordsworth is, indeed, boasting of his "quiescence." Any idea of opposing the "ill" is undercut by the alternative of patient endurance. Wordsworth is not simply "bidding" (the same word Browning uses in his poem) *himself* "lie still," but the entire nation as well.

It seems that Browning had "The Warning" in mind when he wrote "The Lost Leader." His attack on Wordsworth was not as unfair as some have claimed, and as Browning seems to have feared in later life. Wordsworth may not have deserted the radicals for "a handful of silver," but he certainly *did* "bid crouch whom the rest bade aspire"—in this poem, at least. "The Lost Leader" appeared in 1845, and it would be interesting to know whether Wordsworth was aware of it, and, if so, whether he recognized himself. Daniel Karlin has mentioned this as a possibility.[10] Perhaps the poem contributed to the scorn Wordsworth seems to have felt for Browning. Interestingly, though, in a manner uncharacteristic of him, Browning was unable to leave the poem alone. Woolford and Karlin describe this curious act of ongoing revisionism in some detail; overall, the changes progressively moderate the poem's attack on Wordsworth.[11] Woolford and Karlin also point out a strange anomaly: the text of the poem as printed in Browning's *Selections* of 1872, although mostly retaining the "softened" readings adopted in earlier editions, *strengthens* the attack on Wordsworth by printing "one more devil's triumph and sorrow to angels" where earlier versions had referred to devils in the plural (i.e., Wordsworth's apostasy causes rejoicing in Hell), rather than implying, as this version does, that Wordsworth is a or even *the* devil.[12] This version of the poem seems to indicate a lingering ambiguity toward Wordsworth even at this stage: "the more truculent 1845 version symbolically survives as a kind of ghost behind the arras in the line intercalated from it."[13] These revisions are broadly in accordance with Browning's changing attitude toward Wordsworth throughout his career; from 1840 onward, Browning would find his attempt to "erase" Wordsworth's influence harder and harder, and he would eventually reach a sort of reconciliation—at precisely the time he was assembling the 1872 *Selection*, curiously enough. Perhaps the 1872 version of "The Lost Leader" is the product of this turmoil.

Nevertheless, poems like "The Warning" suited the immediate purposes of the post-1840 Browning, since they displayed the reactionary side of Wordsworth that Browning needed to emphasize in order to keep the genie in its bottle. By keeping this image of Wordsworth in front of his eyes—and those of his readers—Browning could avoid reminders of the poet of *The Excursion*, and his influence on *Paracelsus*. A considerable degree of the animosity displayed toward Wordsworth in this period seems to stem from Browning's suppressed consciousness of his aesthetic debt. The attacks can be interpreted as a desperate use of all available materials in an attempt to make Wordsworth look as ridiculous, and insignificant, as possible.

Browning's Explicit Attacks on Wordsworth

At around the period that Wordsworth became poet laureate, Browning mounted one of his most wounding attacks on the old poet in a letter to R. H. Horne.[14] Indeed, so cruel was the attack that Browning asked Horne not to publish it. Horne had asked Browning for a suitable epigraph for his chapter on Wordsworth in his *New Spirit of the Age*, and Browning brutally suggested the following lines from book 10 of *Paradise Lost* (omitting 444):

> He, thro' the midst unmarked,
> In show plebeian angel militant,
> Of lowest order, passed: and from the door
> Ascended his high throne, which, under state
> Of richest texture spread, at the upper end

Was placed in regal lustre. Down awhile
He sat, and round about him saw unseen.
At last, as from a cloud, his fulgent head
And shape star-bright appeared, or brighter, *clad*
With what permissive glory since his Fall
Was left him, or false glitter. All amazed
At that so sudden blaze, the *Stygian throng*
Bent their aspect [Browning's italics].

Browning followed the quotation with the sardonic comment "as Jeffrey does in the reprint of his review of the Excursion: this is too good a bit, I fear: take the kinder side of the matter and give him some or all of your own fine sonnet."[15] This is the most vicious attack Browning ever mounted on Wordsworth; *Sordello* condemned him as useless, but did not ascribe active calculation or malice to him. The slighting references to Wordsworth in Browning's correspondence with his future wife smack more of disappointment than the cold accusation found here. Browning is declaring that the entirety of Wordsworth's career has been a sham. His early years of obscurity, of writing unpalatable poetry "in a selection of the language really used by men", had simply been a way to move "unseen" in "plebeian" guise until he saw his moment. His sympathy for the oppressed was merely an assumed disguise. His recognition as the leading poet of the age, and acceptance of public office, is the result of a sordid betrayal of his erstwhile companions—all the honors heaped upon him are "*false glitter*," and his "*Fall*" from grace leaves him only the "*permissive glory*" his new masters grant him. Browning also strikes out at those (like Jeffrey) who had long derided Wordsworth, only to praise him when it became fashionable to do so and pour fuel onto the "sudden blaze" of Wordsworth's fame.

Browning continued to attack Wordsworth in his correspondence with Elizabeth Barrett, notwithstanding Elizabeth's own continued admiration for the older poet. Simply abusive are Browning's references to the bald old poet appearing at court in Samuel Rogers's borrowed "bag-wig"—"to the manifest improvement of the Laureate's pocket, but more problematic improvement of his person, when one thinks of the astounding difference of 'build' in the two poets"—and flopping pathetically down on his knees before the queen "to be picked up by two lords-in-waiting."[16] Much more interesting is a sudden explosion of rage against Wordsworth that comes in response to Elizabeth's description of a letter from Harriet Martineau describing Wordsworth's domestic situation at Rydal Mount. Martineau found it all rather cozy and charming, but Browning finds it anything but:

> She plainly sees the proper use and advantage of a country-life; and *that* knowledge gets to seem a high point of attainment doubtless by the side of

> the Wordsworth she speaks of—for *mine* he shall not be as long as I am able! Was there ever such a "*great*" poet before? Put one trait with the other—the theory of rural innocence—alternation of "vulgar trifles" with dissertating with style of "the utmost grandeur that *even you* can conceive" (speak for yourself, Miss M.!)—and that amiable transition from two o'clock's grief at the death of one's brother to three o'clock's happiness at the "extraordinary mesmeric discourse" of one's friend. All this, and the rest of the serene and happy inspired daily life which a piece of "unpunctuality" can ruin, and to which the guardian "brings" as crowning qualification the knack of poking the fire adroitly—of this—what can one say but that—no, best hold one's tongue and read the "Lyrical Ballads" with finger in ear. Did not Shelley say long ago "He had no more *imagination* than a pint-pot"—though in those days he used to walk about France and Flanders like a man? *Now*, he is "most comfortable in his worldly affairs" and just this comes of it! He lives the best twenty years of his life after the way of his own heart—and when one presses in to see the result of the rare experiment . . . what the *one* alchemist whom fortune has allowed to get all his coveted materials and set to work at last in earnest with fire and melting-pot—what *he* produces after all the talk of him and the like of him; why, you get *pulvis et cinis*—a man at the mercy of the tongs and shovel![17]

The roots of this outburst lie in the admiration of Wordsworth that characterized *Paracelsus*. The attack is akin to the rage of a disappointed lover. Browning begins his litany of disappointment with a list of Wordsworth's less appealing personal traits, as displayed in Martineau's letter. Wordsworth's "theory of rural innocence" and his droning "personal" talk are merely irritating, and his ability to swiftly forget his brother's death in the course of an afternoon is an indication of his self-centeredness; rather more upsetting to Browning is Wordsworth's allowing himself to sink into a "serene and happy inspired daily life," tended continually by a subservient wife. Browning would certainly have found this reduction of Mary Wordsworth to the status of housemaid repugnant, but there is a deeper reason why this vision fills him with disgust. De Quincey resented the way that Wordsworth had been granted a largely free and untroubled life, in contrast with his own; all the same, there is no indication in his articles that he felt that Wordsworth had wasted the opportunity this period had granted him to produce a really important body of work. Browning, however, feels resentment of Wordsworth's good fortune for aesthetic, not personal, reasons. He is angry with Wordsworth *as a poet*. What really infuriates him is the way he had failed in his duty to produce work worthy of him in the "best twenty years of his life." The Wordsworth of 1846 is, as well as being a selfish old bore, a rotten poet; granted what almost no other poet has ever had—ideal working conditions, good health, a loving and subservient wife and few distractions—the sage of Rydal Mount, like the servant in the parable, buried his talent/talent instead of using it. Wordsworth has squandered his "rare experiment" and ended up sitting amidst dust and ashes, when he *ought* to have produced work for the whole world to marvel at.

This attack clearly indicates that even in 1846, six years after the publication of *Sordello*, Browning was still deeply troubled by Wordsworth. The *Sordello* dismissal of Wordsworth was calculated to render him contemptible. Browning's sneering remarks about Wordsworth's bag-wig, and so on, are in this vein, but this impassioned attack is another matter entirely. It was necessary in *Sordello* to devalue the entirety of Wordsworth's achievement, and Browning specifically held up the older poet's *early* nature poetry for derision in the lines that have "Wordsworth" pontificating about his "madrigal o' the mugwort." According to the Browning of 1840, Wordsworth was spouting nonsense from the start. In his letter to Elizabeth Barrett, however, Browning concedes that Wordsworth's early work was worthy of admiration; one should try to remember his earlier days by blotting out the present and reading the "'Lyrical Ballads' with finger in ear." However poor Wordsworth's later poetry, Browning is unable to forget the power and influence of his earlier work, and the sad contrast it makes with his later efforts. The failure on Wordsworth's part to produce *The Recluse* is being alluded to here. In losing his temper with Wordsworth in this letter Browning exposes the inner consciousness of his debt that will explode again, with far more devastating impact, after *The Ring and the Book.*

Browning's image of Wordsworth sitting by a burnt-out hearth may have a source in Wordsworth's own poetry; Browning may have been turning Wordsworth's professed preference for isolation against him. In the poem "I am not One who much or oft delight" (also known as "Personal Talk") Wordsworth dismisses the attractions of what he regards as gossip (and what normal human beings would see as everyday social interaction), saying,

> Better than such discourse doth silence long,
> Long, barren silence, square with my desire;
> To sit without emotion, hope or aim,
> By my half-kitchen my half-parlour fire,
> And listen to the flapping of the flame,
> Or kettle, whispering its faint undersong.
>
> (lines 9–14)

Browning may well have been ironically alluding to this rather bleak poem in his letter, and implying that he finds Wordsworth's corpselike lack of "emotion, hope, or aim" grimly symptomatic of his burnout as a poet, as well as a man.

There is another potential source for this image in De Quincey's articles on Wordsworth. De Quincey describes Wordsworth as "burned out": "[S]ome people, it is notorious, live faster than others; the oil is burned out sooner in one constitution than in another—and the cause of this may be various; but, in the Wordsworths, one part of the cause is, no doubt, the secret fire of a temperament too fervid; the self-consuming energies of the brain, that gnaw at the heart and life-strings for ever."[18] Browning may well have remembered this image while writing his letter, since, by this stage, his view of Wordsworth had grown very close to that of De Quincey, who also felt that Wordsworth had "lived too long."

Browning also drags Shelley into the fray, in order to have another ally in his attack on Wordsworth's aesthetic failure. He quotes Shelley's scathing remark that "he had no more *imagination* than a pint-pot" (from Shelley's satirical attack on Wordsworth, *Peter Bell the Third*), but there appears to be another allusion to Shelley in these lines. Browning's final image of Wordsworth as a failed alchemist sitting among *pulvis et cinis* is reminiscent of Shelley's lines in *Alastor*:

> O, that the dream
> Of dark magician in his visioned cave,
> Raking the cinders of a crucible
> For life and power, even when his feeble hand
> Shakes in its last decay, were the true law
> Of this so lovely world!
>
> (lines 681–86)

By referring to these lines in his letter to Elizabeth Barrett (who would certainly have spotted the reference), Browning demonstrates the intensity of his desire to blacken Wordsworth's name. Bloom, in pointing out some allusions to Wordsworth and Coleridge in *Adonais*, also supplies some more possible Shelleyan sources for this vision; he suggests that Shelley is thinking of one or both of the aging first-generation romantics when he says of Keats that

> From the contagion of the world's slow stain
> He is secure, and now can never mourn
> A heart grown cold, a head grown grey in vain;
> Nor, when the spirit's self has ceased to burn,
> With sparkless ashes load an unlamented urn.
>
> (lines 356–60)

Bloom also points out how Shelley seems to chide his predecessors with a reference to their continued earthly existence, as opposed to Keats's escape into eternity:

He wakes or sleeps with the enduring dead;
Thou canst not soar where he is sitting now:—
Dust to the dust! But the pure spirit shall flow
Back to the burning fountain whence it came,
A portion of the Eternal, which must glow
Through time and change, unquenchably the same,
Whilst thy cold embers choke the sordid hearth of shame.
(lines 336–42)[19]

Browning would have known these lines well, and it is likely that they, too, contributed to his description of Wordsworth as a burned-out alchemist. Browning's desire to attack Wordsworth is so strong that he is forced to reach into the past and disinter Shelley (another romantic "dreamer") in order to have his support against Wordsworth. Nevertheless, Browning's attitude toward his predecessor, like De Quincey's, retained a strong tincture of frustrated love. Despite his assertion that he could not find the energy to cross the room if "at the other end of it all Wordsworth, Coleridge and Southey were condensed into that little china bottle yonder," the old man would not lie still.[20]

The "Essay on Shelley"

After 1840 Wordsworth was essentially dismissed. This pattern of erasure would persist in Browning's poetry until *Balaustion's Adventure* appeared in 1871; Browning was concerned to avoid returning down the romantic path. Nevertheless, there is one odd departure from this pattern; Browning's "Essay on Shelley," written in 1851 and published in 1852 as the preface to a collection of what were thought to be some of the poet's letters (the book was swiftly withdrawn when the letters turned out to be spurious). The "Essay" does not explicitly mention Wordsworth, but it indicates a continued ambivalence on Browning's behalf toward romanticism. It demonstrates a more tolerant attitude toward the brand of idealistic romanticism embodied by Shelley (and by Aprile in *Paracelsus*) that Browning had dismissed in *Sordello*. Woolford maintains that Browning, in the "Essay," is aware of the "essential solipsism of Romanticism," but believes that its aims are essentially laudable and not entirely to be condemned.[21] Nevertheless, the "Essay" does not represent a volte-face. Browning makes it clear that he has not altered his belief that the poet must concern himself with the real world: "[I]f the subjective might seem to be the ultimate requirement of every age, the objective, in the strictest sense, must still retain its original value. For it is with this world, as starting point and basis alike, that we shall always have to concern ourselves; the world is not to be thrown aside, but reverted to and relearned."[22] It would be strange indeed if the Browning of 1851 should argue in favor of anything but the "objective" program he had embraced in 1840, and which would lead to *Men and Women* four years later. Nevertheless, there is a definite mellowing toward the idealistic romantic poet, as exemplified by Shelley, that is not perceptible in the poetry of this period. When Browning describes the way the "subjective" poet struggles toward "not what man sees, but what God sees—the 'Ideas' of Plato, seeds of creation lying burningly on the Divine hand," he is not holding up the poet's metaphysical quest to ridicule in the way he mocked the "Wordsworth" poet's "madrigal o' the mugwort."[23] This is Browning's first published mention of Plato for almost twenty years—since the speaker in *Pauline* declared that Plato gave him the "key to life" (line 435). The mention of Plato here indicates a return to a more tolerant attitude toward metaphysical idealism. The seeds of Browning's later swing back to romanticism seem already present in the "Essay." There is no clearer indication of this than in a passage in which Browning depicts Shelley as the embodiment of a *synthesis* of "subjectivity" and "objectivity," not purely as the exemplar of the "subjective" poet. Shelley's idealism, says Browning, is thoroughly humanistic, since it constructs an "ideal man" toward whom other men can aspire. Browning describes Shelley as possessing

> the whole poet's virtue, I repeat, of looking higher than any manifestation yet made of both beauty and good, in order to suggest from the utmost actual realization of the one a corresponding capability in the other, and out of the calm, purity and energy of nature, to reconstitute and store up for the forthcoming state of man's being, a gift in repayment of that former gift, in which man's own thought and passion had been lavished by the poet on the else-incompleted magnificence of the sunrise, the else-uninterrupted mystery of the lake,—so drawing out, lifting up, and assimilating the ideal of a future man, thus described as possible, to the present reality of the poet's soul already arrived at in the higher state of development, and still aspirant to elevate and extend itself in conformity with its still-improving perceptions of, no longer the eventual Human, but the actual Divine.[24]

Is there a subtle criticism of Wordsworth in this passage? The poets who have "lavished" their genius on the "magnificence of the sunrise" or the "mystery of the lake" certainly sound like the mature Wordsworth. Shelley would thus be an embodiment of "the next step" in poetic evolution; his poetry is concerned with bettering the state of men, while that of Wordsworth is limited to eulogizing the beauty of nature. This idea could be seen as a subtler version of the vision of Wordsworth and the Israelites in the desert in *Sordello*. But here there is no ambivalence toward Shelley, whose existence hints at man's potential. "The ideal of a future man," dismissed in *Sordello*, is here depicted as a legitimate target. Woolford argues that Browning is attempting here to both "do homage to what he sees as the Romantic achievement" and "construct a centre for his own poetic activity."[25] This version of Shelley can serve as a model.

Browning's Shelley is a representative figure; he demonstrates the possibility of a purified romanticism of the kind Browning sought in *Paracelsus*. Later in his career Browning would seek out several such figures—Wordsworth's Dion, in particular, resembles Browning's Shelley in his intimations of human potential.[26] The "Essay on Shelley" presages Browning's later return to romanticism by almost twenty years. There is another hint of what is to come in the following passage: "[S]uch was the spherical poetical faculty of Shelley, as its own self-sufficing central light, radiating equally through immaturity and accomplishment, through many fragments and occasional completion, reveals it to a competent judgement."[27] Browning would later come to regard the idea of "self-sufficiency" in a negative light.[28] In the "Essay" Browning uses the term "self-sufficing" in an approving sense; Shelley's "spherical" genius has been turned to humanistic use. Shelley has a tendency to see *beyond* the corporeal world: "[N]ot with the combination of humanity in action, but with the primal elements of humanity he has to do; and he digs where he stands,—preferring to seek them in his own soul as the nearest reflex of that absolute Mind, according to the intuitions of which he desires to perceive and speak."[29] Nevertheless, he makes his insights available to all in a democratic fashion. His "self-sufficiency" is both humanistic and idealistic, and thus to be approved.

Men and Women and the Letter to Ruskin

This softening of attitude was not to last. Though *Men and Women* contains positive allusions to Shelley and Keats (in "Memorabilia" and "Popularity," respectively), Wordsworth—and his influence—is almost entirely absent. One possible allusion comes in "Transcendentalism: A Poem in Twelve Books," in which an unnamed poet is attacked for being overly prosy:

> Stop playing, poet! May a brother speak?
> 'Tis you speak, that's your error. Song's our art:
> Whereas you please to speak these naked thoughts
> Instead of draping them in sights and sounds.
> —Thoughts, good thoughts, thoughts fit to treasure up!
> But why such long prolusion and display,
> Such tuning and adjustment of the harp,

And taking it upon the breast, at length,
Only to speak dry words across its strings?

(lines 1–9)

This *could* be Wordsworth; Browning may be thinking of *The Excursion*, whose "Prospectus" may be considered a "long prolusion and display" to nine books of "dry words." He may also have been thinking of *The Prelude*—a long "prolusion" indeed. This hypothesis is strengthened by Browning's later depiction of the way John of Halberstadt makes visible the visions Boehme and his ilk merely describe:

He with a "look you!" vents a brace of rhymes,
And in there breaks the sudden rose herself,
Over us, under us, round us every side,
Nay, in and out the tables and the chairs
And musty volumes, Boehme's book and all,—
Buries us with a glory, young once more,
Pouring heaven into the shut house of life.

(lines 39–45)

This may be an allusion to Wordsworth's "Immortality" Ode, in which "shades of the prison-house" enclose the "growing boy" and separate him from the "celestial light" of his infancy.[30] If this is the case, Wordsworth's prosy late works are being condemned for their tendency to *distance* their readers from the "glory" he spoke of in the Ode. Critics have, however, suggested other potential sources, including Browning's own younger self.[31] Apart from this poem, however, Wordsworth—as a person—is almost entirely absent from the pages of *Men and Women*, as one ought to expect.[32]

Nevertheless, critics have pointed out the use of a particular Wordsworthian idea—that of the "spots of time," as described in *The Prelude*—in "By the Fireside." Ashton Nichols believes that the moment of "epiphanic fulfillment" in this poem can be seen as Wordsworthian, while Lawrence Kramer suggests that poems like "By the Fireside," "Love among the Ruins," and several later lyrics attempt, not entirely successfully, to achieve the restorative relationship with Dorothy that Wordsworth describes at the end of "Tintern Abbey."[33] Kramer argues that unlike Wordsworth, whose egotism allowed him to internalize Dorothy and turn her into a "self-object," Browning can only see his beloved as an external object (a "defensive and unreliable replacement of the self by the other").[34] Browning would thus have been rewriting the conclusion of "Tintern Abbey" in the pessimistic fashion characteristic of much of his love poetry. Another critic, Lawrence Poston, also believes that Browning is revisiting Wordsworthian topoi in this volume; he suggests that in "By the Fireside" and "Childe Roland to the Dark Tower Came" Browning is revising Wordsworth's view of the relationship between man and Nature in an altogether less positive fashion.[35] He argues that in "By the Fireside," nature is seen as "not a perpetual teacher, only a momentary contributor to the lovers' union," despite the "spot of time" the poem describes; and that Browning in "Childe Roland" provides "a natural order that is both a horrifying and a grimly comic inversion of the Wordsworthian view."[36] Browning would thus be suggesting that Wordsworth's view of the relationship between man and nature needed revision in a doubt-ridden era; "the narrator's troubled vision of Nature in 'Childe Roland' seems finally to reflect a sense that romantic humanism and Christian belief alike required redefinition if they were to survive as sources of value for the errant pilgrim."[37] Poston also makes the interesting suggestion that the Childe's fear that the "mere ugly heights and heaps" have stolen into view to entrap him may have its source in the "boat-stealing" episode in book 1 of *The Prelude*.[38]

Browning may indeed have been thinking of these Wordsworthian topoi while writing these poems, but none of these critics suggest that by using them he was *struggling* with the influence of his predecessor. His "defeat" of Wordsworth in 1840 would have left him feeling free to "borrow" Wordsworth's ideas if he liked, without any concern that such borrowing would impose a burden. He could treat Wordsworth in exactly the same way as he would treat any other writer whose influence was not a threat. Allusions were no longer being used as weapons.

Like many contemporary critics, John Ruskin found much of *Men and Women* every bit as baffling as *Sordello*. On December 2, 1855, he wrote to Browning asking for an explanation of "Popularity"; in response, Browning snapped, "I cannot begin writing poetry until my imaginary reader has conceded licences to me which you demur at altogether. I *know* that I don't make out my conception by my language; all poetry being a putting the infinite within the finite. You would have me paint it all plain out, which can't be; but by various artifices I try to make shift with touches and bits and outlines which *succeed* if they bear the conception from me to you. You ought, I think, to keep pace with the thought tripping from ledge to ledge of my 'glaciers', as you call them; not stand poking your alpenstock into the holes, and demonstrating that no foot could have stood there;—suppose it sprang over there?"[39] Tucker has pointed out that Browning's ideas about the "infinite" seem oddly close to those of Wordsworth in book 6 of *The Prelude*:

> Our destiny, our being's heart and home,
> Is with infinitude, and only there;
> With hope it is, hope that can never die,

Effort, and expectation, and desire,
And something evermore about to be.

(6.604–8)

In pointing out this parallel Tucker is more concerned to illuminate the nature of Browning's own quest to preserve the "conviction of endlessness" that he (Tucker) believes is the mainspring of Browning's creative urge—his continual desire to begin again, to "have more to say"—than he is to demonstrate the influence of Wordsworth on the poet.[40] In the light of the fact that Browning had been sent a copy of *The Prelude* five years before, it seems probable that the lines were in Browning's mind as he wrote to Ruskin.[41] What could Browning have meant by alluding to Wordsworth in this positive way? Tucker believes that Browning and Wordsworth were working in a parallel fashion in their attitude toward the sublime.[42] If this is so, it is extraordinary that Browning would confess it in a letter that would contain his most ringing denunciation of the poetic dreamers who neglected the "real" world in favor of "impossible" visions of sublimity. Even at this stage of his career Browning's feelings toward the erased Wordsworth were deeply ambivalent—he was only too aware of the impressive nature of Wordsworth's humanist achievement.

Even in 1855, at the height of the period during which he habitually painted the romantics as dreamers, Browning could not escape the realization that his enterprise owed much more to these poets—and Wordsworth in particular—than he could admit. Added to this consciousness was his knowledge of Wordsworth's humanism as revealed in *The Prelude*, though it would take him until much later in his career to admit he had been wrong. These pressures contributed to the ferocity of the attack on "romantic" views of poetry that comes later in the letter. Woolford has described the way the letter is a compressed and rather desperate mixture of "Socratic" (in Schlegel's terms) and "Shakespearean" irony that simultaneously displays Browning's "didactic hegemony in self-sufficient isolation" and his consciousness of a "select circle" of more intelligent literary critics/professional reviewers who will "react upon the rest," if instructed how to do so; the letter thus displays the mixture of contempt for and concern with others that characterized Paracelsus and Sordello.[43]

Browning goes on to declare that poetry has a didactic duty to "teach" its audience, and that such "teaching" will inevitably baffle many of its unprepared readers: "[D]o you think poetry was ever generally understood—or can be? Is the business of it to tell people what they know already, as they know it, and so precisely that they shall be able to cry out—'Here you should supply *this—that*, you evidently pass over, and I'll help you from my own stock'? It is all teaching, and the people hate to be taught. They say otherwise,—make foolish fables about Orpheus enchanting stocks and stones, poets standing up and being worshipped,—all nonsense and impossible dreaming. A poet's affair is with God, to whom he is accountable, and of whom is his reward: look elsewhere, and you find misery enough."[44] Browning is ceremonially burying the dreams of Paracelsus and Sordello, both of whom fantasized about "standing up and being worshipped"—as well as those of his younger self in *Pauline*. The duty of the poet is to "teach" that small portion of his audience amenable to didactic instruction. The romantic vision of the poet as priest-prophet is dismissed, much as Wordsworth was in *Sordello*.

Dramatis Personae and *The Ring and the Book*

Browning's next volume of poetry—*Dramatis Personae*—shows little more indication of Wordsworth's influence than *Men and Women*. Browning was still engaged on the "humanistic" mission he had embraced on the palace step in Venice, and his pursuance of this path demanded the continuing misrepresentation and erasure of the romantic poets, particularly Wordsworth. Browning's determination to produce a "realistic" and "humanistic" poetry stripped of romantic trappings can be seen as a sort of kenosis. In this light, the "antiromantic" nature of the works Browning produced between 1840 and 1869 can be seen as part of his struggle to free himself from Wordsworth's influence.

There is evidence in *Dramatis Personae* that Browning's ongoing "dispute" with the "Immortality" Ode still rumbled on; Anya Taylor has pointed out how, in stanza 3 of "Rabbi Ben Ezra," Browning repeats "not only the argument but [also the] sentence structure and meter" of the second sentence of the Ode's ninth stanza.[45] (Taylor contends that Browning's poem is influenced by Wordsworth's argument for immortality in the Ode.) However, the most curious glance toward Wordsworth comes in the volume's "Epilogue," in which the "Third Speaker" (usually viewed as Browning himself) sounds oddly Wordsworthian in his response to the fervor of David and the doubt of Renan. Browning's vision of the world is profoundly humanistic (and democratic); he describes the way his poetry allows him to take the "least man of all mankind" (line 69), and, through examining his "head and heart" (line 70), "find out how and why / He differs from his fellows utterly" (lines 70–71). This is consistent with Browning's desire to avoid romantic fantasy. However, as Browning goes on to describe the way the world "dances" about each individual as though its sole purpose was to "enhance / His worth" (lines 89–90), and grant him "the life, his product" (line 90), the poem begins to echo the Wordsworthian humanism he had found so influential in writing *Paracelsus*. Browning has not changed his view of the poet's mission, but in this poem he seems to acknowledge that Wordsworth's achievement is far from being incompatible with this view. Wordsworth's influence on this poem is particularly evident in Browning's emphasis of the term "nature": "then, like me, watch when nature by degrees / Grows alive round him" (lines 72–73) and "when you see what I tell you,—nature dance / About each man of us" (lines 87–88). These references to "nature" as a living entity with an intimate relationship with each individual are entirely consistent with Wordsworth's own view. Browning is not generally thought of as a poet particularly interested in the natural world; here, though, he seems to embrace Wordsworth's recognition of nature as a profound influence on mankind. Indeed, as the poem moves toward its conclusion, Browning comes very close to adopting a Wordsworthian "pantheism" of the sort he hinted at in *Paracelsus*:

> Why, where's the need of Temple, when the walls
> O' the world are that? What use of swells and falls
> From Levite's choir, Priest's cries, and trumpet-calls?
> (lines 96–98)

This riposte to David's fervor is in accordance with Browning's own increasingly unorthodox attitude toward Christian worship in his later years (he gave up regular attendance at any individual church), but it is also indebted to Wordsworth in two ways. Firstly, the declaration that the "walls / O' the [natural] world" are the true "Temple" in which to worship the Deity is almost certainly something picked up from Wordsworth; secondly, the stanza resembles, in its dismissal of the excesses of David's worship, Wordsworth's dismissal in his "Prospectus" of the visionary aspects of *Paradise Lost.* Browning is confessing, in a rather strangled way, that, far from being anathema to his post-1840 work, Wordsworth's poetry had more aims in common with it than he could comfortably admit. Despite Browning's kenosis, the "Wordsworth problem" would not simply go away. The concentrated Wordsworthian ambience of this poem is unique in the 1840-69 period; it is as if, for the brief period of writing the "Epilogue," Browning felt himself free to return to the view of his predecessor he had held in the 1830s, before his longing for self-definition led to an act of poetic "parricide."

What can explain this isolated example of a return to a sort of "disciple-master" relationship between the two poets? It cannot be argued that the "Epilogue" is the first sign of a profound change in Browning's attitude toward Wordsworth, since, upon completing *Dramatis Personae*, he was to throw himself into work upon his utterly un-Wordsworthian masterpiece, *The Ring and the Book*—a poem that, in its obsession with the verity of its source material, seems to have been written in direct opposition to the sort of romantic poetry condemned in *Sordello*; as he wrote to Julia Wedgwood, "the business has been, as I specify, to explain *fact*."[46] Why turn back on himself, however briefly, in the "Epilogue"? It is impossible to say for certain, since the circumstances behind the writing of most of Browning's individual poems are unknown; very little is known, for example, of the poetry or other works he was reading at the time he wrote each poem, and one can only speculate on the basis of internal evidence. In the case of the "Epilogue," perhaps he had been rereading the "Prospectus," in much the same way as a rereading of the "Immortality" Ode may have influenced "Rabbi Ben Ezra." There is another clue, though, that comes in the final stanza of the poem:

> That one Face, far from vanish, rather grows,
> Or decomposes but to recompose,
> Become my universe that feels and knows!
>
> (lines 99–101)

Browning describes the "Face" (which, according to Alexandra Orr, was the face of Christ) as continually "decomposing" and "recomposing." This process of decay and renewal is an organic one that has much in common with the "pantheism" Browning flirts with earlier in the poem, but it also prefigures an idea to which he will return in the visionary conclusion of *Fifine*, a poem that embraces a very similar vision of eternal recurrence.[47] Woolford has pointed out that the "Epilogue" seems to owe something to the lines in *The Prelude* in which Wordsworth describes a moment of mystical insight derived from the landscape he saw while he was descending the Simplon Pass:

> The immeasurable height
> Of woods decaying, never to be decayed,
> The stationary blasts of waterfalls,
> And in the narrow rent at every turn
> Winds thwarting winds, bewildered and forlorn,
> The torrents shooting from the clear blue sky,
> The rocks that muttered close upon our ears,
> Black drizzling crags that spake by the way-side,
> As if a voice were in them, the sick sight
> And giddy prospect of the raving stream,
> The unfettered clouds and region of the Heavens,
> Tumult and peace, the darkness and the light –
> Were all like workings of one mind, the features
> Of the same face, blossoms upon one tree;
> Characters of the great Apocalypse,

The types and symbols of Eternity,
Of first, and last, and midst, and without end.

(6.624–40)[48]

These lines are essentially pantheistic; at the very least, they display a sort of natural theology at work. God's "face" is perceptible through the natural world. *The Prelude*, as will be shown, was profoundly influential on Browning's opinion of Wordsworth, and *Fifine*'s conclusion demonstrates that Browning knew the poem well by 1871.[49] The fact that the epilogue to *Dramatic Personae* is so reminiscent of this passage indicates that it may have been a rereading of *The Prelude* that stimulated him to briefly assume a more tolerant—indeed, almost apologetic—attitude toward Wordsworth in this poem.

Whatever the reason for this mellowing, it would be swiftly forgotten in the writing of *The Ring and the Book*—a work that would simultaneously stand as the culmination of his effort to transform his work in accordance with a realist/humanistic aesthetic and become his first truly popular book. In fact, as Woolford has argued, the entirety of Browning's career between 1840 and 1869 can be seen as a search for a way to write popular poetry, and with *The Ring and the Book* he seemed to have achieved this aim. Nevertheless, there is evidence that upon the completion of this work, Browning felt an odd sense that this achievement was in fact meaningless, not (to quote the "Essay on Chatterton") to the "true purpose." The first hint of this dissatisfaction comes in a letter from Browning to Julia Wedgwood, in which, responding to an inquiry on her part about the fidelity of *The Ring and the Book* to its source materials, he replies rather testily that "the business has been, as I specify, to explain *fact*—and the fact is what you see. . . . Before I die, I hope to purely invent something,—here my pride was concerned to invent nothing."[50] Browning is at pains to emphasize the fidelity of his latest poem to his desire to depict the world as it is, rather than as it ought to be—"fact is what you see." He has not "created" anything—he has, like his Chatterton, set to work using "the poorest possible materials" as "stuff for transmuting." Whatever of the beautiful and true the poem displays was there all along. However, though he has written his latest poem in accordance with these rules, in this letter, for the first time, he seems to demur at them with the statement that "before I die I hope to purely invent something." "Invention"—the creation of something out of the poet's imagination alone—is a *romantic* trait, and, as such, incompatible with the sternly antiromantic aesthetic embraced by Browning from 1840 on.

Is this almost parenthetical admission of a continued instinct for "creation" merely a blip, or is it the first sign of a profound change on Browning's part in his whole aesthetic conception of the poet's role, and, indeed, of the very nature of the poet? An examination of his next published poem demonstrates that Browning had been forced to reevaluate the poet's powers and mission. In this reevaluation Wordsworth, as one of the greatest influences on Browning, could not but play a very major part.

Balaustion's Adventure: Romanticism Reassessed

Balaustion's Adventure was written in May 1871, and was Browning's first published work since *The Ring and the Book.* That poem had been the culmination of Browning's whole post-1840 drive to remold himself into as antiromantic a poet as possible. If he were to proceed any further in this direction, he would surely cease to be a "poet" altogether and become the producer of something much closer to the "naturalist" novels of Zola, with their obsessive concern for verifiable empirical detail (like the "Old Yellow Book"). The desire to "invent nothing" that Browning described as having been the mainspring of *The Ring and the Book* was inimical to romantic conceptions of inspiration, and even poetry itself. In this light, *Balaustion* contains some extraordinary passages. Sometime between 1869 and 1871 Browning underwent a crisis—not, as some critics have argued, a simply biographical one having to do with Lady Ashburton or anyone else, but an *aesthetic* one linked with his realization that if he were to be a poet at all, he would have to return to a sort of romanticism.[51] The Browning of 1855 maintained that the business of poetry was "all teaching," a hard-nosed program that spurned metaphysical mumbo jumbo in the romantic vein. In *The Ring and the Book* he would sum up this attitude in the words of an inquirer who talks of "poetry, make-believe, / And the white lies it sounds like" (1.455–56). Yet in 1871 the same poet could declare, through the lips of Balaustion in *Balaustion's Adventure*, and with no irony at all,

> Then, because Greeks are Greeks, and hearts are hearts,
> And poetry is power,—they all outbroke
> In a great joyous laughter with much love.
>
> (lines 235–37)

The *poetry* of Euripides has the *power* to make the Syracusans welcome Balaustion and her friends into harbor. The idea of poetry having a material ability to influence events in the "real" world is not absurd; Euripides' verse is vital in sparing the boatload of refugees the horrors of slavery. Poetry, in this instance, has a humanistic purpose. One must also remember that the story is based on historical fact—on a story told in Plutarch's *Life of Nicias*, in which the Roman historian declares that some captured Athenians were "spared for the sake of Euripides." Plutarch even seems to mention the very boat in which Browning has placed Balaustion.[52] Paradoxically, in returning (via the idea of "poetry as power") to a quasi-romantic aesthetic, Browning uses the "objective" and "realistic" technique of basing his story on attested *fact* to lend it validity—the same method he had claimed to be using in *The Ring and the Book*. Here, the method is being used to support a "romantic" rather than purely humanistic thesis. The tools Browning used to build his poetic edifice of 1840–69 are now being used to begin its dismantling.

Towards the end of *Balaustion* Browning returns again to the question of whether poetry has "power," and again returns an affirmative answer. This time, though, the assertion has no basis in "factual" evidence, and is much closer to the romantic "dreaming" he had condemned since 1840; it sounds almost like a systematic denial of all he had asserted to Ruskin in 1855:

> Ah, that brave
> Bounty of poets, the one royal race
> That ever was, or will be, in this world!
> They give no gift that bounds itself and ends
> I' the giving and the taking: theirs so breeds
> I' the heat and soul o' the taker, so transmutes
> The man who only was a man before,
> That he grows godlike in his turn, can give—
> He also: share the poets' privilege,
> Bring forth new good, new beauty, from the old.
> (lines 2416–25)

In 1855 poetry was described as "all teaching," and the "people" remained recalcitrant. All other claims about the "power" of poetry were false. Now, in 1871, the poet is described, not as a dogged teacher, like the preternaturally patient Rabbi Perida, but as a vessel of quasi-divine fire.[53] Balaustion crowns the poets as "royal," and declares them unique in this quality. Browning seems to retain his "republicanism," but with an important modification: his earlier "republicanism" was clear-sighted and humanistic, and this new version has assumed a dreamily "romantic" cast, with the previously derided quality of "royalty" given to the poets. These poets have "power" indeed—power that verges on the divine, since Balaustion says that they can make ordinary men "godlike" like themselves. Their finest quality is their ability to "transmute" the listener into a poet himself, enabling him to "share" their "privilege," to bring forth "new good, new beauty, from the old." Thus, the 1871 program is less elitist than it might appear, and more consistent with Browning's avowed humanism since *Sordello*.

Though the poets seem to have an elite status in that they are a "royal race," the fact that all can share their gift lends a democratic spirit to the scheme. Balaustion's attempt to unite romantic idealism with practical realism marks the beginning of a return on Browning's part to the attempts he made to construct a similar synthesis in his poetry of the 1830s.

Browning knew that one of the main stumbling blocks in the romantic program was the ever-present danger of falling into a blind and useless utopianism; he had used this supposed tendency to blacken Wordsworth in 1840. The lines in *Balaustion* steer clear of this pitfall by recognizing that any "new world" must be built out of the materials at hand; the "poet's privilege" is to "bring forth new good, new beauty, *from the old*" (italics added). The romantic desire for creation is tempered by a realization that one must not descend into fantasy. Browning is not yet openly admitting that he had been wrong to condemn Wordsworth as a dreamer, but he is moving back toward a more "romantic" view of the poet's role. Browning uses the poem *Balaustion* itself to exemplify the process; in her rewriting of the *Alcestis* Balaustion is an example of the way nonpoets can be inspired by poets to their own creative feats:

> For I have drunk this poem, quenched my thirst,
> Satisfied heart and soul—yet more remains!
> Could we too make a poem? Try at least,
> Inside the head, what shape the rose-mists take!
>
> (lines 2431–34)

Balaustion rewrites the play in order to make Admetus an ideal monarch, unwilling to let his wife die for him; his nobility, united with that of his wife, is strong enough to force Hades to send Alcestis back to earth. Balaustion herself brings forth "new good, new beauty, from the old"; the rewritten *Alcestis* would have appealed to Browning's chivalrous instincts, and thus have seemed superior to the more pessimistic original. Balaustion has played her part in poetry's march toward perfection, and has participated in a democratic sense in the "royalty" she ascribes to poets. For the period in which she rewrites the *Alcestis*, she, too, is a member of the "royal race."

All this is in complete contradiction of all Browning had maintained in 1855. Now, in 1871, Browning uses Balaustion to suggest that poets are indeed worthy of "standing up and being worshipped." He does not claim Orphic powers for them, but, nevertheless, he has turned his back on the aggressive rejection of romantic idealism he offered Ruskin in 1855, and has begun to preach something very close to the doctrine he had cast aside in 1840. This reconsideration of the romantic program would have important repercussions as far as Browning's attitude to Wordsworth was concerned.

Woolford has pointed out that Browning's source-story from Plutarch appears in canto 4 of Byron's *Childe Harold's Pilgrimage*.[54] Browning's relationship with Byron was almost as tangled as his relationship with Wordsworth. He disliked what he saw as Byron's contempt for his fellow men, and one particular passage seemed, to Browning, to encapsulate this: it comes in cantos 179 and 180 of *Childe Harold's Pilgrimage*, when Byron belittles humanity in comparison with the ocean (4.1604–20). Browning found these lines particularly irritating, and in book 6 of *Sordello* (and thereafter in *Prince Hohenstiel-Schwangau*, *Fifine*, and *La Saisiaz*) he attacked Byron for writing them.[55] He believed that Byron's antihumanism was a cynical pose; referring to comments upon his attack on Byron in *Fifine*, he wrote to Annie Egerton Smith, "[I]n the *Spectator* that came yesterday, someone repeated that foolish lie that I called Lord Byron "a flat-fish" . . . I never said nor wrote a word against or about Byron's poetry or power in my life; but I did say, that, if he were in earnest and preferred being with the sea to associating with mankind, he would do well to stay with the sea's population; thereby simply taking him at his word, had he been honest—whereas it was altogether dishonest, seeing that nobody cared so much about the opinions of mankind, and deferred to them, as he who was thus posturing and pretending to despise them."[56] Bearing this in mind, it is bizarre that Browning chose to write *Balaustion* around a story that appears in the midst of the passages that so infuriated him in *Childe Harold's Pilgrimage*. However, Woolford has pointed out that the passage demonstrates that Byron not only felt for the suffering, but put forward the power of poetry as a potential tool for their liberation from bondage:

> See! as they chant the tragic hymn, the car
> Of the o'ermastered victor stops, the reins
> Fall from his hands, his idle scimitar
> Starts from its belt – he rends his captives' chains,
> And bids them thank the bard for freedom and his strains.
>
> (4.140–44)

Woolford suggests in "Life—That's Venice!" that writing *Balaustion*—and remembering the tale's connection to Byron's poem—may have indirectly prompted Browning to conclude *Fifine*'s exploration of the same issues in a Venetian setting.[57] This is almost certainly correct; nevertheless, there is more to this linkage. Browning may not have been entirely straightforward in his attacks on Byron in these years. The period 1869–71 marked a profound reconsideration of romanticism, and Wordsworth in particular, which led Browning to veiled admissions that his earlier misreading of Wordsworth had been unfair and misconceived. Browning may have felt his attacks on Byron to have been equally misplaced. The "hidden" reference back to evidence of Byron's humanism in *Balaustion* and the pervading "Byronic" ambience of *Fifine* could thus mean more than all of the attacks on Byron combined; they might be covert admissions that this demotion of Byron to the position of "whipping boy" for Browning's postromantic aesthetic was unfair, though necessary. By continuing to attack Byron for his lack of humanism, Browning could keep up the facade of contempt for romanticism he had erected in 1840 while making amends for his earlier misreading through more oblique references to Wordsworth. The attacks on Byron would receive more attention because of their obvious nature, while the fundamental reconsideration of Wordsworth went unnoticed.

Browning's relationship with Byron was loose enough to be turned to Browning's advantage in this way; Wordsworth would prove somewhat less pliable. It is to Browning's return to the fray with Wordsworth that this study must now turn; this return comes in *Fifine*, but it can only be fully understood in the light of Browning's correspondence with William Knight, president of the Wordsworth Society. This correspondence must be examined in some detail.

6

The Browning-Knight Correspondence: Wordsworth Disinterred

WILLIAM KNIGHT, WHO HAD BEEN BORN IN 1836, WAS PROFESSOR OF MORAL PHILosophy at St. Andrew's University; his interest in Wordsworth was an obsessive sideline. In 1879 he wrote to Wordsworth's descendants, asking to publish a collected scholarly edition; he eventually triumphed, according to Stephen Gill, "through perseverance and courteous assiduity" (a pattern of behavior he would repeat in his correspondence with Browning).[1] In Gill's words, he was a "zealot for Wordsworth," and this zeal led him to Herculean labors: "[A]s Wordsworthian discoverer, enabler, and publicist he towered above contemporaries."[2] His eleven-volume collected edition stands as a landmark in Wordsworth scholarship, and was the first collection of Wordsworth to publish the poems in their chronological order.

Knight's passion for Wordsworth was of the evangelical temper that desires converts; he thus founded the Wordsworth Society, which had its first meeting at Grasmere on September 29, 1880. The constitution declared that the society was to act as "a band of union amongst those who are in sympathy with the general teaching and spirit of Wordsworth" and was also to carry out scholarly work.[3] Knight persuaded many eminent people to join, according to Gill, mainly "middle and upper class and predominantly mainstream Anglican."[4] The annual meetings were not exciting affairs; many of the society's members were rather elderly, and Matthew Arnold grumpily remarked to his wife that "the grave would have been cheerful compared to the view presented by the Westminster Chamber and the assembled Wordsworth Society . . . the Society is not composed of people of a festive type."[5] One wonders what manner of bacchanal Arnold expected; all the same, as Gill points out, the fact that many of the older members had the depressing habit of referring continually to their own impending demise cannot have helped.[6] Unsurprisingly, considering the funereal atmosphere of the whole enterprise, the society fizzled out in 1886;

nevertheless, during the six years of its existence Knight worked furiously, publishing a great deal of scholarly work. He also struggled to assemble a Wordsworth selection during this period, at least initially with the assistance of those of his fellow members who could tear their thoughts away from the approaching grave.

Browning was one of the Victorian worthies asked by Knight to join the society. Evidently, to accept would amount to recognition on Browning's part of Wordsworth's achievement as a poet, if not as a human being; that Browning could be troubled by moral rather than aesthetic scruples is evident from the way his disgust at Shelley's treatment of his first wife led him to decline a request to join the Shelley Society.[7] No such compunction apparently worried Browning in the case of Wordsworth; he accepted the offer of membership, declaring in a letter of May 17, 1880, "I keep fresh as ever the admiration for Wordsworth which filled me on becoming acquainted with his poetry in my boyhood: and the proposed club will contain the name of no more thorough lover of his memory than [Robert Browning]."[8] (How irritating Knight found it to have his society branded a "club" is not recorded).

Having persuaded Browning to join his society, Knight set about attempting to find out what he *really* felt about his predecessor. One cannot imagine him having known *Sordello* well enough (if at all) to detect the dismissal of Wordsworth in that poem (indeed, it does not seem that *any* of Browning's contemporaries noticed this), but he would certainly have known of "The Lost Leader." Browning had had to field inquiries about the origins of this poem for years; there had also, between December 1873 and April 1874, been an exchange of notes in *Notes and Queries* in which it was openly debated whether Wordsworth was the model for the Lost Leader; Walter Thornbury and Jonathan Bourchier both declared that Browning himself had confessed this to them.[9] Nevertheless, by 1880 Browning was openly praising Wordsworth. Knight must have known of this change of attitude, and set about attempting to elicit a more detailed critique of Wordsworth from Browning. He was to prove persistent in his investigations; he proceeded, over the next decade—until the end of Browning's life—to bombard the poet with letters inquiring about Wordsworth.

Knight began, later in 1880, by asking Browning whether he thought he should use Wordsworth's original text as a starting point for the variorum edition he was editing, or a later, much revised text. Browning's reply, printed (like the bulk of his correspondence with Knight) in Knight's 1904 volume *Retrospects*, condemned Wordsworth's violation of his earlier achievement: "[Y]our method of giving the original text, and subjoining in a note the variations, each with its proper date, is incontestably preferable to any other . . . in every case, the change is sadly for the worse: I am quite troubled by such spoiling of passage after passage. . . . If ever diabolic agency was caught at tricks with 'apostolic' achievement—and 'apostolic', with no 'profanity' at all, I esteem these poems to be—surely you may bid it 'aroint' 'about and all about' these desecrated stanzas."[10] Browning's anger at Wordsworth's revisions is more than purely aesthetic. Not only does he attack *all* the revisions—and, by implication, the older Wordsworth's "diabolic" poetic instinct (the "diabolism" is reminiscent of the comparison to Satan in the letter to Horne)—but his irritation shows the reverence in which he held Wordsworth's early achievement; it is described as "apostolic." This seems to indicate a profound change in Browning's attitude toward Wordsworth—back to the positive attitude displayed in his poetry of the 1830s. The older Browning resents the way that Wordsworth's "great language," as he had called it in "The Lost Leader," had been perverted and warped—both in new poems like "The Warning" *and* through brutal revisions to his earlier works. The revisions have become, to Browning, analogous to the "regular about-face of his special party" Wordsworth performed. Browning has swung back to his earlier view of Wordsworth's early work, as if the passage mocking a quasi Wordsworth in *Sordello* had never been written.

What had provoked this reassessment? I will go on to theorize that it had its origin in an unease Browning felt with his "misreading" of Wordsworth, but were there any external, historical factors that made him reassess Wordsworth when he did? Browning certainly grew more conservative as he grew older; the "republicanism" of his youth had been toned down, if not entirely discarded. He told Alexandra Orr that he was a "passionate Unionist" and, bizarrely, contemplated writing a play in opposition to female suffrage.[11] Even if these declarations were not entirely serious, Alfred Domett records Browning, in March 1872, expressing disgust at a socialist rally in Hyde Park.[12] He consistently avoided any public exposition of his political beliefs, unlike his younger self. The entire pattern of his later life also points to an increased conservatism. He embraced fame with open arms, becoming an inveterate "diner-out," moving in the most elevated of circles, and counting aristocrats among his closest friends. He was always immaculately dressed and, unlike the shambling Tennyson, utterly unlike the public perception of a "poet." It is easy to forget that Elizabeth Barrett's money, and the income generated by the sales of his later works, made him a very wealthy man. A symbolic moment came in March 1869, when the former "republican" was presented to the queen he had imagined, thirty years before, joining the peasants in *Sordello*.[13] Had Tennyson died before 1889, Browning would almost certainly have been offered the post of poet laureate. Betty Miller's biography goes too far in her condemnation of Browning as a mercenary social climber, but there is a degree of truth in her argument. All these factors would have colored Browning's view of Wordsworth's own metamorphosis. The lifestyle of the later Wordsworth had not been so different from that of the older Browning; Wordsworth's, indeed, was the more obviously "poetical," since he spent most of the year in rural seclusion. The Browning who had become an establishment figure could hardly condemn Wordsworth for having done the same.

Another factor affecting Browning's opinion of Wordsworth would have been the older poet's gradually rising reputation. Wordsworth's death was followed by a period of critical neglect; most critics who wrote on Wordsworth during this period were content to merely parrot a few received ideas.[14] During these years, Browning was unlikely to be questioned about a poet whose work was being generally ignored. Nevertheless, as the 1860s turned into the 1870s, there was what Gill calls a "Wordsworth Renaissance": an increasing realization of Wordsworth's importance and a growing public debate about the nature of his achievement.[15] This "renaissance" led to the foundation of the Wordsworth Society. It is intriguing that Browning's "reconsideration" of Wordsworth took place at the exact moment when this renaissance was beginning to pick up speed, at the cusp, as it were, of change in Wordsworth's critical reception; R. H. Hutton's influential 1857 essay on Wordsworth, for example, was reprinted as "Wordsworth and His Genius" in his *Essays, Theological and Literary* in 1871, the year of *Fifine*. Wordsworth's return into the arena would make the old poet a far more formidable "adversary." Since the renaissance took place *after* Browning wrote *Fifine*, it cannot be argued that it forced Browning to a reconciliation; however, it is likely that Browning's awareness of Wordsworth's steadily rising reputation contributed to his decision to come to terms with his predecessor. Wordsworth's rising reputation also coincided, oddly enough, with that of Browning; as a literary lion, he could not denigrate a respected predecessor without seeming crass. The weight of this burden would have increased as the years went on; Wordsworth continued to rise in critical estimation, and Browning's own social standing increased. Browning's reconciliation with Wordsworth may have been, at least in part, a political decision. It must also be remembered that Wordsworth had, by 1871, been dead for over twenty years. It would have been difficult for Browning to retain the resentment he had felt against Wordsworth for all that time; the struggle may have ultimately proved more wearisome than painful.

As the correspondence continues, one perceives a more or less continual evasiveness on the poet's part. He attended a fair number of Wordsworth Society meetings, but always stubbornly refused to speak at them. Knight attempted to persuade him to "say something" about Wordsworth at the meeting in 1883, but, after eight months' prevarication, Browning told Knight in a letter of March 21, 1883,

> I so hate saying "no" to a request from you—the kinder and more gracious the request, the harder its evasion or refusal,—that I have let the days go on until, being forced to reply to a somewhat similar demand just made on me, I asked myself whether it would not be a wise economy of pain to at once assure you that, for many reasons, I am quite unable to do even the poor little service to that great memory of Wordsworth which you honour me by supposing I might render. I do increasingly feel (cowardly as seems the avowal) the need of keeping that quiet corner in the world's van which I have got used to for so many years. "This comes too near the explaining of myself"; and you will therefore let me begin, and end, by saying, with all severity, that I am gratefully and humbly, yours ever, [Robert Browning].[16]

This is extraordinary, even for Browning, who could be every bit as convoluted in his prose as in his poetry, when pressed. Could he not have simply declined? He does not make the reasons for his reluctance at all clear; after a brief reference to "many reasons" he speaks of a need for "retirement." Aside from the fact that far from "keeping that quiet quarter in the world's van" he had for over twenty years been a ubiquitous socialite, the way Browning tries to wriggle off Knight's hook has something desperate about it. His comment about the "explaining of [him]self" is a (mis)quote of Portia's "this comes too near the praising of myself" in *The Merchant of Venice* 3.4.22; it is also eerily reminiscent of the "revealment of myself" that Hohenstiel-Schwangau promises his imaginary companion in a previous Browning poem—a "revealment" that only serves to reveal the complete absence of any identifiable personality, or one that has utterly disintegrated (*Prince Hohenstiel-Schwangau, Saviour of Society*, line 22). Could Browning have feared such a cataclysmic outcome to any attempt at self-revelation? It sounds melodramatic, but the idea horrified him. This refusal to speak about Wordsworth was *not* merely a manifestation of the shyness that always handicapped any efforts he made to speak in public, but a recognition that to explain *why* he had returned to a positive view of Wordsworth would leave him open to precisely the same allegation of apostasy that he had leveled at Wordsworth many years before.[17] Browning had performed his own "regular about-face," though not of as obvious a character as that of Wordsworth or Southey.

Knight's "pursuit" of Browning continued as the years rolled on. Browning managed to avoid the 1883 meeting; he did turn up the following year, but again declined the opportunity to speak. Things seem to have settled into an acceptable pattern for Browning—the occasional meeting, at which he could sit in benign silence, was perfectly endurable (though not, perhaps, much more than that). However, in 1885, Knight found another line of attack: he requested a list of Browning's favorite Wordsworth poems. This should have been a straightforward task, necessitating only a trip to his bookshelves: he owned several Wordsworth volumes, including the collected *Poetical Works* of 1836–37, inherited from his wife.[18] Browning accepted this task; in a letter of August 10, 1885, he tells Knight that he will "attempt to pick out the twenty poems which strike me (and so as to take away my breath!) as those worthiest of the master."[19] Nevertheless, reticence seems to have set in. He failed to turn up for the 1885 society meeting, and over three months later he still had not supplied a list. In a convoluted letter of November 10 he offers the excuse that "at Venice—where was a complete edition of Wordsworth to be found, or even hoped for? and, without such a necessary assistance, I was unable to comply with your request."[20] Later in the letter he declares that "plenty of matters" have claimed his "prompt attention" and that "an off-hand profession of choice" would be "too foolishly presumptuous."[21] Even so, he declares that he will use his wife's "pencil-marked" edition of Wordsworth to assist him in making his choice, "whatever may be its worth."[22] It is as if he were letting Knight know that the selection might not be purely his own, thus diluting any impact his decisions might have.

Nevertheless, in a letter of February 24, 1886 (over *six months* after the original request), Browning set about trying to tell Knight why he could not, ultimately, make the selection at all. He touches upon a central concern of his career, the question of audience: "[O]ne remembers few more commonplace admonitions to a poet than that he would wiselier have written but a quarter of the works which he has laboured at for a lifetime; unless it be this other, often coupled with it; that such works ought to be addressed to the general apprehension, not exclusively suited to the requirements of a (probably quite imaginary) few. Each precept contradicts the other. Write, on set purpose, for the many, and you will soon enough be reminded of the old *quot homines* and write as conscientiously for the few—your idealised 'double' (if it comes to that)—and you may suit him with the extremely little that suits yourself."[23] Browning uses this conflict to explain his reluctance to make a Wordsworth selection; it applies with equal perplexity to the job of a selector. He asks, "[I]n view of which of these objects should the maker of a selection of the works of any poet worth the pains begin his employment?"[24] Any such selection, he argues, must be purely *personal*, and it is impossible to make one upon which all readers will agree—one, that is, from which all traces of the *selector's* personality, likings, and idiosyncrasies have been eliminated.[25] To make a selection would therefore bring him perilously close to the "revealment" of himself he found so disquieting; he declines the task, preferring to leave "each recipient his own selector" in the business.[26] He had no intention of letting Knight (or anyone else) view *his* "idealised double."

Thus, in order to escape the duty of making a Wordsworth selection, Browning tried to deny the validity of making any selections at all. Interestingly, though, he says that "it is quite another matter of interest to know what Matthew Arnold thinks most worthy in Wordsworth."[27] Arnold had published his influential selection of Wordsworth's poetry in 1879, and had sent Browning a copy.[28] Browning is therefore elevating Arnold's reliability as a selector and critic of Wordsworth far above his own; Arnold must somehow possess the remarkable ability to *transcend* his own prejudices and opinions when acting as a selector. Browning was not, however, always so confident about Arnold's abilities as a selector of poems: in a letter of August 24, 1881, to W. Hale White (Mark Rutherford) he asks White if he thinks that "Matt. Arnold's selection of passages and poems from Byron was a poor one? I—at all events—do not so 'select' when I go over his works in memory—where they pretty nearly all are."[29] The fact that Browning could be so dismissive of Arnold's skill as a selector five years before the letter to Knight raises some doubts as to how genuine his professed admiration for Arnold actually was. Perhaps Arnold was merely being used as a kind of human shield against Knight's probing.

Browning provides a few crumbs for Knight, but only of the most commonplace sort. Emphasizing his incompetence as a critic with rather forced modesty (he refers to "such a one as myself"), he tells Knight that he admires "every poem written during about the first twenty years of the poet's life: after these, the solution grows weaker, the crystals gleam more rarely, and the assiduous stirring-up of the mixture is too apparent and obtrusive."[30] Knight tells us that the poet cannot have meant "the first twenty years" of Wordsworth's life, since during that period Wordsworth produced only juvenilia; he says that Browning really meant the first twenty years of what he calls Wordsworth's "poetic life," which would span the period of Wordsworth's greatest poetic achievement—roughly 1793–1813/4.[31] There is a hint in these lines of the old frustration Browning felt at Wordsworth's squandering of his talents; the image of Wordsworth stirring up his weakened "solution" in search of the odd crystal is reminiscent of Browning's 1846 depiction of him as a failed alchemist. The 1886 criticism is, however, much less scornful. By 1886 it was widely acknowledged that Wordsworth's later works are inferior to the earlier poems; Arnold, for example, had voiced this idea in the preface to his Wordsworth collection of 1879.[32] Browning is thus uttering a critical truism.

Nevertheless, Knight eventually managed to force something approximating to his "selection" out of the old poet. Having composed his *own* selection, he sent Browning a list of all those he had chosen, to find out what he made of them. Browning "went over them with minute care, marking all those which he specially liked, and adding several which [Knight] had omitted."[33] On March 23, 1887, he wrote to Knight (presumably including the annotated list with his letter),

> I have seemed to neglect your commission shamefully enough, but I confess to a sort of repugnance to classifying the poems as even good and less good, because in my heart I fear I should do it almost chronologically—so immeasurably superior seem to me the "first sprightly runnings."[34] Your selection would appear to be excellent, and the partial admittance of the later work prevents one from observing the too definitely distinguishing black line between supremely good and—well, what is fairly tolerable—from Wordsworth, always understand! I have marked a few of the early poems included in your list: I could do no other when my conscience tells me that I can never be tired of loving them—while, with the best will in the world, I could never do more than try hard to like them. You see, I go wholly upon my individual likings and distastes; that other considerations should have their weight with other people is natural and inevitable.[35]

Even this passage is far more riddled with qualifications than appears at first glance. Browning's emphasis of the superiority of the "first sprightly runnings" is a critical commonplace; he was still being as cautious as possible in what he said to Knight. Later in the passage he qualifies himself still further with the admission that he goes "wholly" upon his own "individual likings and distastes"; this is in accordance with his earlier disparagement of the business of selection, and Browning is implicitly criticizing the Victorian "cult" of selections as epitomized by Palgrave and Arnold. Nevertheless, he implies that a glimpse of the "real" Browning's opinion of Wordsworth may be accorded through this parade of his own "individual likings and distastes."

Alexandra Orr, who reprints the letter in her biography of Browning, resolves a strange ambiguity. In reference to Browning's declaration that he has marked a few of the "early poems" in the list, and "could do no other when my conscience tells me that I could never be tired of loving them—while, with the best will in the world, I could never do more than try hard to like them," Orr tells us that "by 'them' Mr. Browning clearly means the later poems, and probably has omitted a few words which would have shown this."[36] She presumably means the second "them" in the sentence, and her personal acquaintance with the poet makes her solution probable.

What can be learned from the list of "early poems" that Browning added to Knight's selection? Here is the list:

"The Reverie of Poor Susan" (1800)
"Goody Blake and Harry Gill" (1798)
"The Complaint of the Forsaken Indian Woman" (1798)

"The Danish Boy, a Fragment" (1800)
"Rob Roy's Grave" (1807)
"The Farmer of Tilsbury Vale" (wr. 1800, pub.1815)
"Power of Music" (1807)
"Stargazers" (1807)
"Dion" (1820)
"The Eclipse of the Sun, 1820" (1822)
"A Jewish Family" (1835)

Not all these poems are "early," but there is a clear balance in the list in favor of the "first sprightly runnings." The list is almost entirely composed of little-known pieces; this is not an indication of perversity on Browning's part, since the list contains poems Browning *added* to Knight's selection—a list that already contained the poems generally accepted as Wordsworth's finest achievements.

Browning had made it hard for Knight to read much into his selection. By adding a few personal favorites to Knight's list, Browning had acceded to his demands, but in a way that must have left him unsatisfied. Apart from a good knowledge of Wordsworth, what had Browning demonstrated? Knight was not a Browning specialist, and it is unlikely that he had any idea of the struggle with Wordsworth as depicted in *Paracelsus* and *Sordello*. Reading Browning's list would have meant little to anyone who had not studied Browning's poems with Wordsworth specifically in mind.

Before examining the list in detail, it is necessary to consider the final fruit, as it were, of the Browning-Knight correspondence: the Wordsworth selection that Knight published in 1888. In its preface, Knight tells us a good deal about how he assembled the selection. His original plan was to publish lists of Wordsworth's finest poems as chosen by "twenty or thirty" "contemporary poets and men of letters."[37] The plan had to be abandoned—"difficulties stood in the way of its realization"—including, one suspects, the realization that plowing through "twenty or thirty" lists of poems, whoever had compiled them, would be an arduous task even for the Wordsworth fanatic.[38] Knight therefore made his own selection, but sent it to a list of society members for comment; the list, apart from Browning, included Lord Coleridge, Edward Dowden, and Lord Houghton.[39] Knight tells us that he assigned "certain years" to each contributor and asked for his opinion "as to the wisdom of the selection made from those poems written during those years."[40] He says that the contributors had a greater hand in the selection than one might expect; "in some cases, poems which might have been omitted by me have been added by them; and in other instances, those selected by me have been cancelled."[41] Nevertheless, Gill has shown how Knight's attitude towards the selections made by his contributors verged, at times, on the dictatorial; the poet's nephew Charles, bishop of St. Andrews, for example, was essentially (if ever so politely) ordered to choose a selection of *Ecclesiastical Sonnets* that exactly replicated Knight's own.[42] We should therefore take Knight's "democratic" claims with a pinch of salt. Of all the contributors, only Browning, Lord Selbourne, and Russell Lowell are credited with specific critical responses. Selbourne liked "A Jewish Family," but not enough to include it; Lowell, the reader is informed baldly, "approved" of Knight's list.[43] Knight's presentation of Browning's response, though, is of an entirely different character: it is dealt with in great detail. Knight quotes very extensively from Browning's letters, in particular from those of August 10, 1885 (in which Browning accepted the task), November 30, 1885 (Knight quotes the lines in which Browning declares that he will use his wife's annotated edition of Wordsworth), and February 24, 1886 (nearly in its entirety).[44] He thus makes plain to the reader the amount of prevarication in which Browning indulged before delivering the goods. He does omit the 1883 refusal to speak on Wordsworth (with its epic sentence of justification) and Browning's excuses about the dearth of Wordsworth collections in Venice in 1885, but an astute reader could surely have detected something amiss in Browning's ocean of verbiage. As well as laying Browning's troubles open to the world, Knight adds the rather gratuitous comment that "Mr. Browning's reference to Wordsworth in 'The Lost Leader', and his letter to Mr. Grosart on the subject of that poem, are [*sic*] well known."[45] Here there may be a glimpse of Knight's motivation for his pursuit of Browning—he knew full well that Browning had denigrated the Master, and had attempted to justify his attack in unconvincing terms.

Did Knight have permission to quote from Browning's correspondence so extensively, publicly, and revealingly? Browning had consistently refused to "say something" in public about Wordsworth for years; yet here he is, doing just that—or, rather, attempting to explain why he *can't* do just that. Browning had presumably known that Knight would publish his list, but whether he knew his letters would become public property is another matter. As an intensely private man, he is unlikely to have reacted well to someone publishing his private letters. The list is apparently unrevealing; the letters rather less so. Unfortunately, there is no firm evidence as to how Browning saw the publication of the volume. He did not, as far as is known, correspond with Knight after 1887, but this is not necessarily a sign of displeasure. Strangely, though, Knight does not seem to have sent Browning a copy of the volume upon its publication in 1888. As the only one of the contributors to have his list published in its entirety in the book, as well as large sections of his letters, it would surely have been the least of courtesies for Knight to send Browning a complimentary copy. However, there was no copy of the selection in the library put up for sale on Pen Browning's death in 1913. If Knight did not send Browning a copy, why not? Could he have feared Browning's displeasure? Alternately, if he *did* send Browning a copy of the book, what happened to it?

It is impossible to answer these questions with certainty. There is one clue, however. In *The Browning Collections*—which contains a list of all the items put up for sale in 1913—there are a few items that can be connected with the Browning-Knight correspondence. There is a copy of Knight's *The English Lake District, as Interpreted in the Poems of Wordsworth*, published in 1878, and inscribed to Browning by the author, which indicates that the two were at least acquainted before the first letter that survives from their correspondence.[46] There are also copies of the 1904 volume *Retrospects*, in which Knight printed his correspondence with Browning in full, and of a volume Knight edited in connection with Browning's centenary celebration in 1912—inscribed to Browning's daughter-in-law, which would suggest that whatever ill effects the publication of extracts from the letters in 1888 may have had on the poet himself, Knight remained on polite terms with the family.[47] Of more interest, however, are two copies of the *Transactions of the Wordsworth Society* (nos. 1 and 5), evidently sent to Browning by Knight.[48] On the cover of no. 1, published in 1882, someone (presumably Knight) has written "Wordsworth," followed by "To [Robert Browning] Esq from W. K. Specimen of Preface." The words "Robert Browning" have been erased. On the inside front cover is affixed a note by Wilfred Meynell, who bought the lot containing this volume: "Browning's copy sent to him by W(illiam) K(night) B's name erased, I can't guess why. W.M."

Did Browning himself erase his name? Either Fannie or Pen Browning may have done so, after the poet's death. Sarianna, the poet's sister, cannot be ruled out. Despite having the opportunity, though, none of these three had much of a motive for such an act. Perhaps, if Browning had died on bad terms with Knight, any one of them may have scrubbed out his name in an odd act of postmortem revisionism. Pen disliked Orr's biography of his father, and perhaps he felt similarly towards Knight. Nevertheless, it seems more likely that Browning erased his own name. Even in his genial later years Browning was capable of outbursts of fury, the most famous example being the savage way he attacked Edward Fitzgerald in verse in 1889.[49] Browning is also said to have—presumably drunkenly—threatened his friend John Forster with a carafe.[50] It is not unreasonable to postulate a similar, if less public, reaction to Knight's publication of the correspondence. Perhaps Browning's reaction was not dissimilar to that of Edouard Manet upon being presented with a double portrait of himself and his wife by Degas; Manet found the portrait of his wife unflattering and hacked her face out of the painting, much to Degas's mortification.[51] Browning's erasure of his own name from Knight's publication may have served similar ends; by erasing his name, he would have been disclaiming any connection with its editor. The fact that the *Selections* was not put up for sale in 1913 is equally conducive to the theory that Browning was angry with Knight; either Knight did not bother to send Browning a copy (itself an insult) or he did, and Browning, angered by its contents, disposed of it.

One other factor about the 1888 volume may have angered Browning: the fact that, having pestered Browning for years to supply him with a list of favorite Wordsworth poems, Knight failed to print most of them in his own selection. He tells us, "[L]ast year I sent a copy of the poems selected for this edition to Mr. Browning. He went over it, and expressed his approval of all that were proposed to be included, but added the following fifteen."[52] The list then follows. It is intriguing that this list, published in 1888, differs from the one Knight reproduced in his *Retrospects* volume of 1904. It includes four poems that Knight was not to reproduce in the list in 1904: "Lucy Grey," "The Pet Lamb," "'Tis said, that some have died for love," and "The Childless Father," all published in *Lyrical Ballads* (1800). Why are they absent in 1904? Knight may have simply forgotten them, but this would postulate that he could not be bothered to check his original list when he was writing *Retrospects*. This is a minor, yet baffling, puzzle. Even if Knight had somehow wished to exclude these four poems when he published the list for a second time in 1904, the original list was already in the public domain.

The "additional" poems (a misnomer, since they appeared in Knight's *original* list) confirm a bias in Browning's tastes towards the early works. Once they are added to Browning's list and this list is compared with the poems Knight actually decided to print, the reasons why Browning may have felt aggrieved are clearer. Knight, having named the poems in Browning's selection, publishes only *five* of them: "The Reverie of Poor Susan," "The Complaint of the Forsaken Indian Woman," "'Tis said, that some have died for love," "The Eclipse of the Sun, 1820," and "A Jewish Family." This not a declaration of faith in Browning's critical powers; Knight has judged ten of his favorites unworthy of printing. What is insulting is not the way that Knight does not share Browning's judgment about which poems should be printed—he was, after all, the editor—but the way that, by printing Browning's selection, Knight makes it clear that he disagreed with the majority of his choices. The other nineteen contributors are not exposed in this way; the focus of the preface to the 1888 volume is almost entirely on Browning—and not to his credit.

Browning had apparently gained very little by submitting to Knight's pressure and sending him his list. However, a detailed examination of the list reveals that he seems to have decided to issue a *challenge* to his persecutor—a challenge that Knight, a scholar of Wordsworth rather than Browning, was unsuited to accept, or even notice. Some of the poems in the list form strands in a "web of reference" of Browning's own creation. Browning was creating a network in which images, phrases, and ideas in these poems remind the astute reader of other works, including those by Browning *and* Wordsworth. When these strange linkages are examined, the nature of Browning's reluctance to discuss Wordsworth in public becomes clearer and leads to a consideration of a radical change of attitude towards Wordsworth, given expression in *Fifine.* This reconsideration can be treated as a second "creative misreading" of Wordsworth; as in 1840, Browning seems to have wished to keep his misreading as hidden as possible, and therefore published it in a poem that, like *Sordello,* would provoke almost universal bafflement. Knight could hardly have been expected to have understood, or even read, *Fifine*; therefore, he could be offered Browning's "encoded" list of Wordsworth poems. It is only in the course of an extended study of Browning's relationship with Wordsworth that one can perceive that the list is in fact an admission, on Browning's part, of his *second* change of opinion vis-à-vis his predecessor.

7

Browning's Wordsworth Selection

WE WILL FOCUS IN DETAIL UPON SEVEN OF THE POEMS IN THE LIST, BUT ALL OF THE poems—except, perhaps, "The Eclipse of the Sun, 1820"—in some way comment upon Browning's relationship with Wordsworth. The main theme that emerges from the list is that of Wordsworth's *humanitarianism*; in particular, his sympathy for poor, lonely, bereaved, and otherwise suffering figures, from the oppressed Goody Blake to the stoic Timothy in "The Childless Father." None of the poems display Wordsworth's "egotism," or the contempt for the "real" that in *Sordello* metaphysical "nature poets" were condemned for. The Wordsworth of Browning's list is a man profoundly aware of the reality of human suffering, and concerned to grapple with it in his art. All of the poems except "Rob Roy's Grave," "Star-gazers," "Dion," and "The Eclipse of the Sun, 1820" are of this type; their selection is the most straightforward part of Browning's "apology." By choosing them Browning was confessing that Wordsworth had always been aware of human suffering—he displays his humanitarianism in poems written over a thirty-seven-year period, up to the late "A Jewish Family," a poem that would also have appealed to Browning's well-known sympathy with the Jews. The poems display a wide—and balanced—variety of suffering and loneliness; three deal with women ("The Reverie of Poor Susan," "Goody Blake and Harry Gill," and "The Complaint"), three with children ("The Danish Boy," "Lucy Gray," and "The Pet Lamb"), and three with men ("'Tis said," "The Childless Father," and "The Farmer"). It is interesting that in the list supplied by Knight these primarily humanitarian poems are given together, in the first half of the list; it is unclear whether this was Browning's own order, but if it was, the poet seems to have been giving his list a degree of thematic coherence.

The list is also surprisingly deficient, for a list of Wordsworth poems, of "nature poetry." Browning's own work was always far more interested in humanity than nature, and he seems to have chosen poems in which Wordsworth displays a similar interest. Though many of the characters in the poems are country-dwellers, Wordsworth chooses to dwell upon their own lives and (usually) unhappiness rather than upon the natural landscape around them. In "'Tis said," for example, the bereaved speaker, despite dwelling on "Helvellyn's side," cannot take comfort in the natural landscape; indeed, it *torments* him:

> Roll back, sweet Rill! Back to thy mountain-bounds,
> And there for ever be thy waters chained!
> For thou dost haunt the air with sounds
> That cannot be sustained.
>
> (lines 29–32)

The man's human grief overwhelms his appreciation for nature, and the landscape brings him no comfort. The similarly bereaved Timothy, in "The Childless Father," sets out for the hunt in the wild landscape around Skiddaw with a "tear on his cheek" for his lost child, rather than a determination to focus upon natural grandeur (line 20). The characters generally display a very human inability to take "Wordsworthian" comfort from nature. The poems depict a Wordsworth only too aware that nature may not always be enough; even the two characters who are at least temporarily sustained by thoughts of their rural homes, "Poor Susan" and Adam, the farmer of Tilsbury Vale, find this sustenance to be only temporary and remain trapped in the brutally exploitative world of London.

It is also interesting that four of the poems Browning chooses are set in London: "The Reverie of Poor Susan," "The Farmer of Tilsbury Vale," "Power of Music," and "Star-gazers" (the last three appearing—perhaps intentionally—together in the list). Browning was born a Londoner and lived there for much of his life; this may partially account for his interest in these poems (just as his years residing in Italy may have drawn him to the otherwise unimpressive poem "The Eclipse of the Sun, 1820"). However, he may also have desired to depict Wordsworth as a London poet as part of his effort to present a humanitarian Wordsworth, as aware of urban misery and suffering as of its rural equivalent. The stargazers, the blind fiddler's listeners in "Power of Music," Poor Susan, and old Adam are all victims of an exploitative commercial world from which they can only make the briefest of escapes—and the "escape," if it can be so called, of the stargazers seems to render their world even more unsatisfactory.

Browning may also have chosen the poems because he felt them to be of high quality. Of the list, only "The Eclipse of the Sun, 1820" is an inferior effort, and all of the poems taken from the *Lyrical Ballads* and the superb *Poems, in Two Volumes* of 1807 are fine (if not generally well known) works. "Lucy Gray," "'Tis said," and "Star-gazers" are particularly powerful and haunting. All of the poems, except, perhaps, "The Eclipse of the

Sun, 1820," also form part of Browning's "apology" to Wordsworth, but seven are of particular interest, in that their selection has additional motives to those suggested above: "Rob Roy's Grave," "Power of Music," "Stargazers," "Dion," "The Reverie of Poor Susan," "The Farmer of Tilsbury Vale," and "The Complaint."

"Rob Roy's Grave"

Wordsworth published "Rob Roy's Grave" in 1807. He wrote it while brooding over the collapse of the French Revolution into terror, the tyranny of Napoleon, and, ultimately, bloody pan-European warfare. Initially, the poem seems to have little to do with France. Gazing upon Rob Roy's grave, Wordsworth speculates upon his "moral creed" and ironically imagines the outlaw—were he as *wise* as brave—preaching a revolutionary "might-is-right" philosophy. "Books," "statutes," and other regulatory mechanisms are dismissed in favor of an animalistic struggle for survival:

> "the simple Plan,
> That they should take who have the power,
> And they should keep who can."
>
> (lines 38–40)

In fact, this "revolutionary" is preaching a reactionary doctrine; if might is right, then surely the "rents and factors, rights of chace, / Sheriffs, and lairds and their domains" cannot be faulted for their tyranny (lines 69–70). Rob Roy's "revolutionary" message is calculated to excuse his own ambition:

> "Since then," said Robin, "right is plain,
> And longest life is but a day;
> To have my ends, maintain my rights
> I'll take the shortest way."
>
> (lines 53–56)

He inserts the Darwinian proviso that the iron laws of nature forbid "wanton cruelty" and simply ensure that everyone rises—or falls—to the appropriate level (lines 45–48). This rhetoric is cynically deployed; he wants to destroy the existing system in order to establish another—controlled by himself—in its stead. Wordsworth is not in fact presenting the reader with a picture of Rob Roy as he actually imagines him to have been; he explains at the poem's conclusion that the real outlaw loved the "*liberty* of man" (line 104) and was a friend of "all the oppress'd" (line 111). He would, were he living in 1805–6, have "battled for the Right" (line 108). *Wordsworth's* Rob Roy is, in fact, a satirical portrait of Napoleon, who rose to power through similar machinations; Wordsworth's view of Napoleon's career helps to explain his later fear of radicalism and revolution. Men like Hazlitt and Blake, who remained radicals all their lives, remained in a minority during this period; the actions of Napoleon turned most of the admirers of the Revolution into reluctant allies of the status quo.[1]

Wordsworth goes on to "lament" the way Rob Roy was defeated by "Polity." In 1807, with Napoleon as his example, Rob Roy would have been inspired to conquer more territory:

> And to his sword he would have said
> "Do thou my sovereign will enact
> From land to land through half the earth!
> Judge thou of law and fact!
>
> "'Tis fit that we should do our part;
> Becoming, that mankind should learn
> That we are not to be surpassed
> In fatherly concern.
>
> "Of old things all are over old,
> Of good things none are good enough:-
> We'll shew that we can help to frame
> A world of other stuff.
>
> "I, too, will have my Kings that take
> From me the sign of life and death:
> Kingdoms shall shift about, like clouds,
> Obedient to my breath."
>
> (lines 77–92)

His declaration that he, like God, will have obedient kings below him simultaneously describes his desire to usurp the existing power structures and his implicit acceptance of them. He wants to be God. His desire to "shift about" kingdoms is reminiscent of the "wanton cruelty" of tyrants like Marlowe's Tamburlaine—cruelty he had earlier declared impossible in "Nature." In the two middle stanzas he adopts the royal "we," declaring his "fatherly concern" for his subjects and thus adopting the jargon of despotism. Importantly, he also adopts a utopian pose similar to that of the more extreme French revolutionaries. Wordsworth is attacking the rejection of what *is* (in favor of dream visions of what *might be*) that characterized those who initiated the Terror. The fact that Rob Roy's utopianism is a mask for personal ambition adds to the force of Wordsworth's assault.

When Wordsworth wrote this poem, he had seen radicalism go sour; *The Prelude*—and the description of the Solitary's career in *The Excursion*—depicts the traumatic effect of the French Revolution's collapse on its supporters. He had come to recognize that it was safer to throw in his lot with the lesser "tyranny" in Britain. In selecting this poem, Browning was indicating that his dismissal of Wordsworth had been unfair; in "Rob Roy's Grave" Wordsworth proves himself capable of humanism. Browning was implicitly confessing that his earlier admiration of his predecessor's realistic humanism had not been misplaced. He chose several other poems to join "Rob Roy's Grave" in his confessional montage; all of these poems refer back to a moment in Browning's career when he "reversed" his reading of Wordsworth and admitted that he had been "wrong" about him for over thirty years. This moment came in *Fifine*. Browning used the list he sent to Knight as an "index" to his reconsideration of Wordsworth that the determined could decode.

Consider "Rob Roy's Grave" in the light of *Fifine*. The important lines are the stanzas in which Rob Roy expresses the utopianism used by tyrants—specifically, the phrase "we'll shew that we can help to frame / A world of other stuff" (lines 87–88). This belief that a sweeping rejection of things both "old" and "new" could remake humanity was, for the younger Browning, one of the central tenets of romanticism, and one of the main reasons he rejected it. However, Browning began to reconsider his earlier attack on romanticism after he had published *The Ring and the Book*; *Balaustion* shows him adopting a more tolerant attitude towards the wilder claims for poetry put forward by the romantics. It is strange, then, to find these lines in section 109 of *Fifine*, in which the narrator attempts to deduce "the lesson of a life" from his dream vision of the Venetian carnival:

> And—consequent upon the learning how from strife
> Grew peace—from evil, good—came knowledge that, to get
> Acquaintance with the way o' the world, we must nor fret
> Nor fume, on altitudes of self-sufficiency,
> But bid a frank farewell to what—we think—should be,
> And, with as good a grace, welcome what is—we find.
>
> (lines 1879–84)

The lesson is a rejection of utopianism in favor of a decision to deal with the world as it is. The most utopian breed of romanticism, one that arrogantly "frets" and "fumes" on "altitudes of self-sufficiency," is condemned as lacking in humanistic efficacy: the breed of romanticism rejected in *Sordello*, in the person of Wordsworth. In the light of *Sordello*, this attack on extreme romanticism should come as no surprise. What is odd is the way the lines seem to indicate that Browning has turned his back on the more tolerant attitude towards romanticism displayed in *Balaustion*, and returned to the hard-nosed attitude displayed in *Sordello*. This is strange—until the lines are considered in the light of Browning's later choice of "Rob Roy's Grave" as a personal favorite.

The poem contains an ironic attack upon utopians who claim the ability to produce a "world of other stuff"; Wordsworth intimates that if "liberty" is attainable, it is only through a determination to deal with the world realistically. This is the very idea expressed in these lines from *Fifine*. "Rob Roy's Grave" makes it clear that Wordsworth had realized the importance of realistic humanism and the dangers of fantasy back in 1805–6, some years before what Browning saw as his collapse into conservatism. Thus, to condemn Wordsworth for dreaminess in 1840 had been unjustifiable.

Another aspect of the poem would have troubled Browning. The poem demonstrates Wordsworth's realization that utopianism is fruitless, and thus serves to explain why he became a conservative. This would have reminded Browning of his *own* rejection of romanticism. He had come to the conclusion that the only winnable humanistic struggle was that for "youth and strength and health"—*bodily* happiness. The possibility that the whole race could be "dizened out" as "chiefs and bards" was out of the question. Browning had, far from embracing his republicanism anew, *diluted* it in the cause of making it more realistic; he had been forced to compromise. Is this so very different from Wordsworth's rejection of *his* radical excesses? Wordsworth would have argued, like Browning in *Sordello*, that the dreams of his youth were sterile and antihumanistic, as well as being capable of being turned to evil ends. His "betrayal" of the radical cause therefore sprang from reasons uncomfortably close to Browning's own. Browning had come to realize by the time he wrote *Fifine* that Wordsworth knew perfectly well that it was necessary to "bid a frank farewell to what—we think—should be / And, with as good a grace, welcome what is—we find."

"Power of Music"

"Power of Music," also published in 1807, presents Wordsworth's account of a blind fiddler he observed in Oxford Street and the effect of his music upon his listeners. The fiddler's music has "power" indeed—it enchants "twenty souls" and transports them from the squalor of their ordinary lives to a world of happy dreams. Wordsworth explicitly compares the fiddler's power with that of Orpheus, whose music moved trees, animals, and even rocks to dance:

> An Orpheus! An Orpheus!—yes, Faith may grow bold,
> And take to herself all the wonders of old;—

Near the stately Pantheon you'll meet with the same,
In the street that from Oxford hath borrowed its name.

(lines 1–4)

The fiddler's gift for enchanting humans rivals that of his predecessor. Wordsworth particularly emphasizes the way he alleviates the sufferings of working-class people:

What an eager assembly! what an empire is this!
The weary have life, and the hungry have bliss;
The mourner is cheared, and the anxious have rest,
And the gilt-burthened soul is no longer opprest.

(lines 9–12)

His listeners are all poor workers—the "Gibeonites," as Browning called them in *Sordello*, neglected by the quasi-Wordsworth as they thirsted in the desert. Their burdens are emphasized: the "pale-visaged Baker, with basket on back," the "Porter" who "sits down on the weight which he bore," and the "Lass with her barrow." All these people are temporarily relieved of their loads while they listen to the fiddler's music, and given time to breathe:

That errand-bound 'Prentice was passing in haste—
What matter! he's caught—and his time runs to waste—
The News-man is stopped, though he stops on the fret,
And the half-breathless Lamp-lighter he's in the net!

(lines 17–20)

A mother "whose Spirit in fetters is bound" is given a brief taste of freedom, and there is, perhaps, a comic reference to Orpheus's power over the vegetable world in the "tall Man, a Giant in bulk and in height" (line 33) whom "the music stirs . . . like wind through a tree" (line 36). The fiddler does not act out of philanthropy—he fiddles for the "boons" his listeners drop into his hat—but Wordsworth emphasizes his blindness and suggests that his benefactors are well rewarded. They are, briefly, removed from a brutally commercial world in which predatory "Coaches and Chariots" (line 41) "fly" and "pursue" each other (line 44). (The "Coaches and Chariots" will reappear in "The Farmer of Tilsbury Vale.") The fiddler is thus using his aesthetic abilities in a socially beneficent fashion; in his combination of altruism and self-interest he is reminiscent of Paracelsus, who alleviated suffering with hallucinogenic drugs in return for money. Both the fiddler and Paracelsus are *realistic* figures, in comparison with the fantastic Orpheus; neither can enchant "stocks and stones," and the "new world" they conjure up is illusory. All the same, in their more limited ways, both demonstrate the "power" to alleviate suffering and make the world—briefly—bearable.

The fiddler's humanistic program is similar to the realistic one Browning adopted between 1840 and 1869—the fiddler's music cannot save the souls of his audience, but it can, for a period, ease their bodily pains. The crucial difference is that Browning's post-*Sordello* program tended ultimately to the abandonment of "poetry"—the equivalent of the fiddler's music—altogether, and its replacement with something close to "realistic" fiction. Browning's "romantic" nightmare was of the poet simply producing meaningless noise; the fiddler produces noise, but justifies this outpouring by the beneficial effects of his music. He has created a *synthesis* of humanistic romanticism. If Wordsworth's Rob Roy embodied romanticism corrupted, the fiddler embodies romanticism purified through its social benefits. The comparison of the fiddler to Orpheus is particularly interesting; in 1887 a Wordsworth poem describing the granting of quasi-Orphic powers to a blind fiddler is seen by Browning as entirely justifiable, rather than as insane fantasy (as he had said to Ruskin in 1855). By choosing this poem, Browning is indicating what, in his opinion, a poet ought to be: one whose quasi-Orphic powers are used for humanistic purposes.

Like "Rob Roy's Grave," this poem's selection leads back to *Fifine*; that poem contains a similar portrait of a "poet" with quasi-divine powers. In section 78 Juan retells the tale of Arion, a semilegendary lyric poet and cithera player who is said to have invented the dithyramb. Herodotus tells of the time Arion was threatened with murder by the sailors transporting him to Corinth, where he lived at the court of the tyrant Periander. Arion played a dirge before leaping into the sea; his music enchanted a school of dolphins, which carried him safe to shore.[2] Browning's use of this tale demonstrates his changing attitude towards the power of music—and of poetry. Juan declares that his tale is "fable, therefore truth" (line 1291). Arion's music has *power*: power to enchant both Periander's court and the dolphins, and thus to save his life. It causes buildings to tremble (lines 1301–3). Indeed, it enchants all Corinth ("one breast / A-throb for song and thee" [lines 1297–98]). Balaustion elevated poets to the unique position of the "one royal race." Juan reiterates this lofty idea of the poet's role: "nay, Periander pressed / The Methymnaen hand, and felt a King indeed" (lines 1298–99). Periander the tyrant is himself "royal"; yet Juan intimates that he is only *confirmed* in his royalty when he presses Arion's hand. This reminds us of Balaustion's vision, in *Balaustion's Adventure*, of poets who have the power to "hand on" their godlike gifts, and thus spread the benefits of their song abroad in a *democratic* sense (lines 2420–25). Arion passes on a measure of his power, and allows Periander to share his "true" royalty. His gift is quasi-divine; he is called "that great mouth of the gods" (line 1300). In presenting the reader with this vision of Arion, Browning is repeating Balaustion's earlier message about the status of poets. Balaustion did not grant her poets Orphic powers, but she did see them as being worthy of "standing up and being worshipped." Here, in *Fifine*, the reader is presented with an example of what, in Balaustion's opinion, a poet ought to be; Periander guesses "how Phoebus' self might give that great mouth of the gods / Such a magnificence of song!" (lines 1300–301). Yet this "mouth" also has the democratic gift of passing on its gift to others.

So far, the Arion story has reiterated the limited vision of the "power" of poetry given in *Balaustion*. Arion's music makes the walls tremble and "transmutes" his listeners, but does not rival that of Orpheus in fantastic powers; yet Juan goes on, in section 78, to retell the story of Arion's miraculous escape in a way that for the first time seems to acknowledge that the tales about Orpheus were *not* fantasies. The poetry of Euripides, as used by Balaustion, had "power" over the Syracusans; but this "power" was explicable in psychological terms. It was also firmly rooted in historical fact, since the original tale was recounted in Plutarch's *Life of Nicias*. Browning was thus moving away from his previous belief that poetry was "all teaching" and toward a synthesis of humanism and romanticism that did not need to go so far as to grant poets Orphic powers. Yet here, less than a year later, the reader meets Arion, an impressive figure, whose performance lends him a regal air: "so stand thou, and assume the robe that tingles yet / With triumph" (lines 1304–5). The "assumption" of the robe reminds us of the investment of a monarch—indeed, the way that Arion seems to draw the robe around "himself" is reminiscent of Napoleon's self-coronation. Arion's majesty is similarly self-created; he is inspired by the gods, but it is emphasized that he is not merely a "great mouth":

> So, standing on the bench o' the ship, let voice expend
> Thy soul, sing, unalloyed by meaner mode, thine own,
> The Orthian lay.
>
> (lines 1307–9)

The dithyramb was, it is said, Arion's invention; he was a "romantic" before the romantics, "expending" his soul and expressing "powerful feelings." Like Wordsworth, Arion had invented a new sort of poetry.[3]

Juan continues to emphasize Arion's "royal" status—he leaps into the sea "from music's lofty throne" (line 1309). Juan concludes with the story of Arion's escape. Orpheus may have been able to enchant animals to dance, but Arion moves them to save his life. The "exquisite sea-thing" recognizes Arion's majesty. In *Balaustion* poetry justified itself through its ability to ease physical suffering; its "power" was seen in a fundamentally *realistic* way. Nevertheless, Balaustion's vision is not entirely in accordance with Browning's earlier vision, which explicitly rejects the democratic vision of the race "dizened out as priests and bards." In *Balaustion* the poet is able to "bring forth new good, new beauty, from the old." More remarkably still, in *Fifine* the reader meets a "poet" who is not only worthy of "standing up and being worshipped," but also gifted with magical powers—as he is carried to shore, Arion, the dolphin, and the sea itself are united into one image of victory and triumph, through music, over the natural world:

> Stem tide, part wave, till both roll on, thy jewelled road
> Of triumph, and the grim o' the gulph grow wonder-white
> I' the phosphorescent wake.
>
> (lines 1315–17)

If his performance before Periander was a coronation, his ride on the dolphin's back is the triumphal progress of a newly crowned monarch.

Browning's use of the Arion myth in *Fifine* demonstrates a return to a "romantic" vision of the poet's role. As with "Rob Roy's Grave," the citation of "Power of Music" allowed Browning to gesture towards *Fifine*. Wordsworth's blind fiddler was to Browning an example of what a truly romantic poet should be; romantic poetry could remain poetry and yet do some good. Before moving on, another fact about the Arion legend must be considered: by alluding to this legend, Browning may also have been alluding to another Wordsworth poem.

Wordsworth published "On the Power of Sound" in the *Yarrow Revisited* volume of 1835; the poem contains a retelling of the Arion myth. First comes a reference to Orpheus that makes the "power" of music clear through his near liberation of Eurydice:

> Hell to the lyre bowed low; the upper arch
> Rejoiced that clamorous spell and magic verse
> Her wan disasters could disperse.
>
> (lines 126–28)

Wordsworth is here recounting a myth in which "music" has supernatural powers that serve a *humanistic* purpose. His reference to Orpheus in "Power of Music" similarly alerts the reader to the fiddler's humanism as well as his power. The lines are followed by a passage in which Wordsworth goes on to retell the story of Arion:

> The GIFT to King Amphion
> That walled a city with its melody

Was for belief no dream; thy skill, Arion!
Could humanize the creatures of the sea,
Where men were monsters. A last grace he craves,
Leave for one chant;—the dulcet sound
Steals from the deck o'er willing waves,
And listening Dolphins gather round.
Self-cast, as with a desperate course,
'Mid that strange audience, he bestrides
A proud One docile as a managed horse;
And singing, while the accordant hand
Sweeps his harp, the Master rides;
So shall he touch at length a friendly strand,
And he, with his Preserver, shine star-bright
In memory, through silent night.

(lines 129–44)

The brief reference to Amphion, who was said to have built the walls of Thebes with his music, has its parallel in *Fifine*. In the latter poem, Browning alludes to the myth of Amphion, who "Mad'st moonbeams marble, didst *record* what other men / Feel only to forget" (lines 1585–86). Rather than any more fantastic power, Juan is praising the power of music to preserve the essence of "feeling" long after its creator has died, but it should be noted that Browning uses one of the very same myths Wordsworth used to illustrate another "power of sound" in his own poem. As in Browning's poem, the powers of Arion are also viewed with approval. Particularly important is Wordsworth's declaration that Arion's powers could "humanise" the "creatures of the sea." They are, therefore, doubly "humanistic": they save Arion's life, and they also imbue the dolphins with a "humanity" of their own. Like Balaustion's poets, Arion has the ability to transfer his gift to his nonhuman listeners in a democratic fashion, and elevate them, however briefly, to his human status.

The importance of this poem to Browning is confirmed by his decision to use the Arion myth to describe his newly "romantic" conception of the poet's role in *Fifine*. The lines are paralleled by Wordsworth's depiction of a similar, if less grandiose, figure in "Power of Music"; "On the Power of Sound" is probably the main source for Browning's decision to use the Arion myth in his poem. By using this myth Browning could allude back to Wordsworth in an apologetic fashion; the allusion to Amphion may serve a similar purpose. Wordsworth had used Arion to illustrate a possible use of the "powers" romantics granted to poets and musicians in a positive and humanistic fashion; through himself using this myth, Browning could acknowledge that his predecessor had preceded him in defining a humanistic romanticism.

"STAR-GAZERS"

"Star-gazers" is an ambiguous poem; Wordsworth offers a number of possible explanations for the apparent disappointment of the "spectators rude, / Poor in estate, of manners base, men of the multitude" (lines 21–22) after gazing at the "resplendent Vault" (line 12) of the Heavens through the showman's telescope, but does not offer any one as "truth." The London setting of the poem would have attracted Browning and offered evidence of Wordsworth's sympathy for urban suffering; but there may also be other reasons for the poem's appeal. Wordsworth's admission that even the urban poor, despite their "base" manners, "thirst for power and majesty," is quasi-democratic in its refusal to condemn the poor for "prostrate" souls, and would have impressed the "liberal" Browning. One potential explanation for the stargazers' disappointment may have particularly appealed. Perhaps, Wordsworth says, the Heavens are simply deficient in humanistic interest, as compared to the world in which we all have, perforce, to live: "is nothing of that radiant pomp so good as we have here? / Or gives a thing but small delight that never can be dear?" (lines 13–14). Wordsworth hypothesizes that the poor, hoping to "escape" from their grueling lives through some sort of mystical experience, are brutally forced to confront the fact (well known to Browning) that humanity can take little comfort in "other" worlds (like the stars)—happiness is only to be found on *this* one. This is a message put forward by Wordsworth in "Rob Roy's Grave," and Browning would have selected this poem for similar reasons.

"DION"

"Dion" was first published in 1820. Dion's story was taken from Plutarch's *Parallel Lives*; he was the brother-in-law of Dionysius I, tyrant of Syracuse. When Plato visited Syracuse in 387 BC, Dion became his disciple; according to Wordsworth, Plato's maxims "softened" his "inbred dignity austere" and ensured

> That he, not too elate
> With self-sufficing solitude,
> But with majestic lowliness endued,
> Might in the universal bosom reign.
>
> (lines 12–15)

Upon the death of the tyrant in 367 and the accession of his extremely unpleasant son, Dionysius II, Dion summoned Plato to the court to educate him. Unsurprisingly, since the new tyrant proved to be a grotesquely sadistic drunkard, this noble venture failed; Dionysius exiled Dion, and Plato returned to the Academy. Wordsworth's poem dwells upon the later stages of Dion's career. In 357, Dion returned to Syracuse and, to public rapture, expelled the hated Dionysius:

> Pure transport, undisturbed by doubt or fear
> The Gazers feel; and, rushing to the plain,
> Salute those Strangers as a holy train
> Or blest procession (to the Immortals dear)
> That brought their blessed liberty again.
>
> (lines 26–30)

The Syracusans saw Dion as an almost divine savior; he wore a "white, far-beaming, corslet" (line 24) and "the general voice" (line 39) invoked his "tutelary care, / As if a very Deity he were" (lines 40–41). Nevertheless, Dion's grandiose ambitions to turn *himself* into Plato's ideal ruler collapsed. The Syracusans, encouraged by his treacherous lieutenant, Heracleides, exiled Dion, then cravenly begged for his return when Dionysius launched a counterattack. When the danger had passed, Dion had Heracleides murdered. Plutarch tells us that Dion was tormented by portents after ordering this assassination, including that of "a woman of lofty stature, in garb and countenance exactly like a tragic Fury, sweeping the house with a sort of broom."[4] Such were his feelings of guilt that, Plutarch says, he "declared that he was ready to die many deaths and to suffer any one who wished to slay him." A follower of his named Callippus took him at his word, and murdered him (line 119).

Wordsworth depicts Dion as a noble figure whose downfall is truly tragic. His Dion is an idealist, but not a dreamer; his Platonic learning, Wordsworth implies, makes him an entirely suitable helmsman of the state:

> For him who to divinity aspir'd,
> Not on the breath of popular applause,
> But through dependence on the sacred laws
> Framed in the schools where Wisdom dwells retir'd.
>
> (lines 46–49)

The quality that Wordsworth satirized in "Rob Roy's Grave" is here presented as laudable, within bounds; he describes a possible unification of the freedom of the idealist and the disciplined intellectualism of the scholar. One *can* transcend one's own humanity, but there is only one way to do this; Dion was

Intent to trace the ideal path of right
(More fair than heaven's broad causeway pav'd with stars)
Which Dion learn'd to measure with sublime delight.
(lines 50–52)

The "ideal path" is not some flickering metaphysical vision but one that can, with care and study, be followed—and, Wordsworth suggests, a path that does ultimately lead to the desired destination. Thus, Wordsworth manages to create a more inspiring vision of Dion's story. In Plutarch, Dion's despair is caused solely by guilt; Wordsworth's Dion has even more cause for regret, in that he has ruled himself out of the possibility of "divine" status. His quest for godhood stems from the humanistic wish to use "divine" powers to help the people of Syracuse. The rules he must obey have no place for murder:

But he hath overleap'd the eternal bars;
And, following guides whose craft holds no consent
With aught that breathes the ethereal element,
Hath stained the robes of civil power with blood,
Unjustly shed, though for the public good.
(lines 53–57)

The blood shed by the revolutionaries in France was, supposedly, shed "for the public good"—Wordsworth is influenced by his own awareness of political reality.

Browning long-standing interest in apostates and failures—as evidenced, for example, in *The Return of the Druses* and *Paracelsus*—would have contributed to Browning's interest in Dion's story, but Wordsworth's presentation of Dion's career and ambitions would also have attracted Browning to this poem. One should note the antidemocratic nature of Dion's ambitions and the path he must pursue; he can only become a god by attending the "schools" where "Wisdom" dwells—a path open only to a select few. Wordsworth's appropriation of such a figure is unsurprising, Browning's more so. There is no evidence that he became a reactionary in his later years; why, then, select, as a particular favorite, a poem that is strongly antidemocratic and elitist in bias?

The web of interconnected images and hints that Browning began to spin between 1869 and 1871, examined closely, exhibits signs of a swing *away* from democracy. In *Balaustion* the presentation of the poet's role displays a blend of democratic *and elitist* qualities. Despite the fact that the "poet's privilege" is a democratic gift, the poets are seen as "royal." By *Fifine*, Arion's power and royalty/divinity are emphasized at the expense of his humanistic ability to make Periander feel "a king indeed." In a similar fashion, Paracelsus, in a moment of inspiration, had cried out "I am priest!"—a concept that *Sordello* was to reject. Now, in *Fifine*, Browning has returned to romanticism; his vision of poetry was becoming one of greater individuality and *personal* inspiration. Though Browning had, to a degree, returned to the aesthetic position he had held in the 1830s, his earlier radicalism had mutated into a more elitist aesthetic.

Wordsworth's Dion would have served as a *model* for Browning, combining romantic aspiration and practical, humanistic instincts. Dion's methodology is very similar to Browning's in his concern to avoid "self-sufficing solitude"; he can only reign "in the universal bosom" by adopting a "majestic lowliness." He is not a poet; but he reminds us of Balaustion's poets and Wordsworth's blind fiddler, otherworldly beings set apart from their fellows yet retaining a desire to *share* their gifts. This desire is reminiscent of Browning's in 1840—his decision to abandon dreaming, "prick up" his "republicanism" and set about "certain engagements I have entered into with myself about that same." Yet Dion's scheme is less pessimistic than Browning's, and does not abandon the romantic vision of a perfectible humanity that concluded *Paracelsus*; it retains it, but with a humanistic cast. The Browning of 1840–69 saw himself as "a man speaking to men," his program growing ever more realistic and his contempt for romantic "idleness" ever more extreme. Dion, on the other hand, follows a path that leads him towards divinity. He is not a demagogue, dependent on "the breath of popular applause," rather an ascetic mystic, strictly adhering to a harsh program that will lead him to his apotheosis as Plato's philosopher-king. Dion fails in his mission through human weakness, but the poem is not a warning against such aspirations; Dion's tragedy is that he *could* have succeeded.

Wordsworth's declaration that Dion was "not too elate / With self-sufficing solitude" would have been of particular interest to Browning. It leads the reader back to *Fifine*, where Juan offers the advice that we must "nor fret / Nor fume, on altitudes of self-sufficiency." This idea of "self-sufficiency," attacked both by Browning and Wordsworth, is consistent with the sort of romanticism dismissed by Browning in 1840; if one is "self-sufficient," one has little motivation for active benevolence. Browning's use of the term in *Fifine*, in the light of Wordsworth's in "Dion," acknowledges that Wordsworth had also recognized this. In *Sordello* Browning attacked a quasi-Wordsworth whose "self-sufficiency" blinded him to others' sufferings. Later in *Sordello,* there is another passage that was, after 1863, revised into an explicit attack on Sordello's own "self-sufficiency":

> What made the secret of his past despair?
> —Most imminent when he seemed most aware

Of his own self-sufficiency: made mad
By craving to expand the power he had,
And not new power to be expanded?

(6.488–91) [5]

It is ironic that later in his career he would be forced to "make amends" to Wordsworth by using this very idea of "self-sufficiency"; he still saw it as a bête noir in 1887, but had to change his emphasis to make it clear that Wordsworth had not himself fallen prey to it.

"The Reverie of Poor Susan"

As Kenneth Johnston has pointed out, the "Poor Susan" of this poem may well be a prostitute who has been forced onto the London streets in the early hours after having been thrown out of her rural family home for sexual misconduct, and who is therefore returning from a night's work.[6] If this is the case, Browning would have been drawn to this poem by Susan's resemblance to the beggar woman or prostitute he met in Venice and described in *Sordello*; both figures are viewed with sympathy rather than moral condemnation. As Susan passes down the ironically named "Wood Street," she hears, in "the silence of morning," the song of a thrush that has sung there for "three years" (lines 1–4). The song of the bird transports her in imagination back to her beloved native landscape:

'Tis a note of enchantment; what ails her? She sees
A mountain ascending, a vision of trees;
Bright volumes of vapour through Lothbury glide,
And a river flows on through the vale of Cheapside.

Green pastures she views in the midst of the dale,
Down which she so often has tripped with her pail;
And a single small cottage, a nest like a dove's,
The only one dwelling on earth that she loves.

(lines 5–12)

Thc "music" of the thrush thus acts upon Susan like a benign drug; it allows her to forget the misery of her London life—for a time. Wordsworth is at pains to make it clear that the bird's song cannot achieve any *permanent* alleviation of Susan's suffering:

She looks, and her heart is in heaven: but they fade,
The mist and the river, the hill and the shade:

The stream will not flow, and the hill will not rise,
And the colours have all passed away from her eyes!
(lines 13–16)

Wordsworth will not allow the poem to end on a note of false consolation; he is not condemning the bird's song as pernicious, but neither is he failing to acknowledge that it cannot bring Susan lasting happiness. He has a *realistic* appreciation of the consolations of "music."[7]

This poem has much in common with "Power of Music" (another London poem)—the fiddler's music also helps its unhappy urban listeners forget their sufferings, if only for a brief period. Browning's selection of "The Reverie of Poor Susan" is in accordance with his newly "realistic" romanticism; it acknowledges that poetry has powers, but recognizes their limits. The thrush's song has, for Susan, much in common with the drugs used by Paracelsus to temporarily ease suffering; it demonstrates the usefulness of romantic "fantasy" in a similarly beneficent way. The danger of fantasy like this is the danger of addiction; Browning's quasi Wordsworth in *Sordello* had fallen prey to such "addiction," and after 1840 Browning came to associate such misuse of fantasy with romanticism in general. The bird's song would have represented a "realistic" vision of the "power" of romantic poetry to Browning: it works temporarily, but cannot entirely free Susan from her suffering. Its place in a Wordsworth poem indicates that Wordsworth himself was equally realistic.

"The Farmer of Tilsbury Vale"

The message of "Poor Susan" and "Power of Music" is essentially repeated in "The Farmer of Tilsbury Vale." The farmer, Adam, like Susan, is forced to live and work in London, and unable to return to his rural home (which he has been forced to flee due to bankruptcy). Nevertheless, his imagination provides him with a degree of consolation; sights like "a wagon of straw" allow him to briefly escape from London (like Susan upon hearing the bird's song, or the blind fiddler's audience):

'Mid coaches and chariots, a wagon of straw,
Like a magnet, the heart of old Adam can draw;
With a thousand soft pictures his memory will teem,
And his hearing is touched with the sounds of a dream.
(lines 77–80)

The "coaches and chariots" were also mentioned in "Power of Music" and seem to have symbolized the bustling predatory world of London to

Wordsworth. Adam's imagination allows his "heart" to escape from this world to Tilsbury Vale, his old home (line 88). Nevertheless, as in "Poor Susan" and "Power of Music," Wordsworth is careful to point out that the consoling power of "imagination" is only temporary; Adam (like Susan) will never be able to return home, except through his reveries. Like the fiddler's music or the bird's song, Adam's "fancy" is viewed in a realistic—though not pessimistic—way; the poem would thus have appealed to Browning for the reasons previously discussed.

"The Complaint of the Forsaken Indian Woman"

Though he does not appear to be suggesting that "The Complaint" was a direct influence on Browning, and is unaware of Browning's Wordsworth list, Park Honan has provided a possible "Wordsworthian" rationale behind Browning's selection of this poem for his list. He cites the poem as an example of a monologue that represents "the poet's assumption of a character not quite his own," but is nonetheless "more expressive of the poet's own feeling than of outward incidents or events" and does not "cause the reader to suspend his awareness of the writer's own presence (as he does in reading a play) and to imagine that someone else is really speaking."[8] Even so, he goes on to say that the poem "represents something of a departure from the rest of his lyric verse, as Wordsworth seems to have written few monologues in which the sole 'speaker' is very clearly not intended to be taken as being the poet himself."[9] Honan is thus suggesting that Wordsworth's "Complaint" is an early precursor of the poetic form that Browning, during what is now taken to be his greatest period, made his own—the dramatic monologue. Perhaps this is why Browning selected the poem as a particular favorite. It is one of the poems on the list to be taken from Wordsworth's much-admired *Lyrical Ballads*; this may well have predisposed Browning in its favor from the start. However, the fact that in this poem Wordsworth seemed to be groping toward the dramatic monologue form may well have attracted Browning's attention. It is impossible to say whether the poem had any real influence on Browning's own development of the form, but the fact that Wordsworth and Browning may have, through this poem at least, been working on parallel paths could well have appealed to Browning enough for him to make a private gesture of acknowledgment towards his predecessor by adding the poem to his list.

Browning chose the poems he was to send to Knight with great care, and for a specific purpose; he wanted to assemble a collection containing poems that pointed back to other poems, both by himself *and* Wordsworth, in which his struggle with Wordsworth is perceptible. Thus, even at this stage (when his relationship with Wordsworth was no longer primarily hostile), Browning was attempting to exercise *power* over Wordsworth, as he had in a cruder way in 1840. By using Wordsworth poems to point towards his own work he was simultaneously acknowledging Wordsworth's importance and influence, and rendering Wordsworth powerless in that he was ransacking his achievement for his own ends. His Wordsworth selection thus served several purposes simultaneously: it was an apology to Wordsworth, a way to assert his control over him, and a challenge to his critics—Knight, in particular. It was, in fact, a coded "confession" of, and index to, the complexity and ambivalence of his relationship with Wordsworth.

A warning: this reading of the rhetoric of Browning's Wordsworth selection should not be taken as indicative of any hard-and-fast theoretical stance towards the practice of selection itself. It would be foolish to deny that *this* selection is in fact some kind of statement. But this is not to say that any other selections made by Browning (or anyone else) can be interpreted in this way; each selection must be subjected to similarly close analysis before any conclusions can be drawn.

Many of the "strands" and motifs identified so far lead to Wordsworth's *The Prelude*. An examination of this poem will prove extremely fruitful in the present context, and will allow us to reach some final conclusions about the nature of Browning's struggle with Wordsworth.

8

Browning and *The Prelude*

THE PRELUDE FIRST APPEARED IN 1850, AFTER WORDSWORTH'S DEATH, THOUGH ITS existence had been known of for some years; De Quincey had alluded to it in some of his articles and quoted passages of it from memory. The poem did not have a particularly good reception; for some years after Wordsworth's death, *The Excursion* continued to be considered as his masterpiece. Nevertheless, it was widely read upon its publication. Considering his interest in Wordsworth, one would expect Browning to have read it as soon as it appeared; there is no need to speculate upon this point, however, because in an unpublished letter of May 9, 1850, Browning wrote to his friend Charles Eliot Norton, calling his "gift of the 'Prelude'" "an excellent omen."[1] In quoting this letter, Antony Harrison hypothesizes that Browning meant that Norton's gift of the new poem by the recently deceased poet laureate may have augured well for his own hopes for that position.[2] This is surely most unlikely; Browning never had any serious hope of the job (there is no evidence that he was even mentioned), and the prospect of the madman who wrote *Sordello* as laureate would have caused mass derision. Browning would have known this as well as (if not—painfully—better) than anyone else; his wife, Elizabeth Barrett, was a more likely candidate (and a far more popular poet), and was actually proposed for the post by the *Athenaeum*. It is more likely that the "excellent omen" referred to the possibility of the publication of further unrevealed works by Wordsworth—in particular, the long-promised *Recluse*. A "prelude" is surely a prelude to *something*; Browning may well have expected a follow-up. (He would have been disappointed in this expectation, since the *Recluse* was never written.) He would, therefore, have been referring to his expectation that Wordsworth's humanist *Meisterwerk* was, at last, about to appear; perhaps Wordsworth would "redeem himself" from beyond the grave. Had the *Recluse* actually appeared, Browning's opinion of Wordsworth would certainly have undergone a swift and radical alteration. As things turned out, Browning was left with only *The Prelude*—a massive achievement in itself—to come to terms with.

The copy of *The Prelude* that Norton sent to Browning in 1850 was put up for sale on his son's death; unfortunately, it seems to have gone missing.[3] We have little idea whether Browning read it immediately upon receiving it; nevertheless, there is a considerable body of internal evidence in his later poems that he not only read and absorbed *The Prelude*, but that he was eventually to revise his opinion of Wordsworth's humanistic achievement in the light of it. Browning would make *The Prelude*, and references to it, the veritable core of his "web of reference." In particular, the poem seems to have helped convince Browning that Wordsworth was a realist as well as a romantic, a poet whose struggles and doubts had led to a thoroughly humanistic perspective. The poem would have helped Browning come far closer to Wordsworth, both as a poet and as a man, than any number of awkward personal encounters with the elderly reactionary of Rydal Mount.

The most important way that *The Prelude* would have influenced Browning is through its presentation of Wordsworth as a humanistic figure. In "Dion" Wordsworth used the phrase "self-sufficing" in a pejorative way that the Browning of 1840 would have recognized and that the Browning of 1871 would return to in *Fifine*—as a sort of coded "apology." The middle-aged Wordsworth who had written "Dion" and the youthful Browning were rather closer than Browning felt comfortable with; Wordsworth's use of the phrase in a poem written some thirty-four years before *Sordello* indicates to us (and must have indicated to Browning) that Wordsworth's own program, even in his later years, was not devoid of realism and humanism. Browning could have discovered this by reading "Dion" at any time after its publication in 1820; he would have had no excuse after 1850, though, since Wordsworth uses the phrase twice, both times in the same way, in *The Prelude*. He first uses the phrase in book 2: speaking of his childhood wanderings during his school holidays, Wordsworth confesses that he "was taught to feel, perhaps too much, / The self-sufficing power of Solitude" (2.76–77). This "perhaps too much" is a startling admission for Wordsworth, whose love for solitude was one of his best-known traits. Wordsworth composed most of his poetry during his solitary walks, and the partial admission that all this lonely brooding may have done more harm than good must have come as a surprise to the reader of 1850. It is the fact that the "power" of solitude is "self-sufficing" that worries Wordsworth. He fears that his youthful isolation may have cut him off from his fellows; at line 75 he describes the "diffidence and modesty" that arose from these wanderings, and speaks of "a quiet independence of the heart" at line 72, but his doubts suggest that he saw this "independence" as potentially arrogant and egotistical. Reading this passage in 1850, Browning would have found Wordsworth hinting at a degree of humanism that made him question the preference for solitude that is clearly put forward elsewhere in his poetry—in the poem "I am not One who much or oft delight," for example, in which he reflects with some satisfaction that "from day to day my little Boat / Rocks in its harbour, lodging peaceably" (lines 49–50). One should bear in mind that Wordsworth would generally climb the Lakeland fells alone (when not in the company of his sister), while brooding and composing poetry. When Browning, in *Fifine*, attacks those who "fret" or "fume" on "altitudes of self-sufficiency," one immediately thinks of soaring birds—but was not Wordsworth, lost in his lonely reveries, equally perched on "altitudes" like Helvellyn or Scafell? This reference would have revealed to Browning that Wordsworth, the solitary wanderer par excellence, shared his own doubts about the humanistic efficacy of such behavior.

Another passage in *The Prelude* may help to explain why Browning chose to include "Dion" in his list. In book 9 of the 1850 *Prelude,* Wordsworth, describing the humanistic ambitions of Beaupuis, compares him to Dion himself:

> Such conversation, under Attic shades,
> Did Dion hold with Plato; ripened thus
> For a Deliverer's glorious task,—and such
> He, on that ministry already bound,
> Held with Eudemus and Timonides,
> Surrounded by adventurers in arms,
> When these two vessels with their daring freight,
> For the Sicilian Tyrant's overthrow,
> Sailed from Zacynthus,—philosophic war,
> Led by Philosophers.
>
> (9.408–17)

The passage uses Dion to highlight the virtues of Beaupuis. Beaupuis was a figure, like others already mentioned, calculated to appeal to Browning's desire to unite idealism and realism. Wordsworth tells us that the Frenchman was an idealist who had a vision of perfectible humanity, which he learned in conversations focused on "rational Liberty, and hope in Man, / Justice and peace" (9.395–96). Even in these lines, however, there is a clear indication that the conversations held between Wordsworth and Beaupuis united an idealist vision with humanistic *practicality*—they talked of "hope *in man*." Man's salvation has to come from inside; it will not be spontaneously donated from elsewhere. According to Wordsworth, though, Beaupuis went even further; he attempted to put his program into *action*. His life was motivated by a passionate concern for the poor and oppressed:

By birth he ranked
With the most noble, but unto the poor
Among mankind he was in service bound,
As by some tie invisible, oaths professed
To a religious order. Man he loved
As man.

(9.302–6)

He recognized the follies and cruelties of humanity, but loved his fellows all the same, falling prey neither to idealistic visions of human goodness nor to Byron's cynical contempt. At the same time, Wordsworth makes it clear that there was something mystical in Beaupuis's mission; his vow to ease the sufferings of the poor was akin to the vocation of a monk or crusading missionary. That Beaupuis did not love humanity in the abstract but, on the contrary, loved individual sufferers is made clear by the famous passage in which, confronted by a "hunger-bitten girl" creeping along a lane, Beaupuis "in agitation" declares "'tis against *that* / That we are fighting" (9.517–18). Browning may have read of this incident in De Quincey's article of 1839, and revisited it—perhaps in ironic contrast—in *Sordello*; his reading of it in *The Prelude*, though, coupled with the extended depiction of Beaupuis as a realistic humanist, would have made the story too important to dismiss as insincere. Wordsworth makes it clear that he sees Beaupuis as a "model" in his active benevolence. In the lines immediately preceding the comparison of Beaupuis and Dion, Wordsworth describes the Frenchman's synthesis of idealism and realism in familiar terms:

one whom circumstance
Hath called upon to embody his deep sense
In action, give it outwardly a shape,
And that of benediction, to the world.
Then doubt is not, and truth is more than truth,—
A hope it is, and a desire; a creed
Of zeal, by an authority Divine
Sanctioned, of danger, difficulty or death.

(9.400–407)

What is this creed but the same one professed by Dion in Wordsworth's poem? Like Dion, the Frenchman has an idealistic vision of the way the world ought to be (his "deep sense")—Dion learned his from Plato—and, also like Dion, Beaupuis attempts to give his vision a practical ("to embody his deep sense / In action") and humanistic ("and that of benediction") reality. Also like Dion, Beaupuis determines to follow Divinely ordained *rules* in his quest—"by an authority Divine / Sanctioned." This compares with Dion's "dependence on the sacred laws / Found in the schools where Wisdom dwelt retired" and his intent to "trace the ideal path of right" (lines 48–50). Both Beaupuis and Dion were thinkers *and* men of action; Wordsworth's reference to "philosophic war" is an attempt to depict a *just* war—the fight against tyranny, both humanistic (i.e., the war will liberate the oppressed) and metaphysical (i.e., it has divine backing). Wordsworth's Dion appealed to Browning in his quest for manifestations of the synthesis he was seeking, and he takes his place in Browning's parade of exemplars of this synthesis. Reading *The Prelude*, Browning would have found in Beaupuis another, whose humanistic practicality actually led to him *dying* in the cause of freedom:

> He perished fighting, in supreme command,
> Upon the borders of the unhappy Loire,
> For liberty, against deluded men,
> His fellow country-men.
>
> (9.424–27)

One cannot more readily display one's faith in a creed than by suffering martyrdom for it; and Wordsworth does not suggest that Beaupuis was deluded. On the contrary, it is his opponents who are described as "deluded men"—their "delusion" results in their servitude of the forces of tyranny. It is also important to note the lines immediately following the description of Beaupuis's death. Beaupuis is

> most blessed
> In this, that he the fate of later times
> Lived not to see, nor what we now behold,
> Who have as ardent hearts as he had then.
>
> (9.427–30)

Wordsworth is not saying that Beaupuis was lucky to die when he did, since his hopes were futile; on the contrary, he is mourning the perversion of the ideals of the Revolution that led to war and tyranny. When he wrote these lines, Wordsworth still believed in Beaupuis's vision and that it could be realized; he retained his "ardent heart," despite the Revolution's failure. The writer of these lines was still grappling with the stark reality of what France had become. He still retained his earlier ideals and was troubled by their failure to manifest themselves in the world; he was not the embittered reactionary that he would later become. Far from reflecting Wordsworth's later collapse, the lines point the reader towards a far richer and more complex picture of his metamorphosis. They are indicative of his growing disillusionment with the Revolution, but, unlike certain later poems, this disillusionment does not seem to spring from a fear of change; on the contrary, its roots lie in the fact that the Wordsworth of 1804–5 was *still* an idealist. His sadness is the result of hope frustrated, yet still present ("who have as ardent hearts as we had then"). The description of Beaupuis offers proof that Wordsworth recognized and desired to imitate his blend of idealistic vision with practical wisdom. Wordsworth may have been more of a pure idealist in his youth, but the whole of *The Prelude* demonstrates how Wordsworth had gained in *practical* wisdom as he grew older.

The publication of *The Prelude* would have produced a crisis in Browning's evaluation of his illustrious predecessor, especially in light of his brutal earlier "misreading." *The Prelude* not only contained evidence of Wordsworth's sophisticated reassessment of his earlier idealism, but also intimated further revelations to come (as Browning seems to have assumed in the letter to Norton). Browning could no longer, in all conscience, continue to brand Wordsworth's romanticism as idle and self-regarding. Wordsworth's youthful radicalism was a deeply held creed that only became "perverted" after long years of struggle. *The Prelude* nowhere admits that Wordsworth's vision had been wrongheaded from the start; on the contrary, it maintains that the Revolution's failure was the fault of human wickedness and folly. The revolutionaries had "overleaped the eternal bars," stained themselves with blood, and rushed headlong into disaster. Had they followed the "ideal path of right," they would have eventually ended up at their destination: a humanist utopia *on earth*, not in some idealist's head.

Wordsworth's "The French Revolution"

"The French Revolution, as It Appeared to Enthusiasts at Its Commencement" was written as part of *The Prelude* in 1804, but first appeared as a separate poem in *The Friend* in 1809 and was reprinted as a separate work from 1815. It would ultimately be reassimilated into its parent poem in 1850, as lines 105–44 of book 11. As a poem dating from the troubled period in which Wordsworth was struggling to come to terms with the failure of the French Revolution, it would doubtless have interested Browning long before 1850. It would be easy to dismiss the poem as an evocation of the idealistic dreams of a young man dazzled by the prospects of liberty held out by the fall of the Bastille. As Wordsworth says in "The French Revolution," "bliss was it in that dawn to be alive, / But to be young was very heaven!" (lines 4–5). Certainly, the poem goes on to delineate the idealism that inspired the young Wordsworth and his friend Beaupuis:

Oh! times,
In which the meagre, stale, forbidding ways

Of custom, law, and statute, took at once
The attraction of a country in romance!

(lines 5–8)

The rapture of the times was that of anticipation, not of fulfillment—"not favoured spots alone, but the whole earth, / That beauty wore of promise" (lines 13–14). However, the poem concludes with Wordsworth's explanation of *why* these few brief months seemed to hold out such promise:

Now was it that both found, the meek and lofty
Did both find, helpers to their heart's desire,
And stuff at hand, plastic as they could wish;
Were called upon to exercise their skill,
Not in Utopia, subterranean fields,
Or some secreted island, Heaven knows where!
But in the very world, which is the world
Of all of us,—the place where in the end
We find our happiness, or not at all!

(lines 32–40)

Events seemed to hold out the promise that those who had dreamed of a perfect society would have the chance to build it on *earth*, and no longer merely in imagination. "Stuff" was "at hand" that could be molded (i.e., it was "plastic") to form a new, "just" society. The *corporeality* of this vision appealed to Wordsworth; the Revolution took place *not* in "Utopia," "subterranean fields," or "some secreted island," but in France. Even Wordsworth's earliest and fieriest radicalism had a solidly realistic and humanistic streak, like that of Beaupuis. Browning would have found these lines unavoidable once they reappeared in the 1850 *Prelude*. Like the lines on Beaupuis, they would have disquieted the Browning who had dismissed Wordsworth in *Sordello*, for they plainly demonstrate the unfairness of his attack. The appearance of *The Prelude* in 1850, far from seeming "an excellent omen," must have been profoundly disquieting.

All the same, it seems to have taken Browning over twenty years—that is, until the crisis of reevaluation that led him to "apologize" to Wordsworth in *Fifine*—to admit to himself that he had been wrong to condemn his predecessor. This does not in any way have anything to do with Browning's dislike of Wordsworth as a *man*; what must have really troubled Browning was the way in which *The Prelude* failed so completely to fit in with his previously negative assessment of Wordsworth as a *poet* and, perhaps even more importantly, as a *political* animal. The poem proved that humanism had been a part of Wordsworth's vision of the romantic program from the very start.

That Browning understood and admitted this is evident from a passage in *Fifine* in which he repeats the conclusion that Wordsworth reached at the end of "The French Revolution." The passage is section 109 of the poem, which has already proved of interest with regard to "Rob Roy's Grave" and because it contains the phrase "self-sufficiency." This passage is a rich source when it comes to seeking out allusions to Wordsworth's poetry, so much so that one cannot doubt that Browning had Wordsworth in mind while writing it. In the present context, the exhortation to "bid a frank farewell to what—we think—should be, / And, with as good a grace, welcome what is—we find" is so reminiscent of the conclusion of "The French Revolution" in its desire to construct a more realistic idealism that it can be no coincidence. To admit that he had been wrong about Wordsworth for so many years must have been painful for Browning; therefore, his "confession" is couched in the obscurest of forms. By referring to, say, certain passages from *The Prelude* in *Fifine*, Browning could thus both assuage his conscience and avoid the intolerable business of public self-exposure.

Section 109 also has another parallel in Wordsworth's poetry: the "Elegiac Stanzas," published in 1807. Wordsworth wrote the poem after the drowning of his brother John in 1806. Browning would certainly have read the poem in his youth; it would only have become truly important to him, however, in the light of his post-1850 discovery of the "idealistic humanism" Wordsworth displays in *The Prelude*.

The "Elegiac Stanzas" describe the way the experience of losing his brother *changed* Wordsworth—for the better, the poet implies:

> I have submitted to a new controul:
> A power is gone, which nothing can restore;
> A deep distress hath humaniz'd my soul.
>
> (lines 34–36)

Wordsworth says that he has been *improved* by this calamity; his soul has been "humaniz'd." This implies that before 1806 he felt he lacked "human" characteristics; lost in his own egotism (the "self-sufficing power of solitude"), he had been unaware of the sufferings and vicissitudes that are incident to the lives of most other men. As previously mentioned, De Quincey had noted rather bitterly that Wordsworth's life had been, on the whole, an uncommonly easy one; Wordsworth had, in fact, been "inhuman." According to the "Elegiac Stanzas," it took John Wordsworth's death to shake the poet out of his complacency, a complacency that is, earlier in the poem, linked to the "dreamlike" quality that Browning had condemned in romanticism. Wordsworth says,

Ah! THEN, if mine had been the Painter's hand,
To express what then I saw, and add the gleam,
The light that never was, on sea or land,
The consecration, and the Poet's dream.

(lines 13–16)

These lines present the "Poet's dream" as delusory. What the poet would add to the picture is described as a "consecration," true, but also as "the gleam, / The light that never was." The poetic vision of "Elysian quiet" would have been just that—a vision. At line 29, Wordsworth describes it as a "fond illusion of my heart." This sort of romantic folly is described as the prerogative of youth. Wordsworth made this clearer in the revision of these lines published between 1820 and 1827, in which they became

and add a gleam,
Of lustre, known to neither sea nor land,
But borrowed from the youthful Poet's dream.[4]

The young poet was a dreamer; the mature poet has been "humaniz'd" and therefore has a realistic view of the world, which unites this grim acceptance with an abandonment of egotism and a recognition of the needs and sufferings of one's fellows. This presentation of Wordsworth as a realistic humanist would have interested—and troubled—Browning, particularly in the light of the passages in *The Prelude* already discussed. The poem's final pair of stanzas would have encapsulated, for Browning, this new vision of Wordsworth:

Farewell, farewell the heart that lives alone,
Housed in a dream, at distance from the Kind!
Such happiness, wherever it be known,
Is to be pitied; for 'tis surely blind.

But welcome fortitude, and patient cheer,
And frequent sights of what is to be borne!
Such sights, or worse, as are before me here.—
Not without hope we suffer and we mourn.

(lines 53–60)

These lines would have meant more to a middle-aged and experienced Browning than to his younger self. Browning looked back on his life with anything but sanguine satisfaction as he approached old age. Famously, in *La Saisiaz*, inspired, like the "Elegiac Stanzas," by the death of a loved one, Browning declared that he "must say—or choke in silence—'howsoever came my fate, / Sorrow did and joy did nowise,—life well weighed,—preponderate'" (lines 333–34). The long years of marriage to an invalid seem to have "humaniz'd" Browning in the same way that John Wordsworth's death "humaniz'd" Wordsworth. Browning's whole change of attitude toward Wordsworth can be seen as a process of maturation; what the youthful Browning had rejected, the older, wiser Browning could accept. It seems likely that a central reason for his extreme reluctance to reveal to Knight his eventual positive assessment of Wordsworth's achievements was the realization of how much he and Wordsworth had in common. Both poets had undergone an aesthetic/political crisis in relation to the poet's role. Both men had grappled with the dispute between idealism and realism. In 1840 Browning had concluded that Wordsworth had lost himself in idealistic speculation, and used this conclusion to back up his plunge into "realistic" poetry. But his later rereading of Wordsworth and exposure to *The Prelude* had instead shown him a Wordsworth who had undergone his *own* crisis. Wordsworth had *recognized* the problem—the need for a poetry both idealistic and realistic—and had tried to solve it himself some years before Browning was even born. Wordsworth *had* failed to achieve the synthesis he was seeking (he had never written *The Recluse*), but at least he had seen the problem and tried to do something about it.

Another passage in *The Prelude* was clearly in Browning's mind as he wrote *Fifine*, and particularly section 109. In book 13 of the 1850 *Prelude,* Wordsworth tells us,

> Long time in search of knowledge did I range
> The fields of human life, in heart and mind
> Benighted; but, the dawn beginning now
> To re-appear, 'twas proved that not in vain
> I had been taught to reverence a Power
> That is the visible quality and shape
> And image of right reason; that matures
> Her processes by steadfast laws; gives birth
> To no impatient or fallacious hopes,
> No heat of passion or excessive zeal,
> No vain conceits; provokes to no quick turns
> Of self-applauding intellect; but trains
> To meekness, and exalts by humble faith;
> Holds up before the mind intoxicate
> With present objects, and the busy dance
> Of things that pass away, a temperate show
> Of objects that endure; and by this course
> Disposes her, when over-fondly set
> On throwing off incumbrances, to seek

In man, and in the frame of social life,
Whate'er there is desirable and good
Of kindred permanence, unchanged in form
And function or, through strict vicissitude
Of life, and death, revolving.

(13.16–39)

This is the most important passage in *The Prelude*, as far as that poem's influence on Browning is considered. In these lines, Wordsworth points towards a way in which the poet *could* achieve a synthesis of the type previously discussed. They read as if they had been extracted from the grand "philosophical" poem *The Recluse* was intended to be. The echoes of phrases and ideas from poems already discussed are numerous in the passage, and indicate that section 109 of *Fifine* uses it as a major source. The faith Wordsworth describes in these lines is a blend of idealism and realism that would have appealed to Browning. Wordsworth reveres a "Power" that is "the visible quality and shape / And image of right reason," and this object of reverence would have enthralled both the idealist Wordsworth and the older Browning. The capitalized "Power" is that of "Nature," but this is not what would have primarily interested Browning. It is the *attributes* of "Nature" that are important here, for they illuminate Wordsworth's romanticism in a way that would have made it very attractive to his successor. The "Power" is a combination of the metaphysical and the physical. As a "Power," there is plainly something otherworldly about it, but it is also the "visible" manifestation of the abstract concept "right reason." Wordsworth is saying that the "Power" of "Nature" is simultaneously part of this world (and thus perceptible through the natural world of trees, mountains, lakes, etc.) and the *image* of an abstract concept—"Reason in her most exalted mood," as Wordsworth calls it later in the poem (14.192). Wordsworth is describing a "Power" worthy of reverence that is both metaphysical (and thus appealing to our idealism) and realistic, in that it at least manifests itself in the "real" world. The "Power" is a part, or reflection, of "right reason"; Wordsworth sounds more like some Enlightenment rationalist than a "romantic" poet, but he is talking about "Reason in her most exalted mood" rather than about some arid calculating power. In book 14 Wordsworth seems to equate it with "Imagination":

This spiritual Love acts not nor can exist
Without Imagination, which, in truth,
Is but another name for absolute power
And clearest insight, amplitude of mind,
And Reason in her most exalted mood.

(14.188–92)

Wordsworth is groping his way toward a grand synthesis. In these lines alone Browning could have found proof that Wordsworth had traveled the same road as himself—and proof, indeed, that he had traveled farther.

Wordsworth goes on to declare that the "Power" of nature "matures / Her processes by steadfast laws," and this reminds the reader of "Dion," in which the hero's aspirations are laudable and achievable aims, providing he "measures" the "ideal path of right." Once again, in *The Prelude*, Wordsworth presents us with a vision of the "ideal" path; the "steadfast laws" that the "Power" adheres to seem analogous to the "eternal bars" that one must not break if, like Dion, one wishes to transcend one's humanity and help others to do so. The evidence that Wordsworth had long been thinking on the same lines as himself would have been mounting steadily, though it would take almost twenty years to force Browning to a humiliating reconciliation.

Wordsworth's next declaration—that the "Power" "gives birth / To no impatient or fallacious hopes"—is an indication that Wordsworth had arrived at an acceptance of the realities of human suffering without descending into cynicism. The "impatient or fallacious hopes" are "what—we think—/ Should be," in Browning's phrase; the dreams that Browning used to condemn *all* romanticism in 1840. Wordsworth has not surrendered his idealism, by any means—he worships an abstract "Power"—but the "Power" does not delude its devotees. In "The French Revolution" Wordsworth called "Reason" a "prime Enchantress"—a pejorative description. Now, the "image of right reason" still draws worship from its acolytes, but it is a *benign* intoxication, one that clears, not clouds, one's vision. It unites "reason" with metaphysical idealism in a synthetic whole; the romantics who cast aside all one would consider "realistic" were just as deluded as "realists" who fail to see beyond the physical world. Beaupuis had molded the visionary and the realistically humanistic in this way. His hopes were not "impatient," neither were they "fallacious," since, as Wordsworth says, they were realizable in the corporeal world, like Dion's. They were wrecked by human greed and ambition, but they were not doomed from the start. Browning, too, condemned both idealism at its worst *and* the sort of pure "realism" that inevitably leads to a grim world of self-interest, cruel tyranny, and spiritual death in which "poets," whatever else they may be, certainly have little part.

In 1840 Browning condemned Wordsworth for being too otherworldly; subsequently, he seems to have seen him as being all *too* worldly. *The Prelude* must have persuaded him that Wordsworth had in fact pursued a *middle* road. Wordsworth makes this clear in the lines where he states that the "Power" provokes him to "no heat of passion or excessive zeal" (i.e., fanaticism) *and* "no vain conceits" (the arrogant assumption of superiority that characterized Byron in Browning's eyes). Wordsworth plainly realized that both extremes blend into each other; they both encourage a separation of the self from awareness of the day-to-day existences of that great suffering mass of people Browning imagined "cuffed and huffed" all over the planet. By 1869–71 it was time for Browning to follow Wordsworth in seeking out the "ideal path" delineated in these lines.

The most striking reference in this passage, in the present context, is Wordsworth's dismissal of "quick turns / Of self-applauding intellect." This reference links in with the idea of "self-sufficiency" that Browning attacks as leading to sterile self-absorption. Through using this phrase in his own work, Browning was acknowledging that Wordsworth had himself recognized the dangers of such self-obsession as early as the time he was writing the 1805 *Prelude*. Browning would have found this dismissal of "self-applauding intellect" leaping off the page at him when he read the passage, declaring plainly that Browning, whatever he thought of Wordsworth personally, had been wrong about the self-absorption of his aesthetics. That Browning continued his "humanistic" program for almost two decades after reading *The Prelude* shows just how hard he must have found it to admit his error.

Wordsworth, after an exhortation to "meekness" and "humble faith" inserted in 1838–39, goes on to describe a stoic endurance in the face of the world that once again unites the ideal with the temporal. The imagery used by Wordsworth here is of particular interest to us, in that it is strongly reminiscent of the visionary conclusion to *Fifine*.

At first, Wordsworth sounds thoroughly metaphysical and, indeed, visionary, when he describes a mind perniciously intoxicated by "present objects, and the busy dance / Of things that pass away." This statement would not seem out of place emerging from the lips of the quasi Wordsworth of *Sordello*. In both cases, Wordsworth (or Browning's parodic version of him) presents the corporeal world as inferior to a metaphysical world—as a passing show unworthy of prolonged consideration. The "busy dance" reminds the reader of "the quick dance / Of colour, lights, and forms" found by Wordsworth in London in book 7 of *The Prelude* (7.154–55). However, what comes next proves that Wordsworth is trying to pull together idealism and realism into a grand humanistic synthesis. Woolford argues that reading *The Prelude*'s examination of the distinction between imagination and reality persuaded Browning that a simple equation of vision or dream with illusion was untenable, and that Wordsworth had attempted to transcend this distinction.[5] This is demonstrated in this passage. Wordsworth tells us that the "Power" of nature holds up "a temperate show / Of objects that endure." Behind the "busy dance" of the merely temporal and transient, there are "objects" that are somehow permanent and unchanging, and it is to these "objects" that we should turn in order to avoid the arrogance that comes of "self-applauding intellect." Wordsworth seems to have plunged even further into metaphysical speculation here (the "objects," simultaneously perceptible and eternal, remind the reader of Plato's Forms), but in the next few lines he abruptly introduces a humanistic argument that he uses to create a final synthesis.[6]

Wordsworth advises us to seek "whate'er there is desirable and good / Of kindred permanence" "in man, and in the frame of social life." He has embraced the humanistic program adopted by Beaupuis, who managed to be actively concerned with the realities of human suffering without jettisoning his idealistic impulses (unlike the Browning of 1840, who believed that the two could not go together). He has become like Beaupuis (who "embodied his deep sense / In action"), Dion, and, to a lesser extent, Arion, Balaustion's poets, and all the other representative figures Browning had come to admire by 1869–71. Wordsworth's program is now thoroughly humanistic (hence the importance of "man" and "social life") but still idealistic. Browning had decided in 1840 that one could save men's bodies but not their souls, but Wordsworth is more optimistic. The baffling "objects" that were both metaphysical and perceptible are now less baffling; this permanent quality Wordsworth seeks is to be found in *man* and in his "social life." If we wish to transcend our own egotism and embrace an ideal, Wordsworth declares, we should not seek it in some world of "other stuff," but within ourselves, in whatever "desirable and good" qualities remain unchanged in the souls of men throughout the ages, untroubled by superficial shifts and changes of language or creed, or the vicissitudes of war and conflict. Wordsworth points to an eternal cycle of birth and death that preserves these qualities within its own continuous process of decay and renewal:

> unchanged in form
> And function or, through strict vicissitude
> Of life and death, revolving.
>
> (13.37–39)

This creed harnesses man's idealistic instincts and turns them to a worthy end—a focusing upon those unchanging manifestations of human goodness that convince one that mankind is worth saving. It is the creed of Beaupuis and Dion, men motivated by a desire to save men's souls, to transform them into something *better*—a goal that Wordsworth did not think false or delusory. Wordsworth is saying that idealism is beneficent and necessary to human progress, but it has to become selfless if it is to avoid becoming perverted into egocentric self-assertion. To be "self-sufficing" is to be of no use to anyone, not even oneself.

THE CONCLUSION OF *FIFINE*

Wordsworth's vision of permanence amid change was a profound influence on the conclusion of *Fifine*. In both *Fifine* and *Paracelsus* the central figure is granted a vision of human progress that seems to illustrate the verities of human existence. In Paracelsus's case, the vision is a radical one of the inevitable march of human progress towards a democratic unity of all humanity. Juan's vision in *Fifine* is more complex, and focuses on the *eternal* verities that lie behind all societies, philosophies, and religions—it is not so much linear as it is circular, a vision of eternal recurrence and of what remains amid the whirl of impermanence. Nevertheless, the visions have a basic democratic impulse in common. The democratic aspects of Paracelsus's vision were deeply indebted to Browning's interpretation of Wordsworthian humanism; however, the details of the vision itself are also indebted to Wordsworth, and, in particular, to the lines in *The Prelude* discussed above.

In concluding his poem with a vision, Browning was adopting a "romantic" technique of the sort he had dismissed in 1840. In *Sordello* he had found the beggar-woman tugging at his sleeve and "waking him up" to reality; thereafter, he had resolved to "prick up his republicanism" and write a humanistic poetry fully engaged with the real world. The visionary was dismissed as pernicious. In *Fifine*, however, the visionary is not condemned. Juan falls asleep after playing Schumann's *Carnaval*, and is granted his vision, but he is not condemned for "dreaming." Woolford has pointed out how Juan prefaces his vision with a "Keatsian disclaimer" that seems to allude to *The Fall of Hyperion*: "a poet never dreams: / We prose-folk always do."[7] He goes on to suggest that this "is a hint at what *Sordello* nowhere concedes: that repudiation of the visionary or transcendent was already part of the romantic program, not an external or retrospective operation to be performed on romanticism."[8] Woolford does not seem to be thinking specifically of Wordsworth here, but the lines are as relevant to Wordsworth as they are to Keats. Browning had concluded *Paracelsus* with a Wordsworthian vision, and would do so in *Fifine*; in these lines, he is suggesting that what Juan sees is not, in fact, a "vision," in the sense of a delusion—it is a vision of the *truth* underlying human existence. Browning's interpretation of the significance and use of dream seems to have become something close to Hartman's interpretation of the way Wordsworth's dream of the Arab in *The Prelude* merges the visionary and the mundane: "The dream is a third kind of experience, sharing existentially the hypnotic and fixating character of apocalyptic moments, but thematically the freer traveler-notion of an experience apparently in time and space."[9] Juan is claiming that it is the *poet* who has the ability to perceive the "truth," and it is the common "prose-folk" who "dream." In *Balaustion* Browning seemed to swing back to a more elitist perception of the poet's role, and here this swing is confirmed. Poets are anything *but* visionaries; the only "visions" they see are of the *realities* that underlie the "busy dance / Of things that pass away." As he had throughout his career, Browning is now attempting—now, once again, acknowledging Wordsworth as his most important predecessor—to fuse visionary idealism with realism. And in the case of Juan's vision, with some success.

Despite his readoption of a Wordsworthian aesthetic, however, Browning had not completely reconciled himself with his predecessor; a particularly striking parallel with *The Prelude* demonstrates how he felt that, on occasion, the older poet's humanism was not as profound as it ought to have been. At the start of the vision, Juan is transported to a "pinnacle" above St. Mark's Square in Venice, from which he views the crowd below with disgust until he decides to take the humanistic option of diving in among them. This is reminiscent of book 7 of *The Prelude*, in which Wordsworth describes his "residence in London."[10] Wordsworth summons up a "vision" of the tumultuous city—like Juan's, a "vision" that seems to *elevate* the viewer:

> Rise up, thou monstrous ant-hill on the plain
> Of a too busy world! Before me flow,
> Thou endless stream of men and moving things!
> Thy every-day appearance, as it strikes—
> With wonder heightened, or sublimed by awe—
> On strangers, of all ages; the quick dance
> Of colours, lights, and forms; the deafening din.
>
> (7.149–55)

But unlike that of Juan in *Fifine*, Wordsworth's "elevation" does not, initially, appear to fill him with disgust, though the description of London as an "ant-hill" does not augur well. Wordsworth goes on to describe the variety of people he observes in the streets:

> the mighty concourse I surveyed
> With no unthinking mind, well pleased to note
> Among the crowd all specimens of man,
> Through all the colours which the sun bestows,
> And every character of form and face:
> The Swede, the Russian; from the genial south,
> The Frenchman and the Spaniard; from remote
> America, the Hunter-Indian; Moors,

Malays, Lascars, the Tartar, the Chinese,
And Negro Ladies in white muslin gowns.
(7.219–28)

The cosmopolitan character of London pleases Wordsworth, and he delights in the variety of nationalities and complexions he beholds. So far, Browning would have found a confirmation of Wordsworth's humanism in book 7. However, as the book progresses, a negative note begins to creep into Wordsworth's descriptions. Browning would have noted the way Wordsworth was content merely to *observe* the goings-on around him, rather like a spectator at a play, and did not choose to participate. Indeed, Wordsworth's avowed liking for theatrical "spectacles" and "exhibitions" confirms this preference for observation over participation. He seems to have taken an equal delight in observing the *audience* at these shows from a stance of amused superiority:

Nor was it mean delight
To watch crude Nature work in untaught minds;
To note the laws and progress of belief;
Though obstinate on this way, yet on that
How willingly we travel, and how far!
(7.274–78)

If Wordsworth's preference for observation would have reminded Browning of Aprile, who was too dazzled by "colours, lights and forms" to have any effect on the world, his detachment would have savored of Byron and Wordsworth's own Solitary during his disastrous American sojourn. At the end of book 7, Wordsworth's distaste for humanity in the mass breaks out into the "hideous blotch" spoken of by Festus in *Paracelsus*; Bartholomew Fair, which in its teeming display of the extremities of human behavior and character ought to fascinate the humanist, fills Wordsworth with horror. The way Wordsworth "implores" the assistance of his muse to allow him to perch above the crowd parallels the way Browning positions Juan at the start of *Fifine*'s conclusion:

For once, the Muse's help will we implore,
And she shall lodge us, wafted on her wings,
Above the press and danger of the crowd,
Upon some showman's platform. What a shock
For eyes and ears! What anarchy and din,
Barbarian and infernal,—a phantasma,
Monstrous in colour, motion, shape, sight, sound!
(7.682–88)

Wordsworth goes on to describe the crowd below him with a nausea that parallels that of Juan; he does not see human beings, but "buffoon against buffoon / Grimacing, writhing, screaming" and a parade of horrific grotesques culminating in an appalled vision of

> All out-o'-the-way, far-fetched, perverted things,
> All freaks of nature, all Promethean thoughts
> Of man, his dullness, madness, and their feats
> All jumbled up together, to compose
> A Parliament of Monsters.
>
> (7.714–18)

Humanity is reduced to some filthy discharge:

> Tents and Booths
> Meanwhile, as if the whole were one vast mill,
> Are vomiting, receiving on all sides,
> Men, Women, three-years' Children, Babes in arms.
>
> (7.718–21)

Browning's description of Juan's initial recoil from the ugliness of the revelers below him is extremely similar to Wordsworth's description of his own disgust. It is true that Wordsworth follows his description of Bartholomew Fair with a description of the way he was able to perceive some permanence amidst the "perpetual whirl / Of trivial objects":

> But though the picture weary out the eye,
> By nature an unimaginable sight,
> It is not wholly so to him who looks
> In steadiness, who hath among least things
> An under-sense of greatest; sees the parts
> As parts, but with a feeling of the whole.
>
> (7.731–36)

This passage, in its resemblance to the passage in book 13 of *The Prelude* already discussed, would have—to a degree—served, for Browning, to alleviate the disgust Wordsworth expressed in his description of the fair. All the same, Wordsworth declares that it was only the "Spirit of Nature" (7.766) that sustained him amidst the "press / Of self-destroying, transitory things" (7.769–70) of London, and this reduction of humanity to the status of "things" would not have appealed to Browning. The similarities between book 7 (and the "Bartholomew Fair" passage in particular) and *Fifine*'s conclusion are extensive. He was, in effect, rewriting Wordsworth's description of the disdain he felt for London and its inhabitants in a way that allowed Juan to substitute, in place of Wordsworth's instinctive revulsion, a bold decision to plunge down *into* the crowd. Juan is a Wordsworth who has overcome the antihumanistic disgust manifest in book 7 and decided to mingle with his fellows rather than remain a "Recluse" or a "Solitary." Even at this late stage, when he had admitted to himself that Wordsworth had been a humanist all along, Browning felt that he needed to be corrected on some points.

Juan's is an "antivision" in that it uses the visionary form to condemn its own potential excesses. Though Juan is dreaming, his dream does not allow him to remain perched on his pinnacle. As he gazes down at the "prodigious Fair" below him, Juan reduces the revelers to a collection of more or less distasteful human characteristics:

> On the other hand,
> I soon became aware, flocked the infinitude
> Of passions, loves and hates, man pampers till his mood
> Becomes himself . . . in the main
> A love, a hate, a hope, a fear, each soul a-strain
> Some one way through the flesh—the face, an evidence
> O' the soul at work inside; and, all the more intense,
> So much the more grotesque.
>
> (lines 1712–21)

This motley assortment of "humours" (line 1727) fills Juan with horror; he has no desire to listen to the "vulgar speech" (line 1733) of these simulacra. In his arrogance, he believes he can dispense altogether with the "voice and vanity / Of speech" (lines 1734–35). However, his decision to dive down into the crowd in order to study them more closely, as if they were laboratory specimens, does not lead to a continuation of this sense of superiority; it in fact reduces him to being a "groundling like the rest" (line 1738). A closer study of his fellow "groundlings" transforms Juan's disgust first to "pity," then to admiration—he recognizes that the diversity of each individual from the "prime design" is useful in that it encourages humans to grow and develop through participation in, rather than disdain for, life's struggle:

> And presently I found
> That, just as ugliness had withered, so unwound
> Itself, and perished off, repugnance to what wrong
> Might linger yet i' the make of man . . .
>
> . . . .
>
> . . . for we must learn to live
> Case-hardened at all points, not bare and sensitive,
> But plated for defence, nay, furnished for attack,

> With spikes at the due place, that neither front nor back
> May suffer in that squeeze with nature, we find—life.
> Are we not here to learn the good of peace through strife,
> Of love through hate, and reach knowledge by ignorance?
> (lines 1765–68, 1777–83)

Like Wordsworth in the "Elegiac Stanzas," Juan has realized that one should "welcome fortitude, and patient chear / And frequent sights of what is to be borne." Browning alludes to that poem earlier in *Fifine*; it is plainly in his thoughts again here, particularly in the idea of life as a "squeeze with nature" against which one ought to fortify oneself without losing one's essential humanity. Indeed, as Wordsworth said in the "Elegiac Stanzas," such "deep distress" can "humanize" the soul. Not only that, but such experiences can make one more aware of the way that the less pleasant aspects of human character are the "hard polished cold crystal environment" (line 1793) that protects the vulnerable soul from the world's ravages, like the solid crystal that surrounds a drop of moisture in a "strange orb" unearthed from a "Druid temple" (line 1794). One should not, therefore, scorn the "soul's casing" in the manner of idealists who scorn the flesh. Juan's desire to neglect neither the world nor the soul is reminiscent of Wordsworth's scheme for *The Recluse*, in which he outlined his scheme to link the "individual Mind" to the "external World"—a scheme that deeply influenced *Paracelsus*. Now, in *Fifine*, Browning has returned to this Wordsworthian scheme, and this is made clear in the next part of Juan's vision.

Juan asks himself why he finds himself in "Mark's Square / Rather than Timbuctoo" (lines 1820–21). Woolford has convincingly argued in his article "Browning Rethinks Romanticism" that Browning used Venice in order to point back towards book 3 of *Sordello* and to rewrite the sequence of the palace steps in a fashion more in accordance with the humanism he had belatedly recognized in romanticism. Nevertheless, Juan goes on to show that the location of his vision is immaterial; what he sees as Venice is in fact representative of anywhere in the world: "in all the maze, no single tenement / I saw, but I could claim acquaintance with" (lines 1855–56). What he "took of late / For Venice was the world" (lines 1857–58). This leads him to a profoundly humanist realization: the "proper ground for wisdom" is "the ground / And not the sky" (lines 1867–68), where he had perched in "pinnacled pre-eminence" (line 1866), and it was only through a closer acquaintance with his fellow humans that he learned the "lesson of a life" (line 1878). This lesson is set out in section 109 of the poem (in which Juan rejects "altitudes of self-sufficiency"), the nexus of the poem's references to Wordsworth.

It is not only the humanistic message of Juan's vision that is Wordsworthian, though. Juan goes on to detail the way in which not merely buildings but also religions, sciences, and all manner of belief structures are in a continual state of flux, eternally collapsing only to rise again in other forms:

> But are they only temples that subdivide, collapse,
> And tower again, transformed? Academies, perhaps!
> Domes where dwells learning, seats of Science, bower and hall
> Which house Philosophy—do these, too, rise and fall,
> Based though foundations be on steadfast mother-earth,
> With no chimeric claim to supermundane birth,
> No boast that, dropped from cloud, they did not grow from ground?
> Why, these fare worst of all!
>
> (lines 1913–20)

Juan inspects time's ravages upon the certainties of history, morality, and art, and reaches the conclusion that "all is change"—the nearest man can hope to get to "Truth" is through one of its imperfect temporal manifestations (lines 1941–56). However, his awareness of the impermanence of mankind's attempts to come to grips with reality does not lead to nihilistic despair. The vision becomes truly Wordsworthian when, to Juan's conclusion that "all is change," a "voice" replies with the gnomic remark, "all is permanence!" (line 2010). The continually shifting kaleidoscope Juan has perceived behind human existence resolves itself into a "Druid monument"—a monument at which Juan and Elvire arrive simultaneously with Juan's description of it as he perceived it in his dream. As Woolford says, "Juan wakes from his dream and finds it true"—dream and reality, far from canceling each other out, are one and the same.[11] The monument symbolizes the permanence behind the swirl of change; in the words of Roma A. King, "[T]hey [i.e., the two stones that comprise the monument] express both the temporal-permanent and the sense-spirit dialectic."[12] Juan's initial conclusion about what he has seen and the "voice" he has heard is resolved into "all's change, but permanence as well" (line 2180). The reader of *The Prelude* is reminded of Wordsworth's own attempt to perceive permanence behind "the busy dance / Of things that pass away" through a determination to make the mind seek it in "man, and in the frame of human life."[13] Browning's menhir seems to symbolize a more complex idea of unity and permanence in diversity, but, like Wordsworth's vision in *The Prelude*, it is focused upon the individual soul and "whate'er there is desirable and good / Of kindred permanence" (13.36–37). Juan quotes Aeschylus to describe the semidivine potentialities that lie behind the "falsehood that is change": man's goal is to reach "God, man, or both together mixed" (line 2188). The lines from *The Prelude* are important, because they retain a humanistic focus while aspiring for something *beyond* humanity, just as Wordsworth's Dion did. Browning had rejected romanticism and Wordsworth in 1840 on the unfair grounds that the romantic program's metaphysical aspirations failed entirely to engage with the common concerns of ordinary men and women; in *The Prelude* Wordsworth demonstrated, from beyond the grave, the unfairness of this calumny.

The appearance of *The Prelude* drove Browning to the elaborate apology to Wordsworth in *Fifine*. For an "apology" is precisely what it is. The poem's concluding vision reminds the reader of the Wordsworthian *Paracelsus*. It also indicates a reconciliation with romanticism, in that Browning now feels able to use a romantic technique he would have condemned only a few years before. He can use the visionary to illuminate the real; as Woolford says, "[H]ere, visionary and real overlap."[14] The *form* of the vision itself has been taken from the lines in *The Prelude* that describe what eternally remains amid the chaos of existence. Browning's symbolic menhir is indeed "unchanged in form / And function" (13.37–38) while life and death revolve about it, and creeds and cultures dissolve and re-form in the elaborate dance of Juan's vision. Wordsworth, like Juan, realizes that human attempts to understand this process are futile, and that one should look elsewhere for "Truth":

> Above all
> Were re-established those watchful thoughts
> Which, seeing little worthy or sublime
> In what the Historian's pen so much delights
> To blazon—power and energy detached
> From moral purpose—early tutored me
> To look with feelings of fraternal love
> Upon the unassuming things that hold
> A silent station in this beauteous world.
>
> (13.39–47)

In Juan's vision he is made to understand that to place too much reliance upon human conceptions of history or religion—the "busy dance / Of things that pass away"—is futile, and that the menhir, holding its "silent station," is a more fruitful object of contemplation, despite its fundamental mystery. Both Wordsworth and Browning emphasize that man cannot understand the workings of the universe, and that a healthy awe is more appropriate; Browning, speaking of the "cold dread shape" one finds if one explores the "caverned passage" within the monument, describes it as a

> shape whereon Learning spends
> Labour, and leaves the text obscurer for the gloss,
> While ignorance reads right—recoiling from that Cross!
>
> (lines 2057–59)

By concluding his poem with such an evident debt to Wordsworth, Browning could finally return to the bosom of his mentor and ask for forgiveness, while confessing that he had been wrong to conclude that humanism was no part of Wordsworth's—or, indeed, romanticism's—program. The sea change that first becomes apparent in *Balaustion* reaches its climax here; through reconciling himself with Wordsworth, Browning has returned to a sort of romanticism. He has not, in fact, "purified" it, but, instead, acknowledged that, at least as expressed in the works of Wordsworth, it was a good deal "purer" to begin with than he had so rashly declared in *Sordello*. Once again, as in *Paracelsus*, Browning was confessing that Wordsworth had been the pioneer; he had commenced the work and laid the foundations for the humanistic romanticism Browning was trying to construct.

Bearing this in mind, it is clear why so many of the poems selected by Browning for his Wordsworth list point towards *Fifine* and its conclusion. Knight had pestered Browning for years in a thinly veiled attempt to find out what he really thought about Wordsworth; in pointing him to *Fifine*, the poet was giving Knight exactly what he had asked for, for, besides *Paracelsus*, that poem contains his most profound engagement with his predecessor. Browning was gambling that Knight would not notice his veiled hints, and he appears to have been correct. Not merely Knight, but *all* Browning's contemporary readers seem to have missed his struggle with Wordsworth entirely. The fight, and Browning's final admission of defeat and reconciliation with his opponent, took place in camera.

After *Fifine*, unsurprisingly, there is little evidence of any conflict with Wordsworth in Browning's poetry. Writing *Fifine* had lanced the boil, and the evident delight and playfulness of the poem is perhaps explained by this relief. The heterogeneous nature of Browning's post-*Fifine* output may owe something to the resolution of this struggle; free of the desire (or need) to confront his predecessor, Browning could write as and when he liked, producing such remarkably disparate works as *Aristophanes' Apology*, *The Inn Album*, and *Ferishtah's Fancies*—poems in which Browning could tackle whatever questions were preoccupying him at the time. Only in the prologue to *Asolando* did Browning return to debate with Wordsworth, and even there in remarkably mellow terms. Perhaps, at the end of his long career, Browning fancied a couple of rounds of sparring with his old opponent—for old time's sake, of course, and pulling his punches.

9
Conclusion

BROWNING'S ENGAGEMENT WITH WORDSWORTH CAN BE BEST UNDERSTOOD IN TWO terms: the struggle and the game. First, the struggle. It is clear that Browning's conflict with his predecessor was an oedipal rebellion—part of Browning's struggle for self-definition. The crushing weight of Wordsworthian influence that weighs so heavily upon *Paracelsus* had to be shrugged off. Wordsworth's influence was so strong that Browning could only free himself from it by means of the decidedly foul tactic of a "misreading" of the older poet that reduced him to a harmless and contemptible figure. If Browning's conflict with Wordsworth is thought of in the terms of a boxing match, he had floored his foe with a punch from behind. Extending the metaphor a little further, it was not in fact a foe he was striking, but the referee.

The trouble with this tactic was that it replaced a living opponent with a mannequin. Browning's struggle with Wordsworth had been one-sided from the start; Wordsworth was largely uninterested in his younger contemporary, and his poetic output is certainly entirely free of Browning's "influence." As far as Wordsworth was concerned, there was no "struggle" at all. Browning was engaged with Wordsworth's *works*, and was free to interpret them in any way he chose, as is demonstrated by the cavalier way in which he felt free to "forget" Wordsworth's humanism after 1840. After *Sordello*, Wordsworth was reduced to the status of sparring partner, or, worse, of punching bag. This emasculation explains the way Browning apparently found it easy to "erase" Wordsworth for almost thirty years after 1840, though his occasional pokes at his predecessor suggest a degree of unease on Browning's part toward Wordsworth's capability to rise again.

If he had so completely managed to rid himself of Wordsworth's influence, why did Browning feel himself forced to "make amends" to his predecessor after completing *The Ring and the Book*? The weakened post-1840 Wordsworth seems incapable of forcing a "strong poet" to such a humiliating reconciliation. There are two possible explanations, neither of which excludes the other. The first is that upon his completion of *The Ring and the Book,* Browning found that he had painted himself into a corner. That poem was, in many ways, a dead end; Browning had emphasized that it was all "fact"—"fact is what you see," he wrote to Julia Wedgwood—fact resurrected and made presentable through the alchemy of poetry, but, ultimately, plain, empirically verifiable fact.[1] How could he continue upon this path without abandoning poetry altogether? In his methods and aims he had become very close indeed to naturalist novelists like Zola, who were also preoccupied with the desire to present "fact." *The Ring and the Book* is arguably more a novel in verse than a poem; to go any further would be impossible without ceasing to cling to any vestiges of "poetic" identity.

Browning's return to a more positive interpretation of the romantics in *Balaustion* and thereafter was therefore a practical decision—a decision that allowed him to go on writing poetry. By returning to the "romantic" interpretation of the poet that he had held in the 1830s Browning could justify continuing to write poetry himself. This would mean coming to some sort of reconciliation with Wordsworth; therefore, Browning forced himself to the distasteful expedient of apologizing to him in *Fifine*.

This cynical explanation has much to recommend it, but it does reduce Wordsworth to the undignified role of puppet, allowed to gather dust in a corner for decades before being picked up again. Another explanation for Browning's volte-face allows Wordsworth to play a rather more animated part in the struggle. Not being aware of Browning's attitude toward him in his lifetime, Wordsworth had little way to contribute blows of his own. However, he did manage—without knowing it—to land one punch from which Browning was never able to recover. This was the posthumously published *Prelude*.

Browning could not have avoided having to come to terms with *The Prelude*'s implications for his opinion of Wordsworth. He possessed a copy by the end of 1850; it is surely significant that he did not apparently go out and purchase the poem himself as soon as it appeared, but waited passively for Norton to send one to him. He would have felt reluctant to come to terms with such a lengthy "new" Wordsworth poem, having performed such a savage misreading of him ten years before. Whether this is the case or not, Browning certainly had a copy of the poem sitting accusingly on his shelf from 1850 on.

Browning's reluctance to come to terms with this poem is attested by the fact that a full twenty years would pass before he would acknowledge Wordsworth's humanism in *Fifine*. The "Essay on Shelley" did indeed demonstrate a curious reconciliation with the romantics which may have been influenced by a reading of *The Prelude*, but it was followed, five years later, by the letter to Ruskin and the publication of *Men and Women*, both of which militated against the romantic aesthetic. It was only in *Balaustion* that a profound change became apparent. It is unlikely that *The Prelude* sat unread on Browning's shelf for twenty years; it is more likely that it took that long for the poem's implications to sink in, or that Browning simply declined to acknowledge them for that period. However, upon the completion of *The Ring and the Book*, Browning was at a quandary as to where to go as a poet; at this stage, an acknowledgment that the older poet was, in fact, still a master to be emulated could be seen as profitable as well as necessary. Thus, in *Fifine*, he used the techniques outlined in the previous chapter to acknowledge that he had indeed read *The Prelude*, and that his reading of that poem had forced him to acknowledge that Wordsworth had, all along, been aware of the need to temper romantic idealism with realism. If the relationship is seen in the terms of a struggle, it seems that Wordsworth managed to snatch victory from beyond the grave.

Browning's engagement with Wordsworth can also be seen as a sort of game. In this case, the game was not with Wordsworth, but with the potential observers of the struggle—the reading public, and, more specifically, William Knight. Browning had little respect for the vast majority of English readers, which is not surprising when one remembers how long it took him to achieve any better reputation than that of the madman who had foisted the unreadable *Sordello* upon the world. It is certainly true that the vast majority of the hardy souls who tackled *Sordello*—of whom there were very few—would have had no idea that the poem contained a sweeping dismissal of Wordsworth and romanticism. There is no contemporary evidence that anyone at all noticed this. People did notice the attack on Wordsworth in "The Lost Leader," but interpreted that poem as an attack upon Wordsworth's political apostasy rather than upon his aesthetics (which it largely was, though not entirely—its reference to "The Warning" indicates that Browning was also angry with Wordsworth's apparent perversion of his poetic abilities for political ends). Apart from this poem, Browning's engagement with Wordsworth went unnoticed, and Browning does not seem to have discussed it on more than a couple of occasions (with Duffy and Forster, and, later in life, with Gosse). When, therefore, Browning came to a reconciliation with Wordsworth, it was almost entirely *private*. He knew that his readers would be baffled by *Fifine*'s complexity—he told Alfred Domett in April 1872 that it was "the most metaphysical and boldest [poem] he had written since *Sordello*" and that he "was very doubtful as to its reception."[2] Nevertheless, the poem was not principally meant for public consumption. He had written it for the express purpose of reconciling himself to his romantic predecessors, and to Wordsworth in particular. What "the public" made of it did not really matter. This is where the idea of "the game" comes in. It is no coincidence that *Fifine* was seen as Browning's most baffling affront to his readers since *Sordello*. Browning was challenging his readers to notice his apology, just as he had challenged them to notice his rejection of romanticism in *Sordello.* He was playing a game in which he held all the cards, gambling that he could keep his self-abasement secret. In fact, he was hoping that his apology would not be noticed—hoping to satisfy *himself* rather than anyone else. In this he was entirely successful. The public recoiled before what they must have seen, horrified, as something akin to *Sordello's Revenge*, and Browning was free to continue his poetic career (and laugh up his sleeve in an almost Paracelsan manner at the idiocy of the common herd—the sort of people Browning was disparaging in the epilogue to *Fifine* entitled "The Householder," in which the weary widower complains to his wife's shade of "all the neighbour-talk with man and maid—such men!" he has had to endure since her death).[3]

Unfortunately for Browning, he had not reckoned with Knight's obstinacy. He would find it necessary to go to quite extraordinary lengths in order to avoid acceding to Knight's demands. The roots of the reluctance Browning felt to discuss Wordsworth with Knight lay in his desire to keep his struggle with the older poet as secret as possible; to openly admit that he had been wrong about Wordsworth and the romantics for so long would expose the entirety of his poetic achievement between 1840 and *The Ring and the Book* as fundamentally misconceived. That it took Browning so long to come to term with *The Prelude* is an indication of how hard he felt it to admit this to *himself*; he felt even more reluctant to admit it to William Knight or anyone else.

Nevertheless, he eventually acceded to some of Knight's demands. The way he chose to answer Knight, though, seems to have been less a surrender than a challenge. An examination of the list Browning sent to Knight shows that, far from being a mere sop or decoy, the list in fact contains a complex series of references that lead the reader familiar with Browning's relationship with Wordsworth to the very core of Browning's reconciliation with him in *Fifine.* Had Knight studied Browning's work and identified the references to Wordsworth therein, the list would have acted as a sort of Rosetta stone. Browning was, in fact, giving Knight exactly what he had been asking for; but, once again, he was playing games. In challenging Knight to decipher his list, Browning was gambling that he would fail, and prove himself every bit as obtuse as the readers who had balked at *Fifine*'s complexities. Browning's gamble was successful; it appears that Knight saw the list as illustrative of nothing except Browning's lack of taste when it came to Wordsworth, judging from the fact that he printed few of Browning's preferred poems in his Wordsworth selection. Knight may have irritated Browning, though, with his publication of the list and large portions of the correspondence in his selection. The fact that Knight does not seem to have sent Browning a copy of his selection, and that Browning appears to have erased his own name from one of the volumes Knight *did* send him, suggests that Browning felt a degree of resentment at even this limited degree of exposure. Nevertheless, Knight had not effected the sort of catastrophic exposure Browning feared; the poet's game-playing had, ultimately, paid off.

Browning's relationship with Wordsworth can thus be understood in the terms of struggle and eventual reconciliation with an overwhelming predecessor, but it cannot be fully comprehended without an awareness of the way Browning used games to avoid publicly revealing all this. The pressures that propelled Browning first to reject, and then to return to, Wordsworth must not be underestimated; they led to a series of aesthetic crises of self-definition in regard to Wordsworth's achievement that forced Browning to confront the fact that a large proportion of his output had been based upon a profoundly unfair representation of Wordsworth. To acknowledge this—even to himself, in the rarefied bell jar of *Fifine*—must have cost Browning a good deal of intellectual pride. All the same, it must not be thought that the conflict with Wordsworth brought Browning nothing but stress and pain; it also gave him an opportunity to "plume up his will" (in Iago's phrase) through his cunning avoidance of the distasteful business of public contrition.[4] The greatest triumph for Browning in his struggle with Wordsworth was the fact that the vast majority of the paying public failed to notice that a struggle was taking place at all.

Notes

A Note on Texts

1. Maynard, *Browning's Youth*, 168–69.
2. Knight, *Retrospects*, 86.
3. See chapter 6.
4. Knight, *Retrospects*, 86, 76. See also chapter 6.
5. Browning to Alfred Domett, July 13, 1842, in Browning and Browning, *Brownings' Correspondence*, 6:32.
6. Peterson, "Unpublished Memoir," 150–51.
7. Woolford and Karlin, *Robert Browning*, 231.
8. Browning, *Poems*, 1:xiii.

Chapter 1. Why Browning and Wordsworth?

1. Here and throughout this book, I mean by "realism" a mode of thought that determines itself to focus squarely upon the so-called real world and, specifically, its inhabitants—in both its pleasant and unpleasant aspects—rather than concern itself with metaphysical or mystical visions of "other" worlds. This does not, of course, make it incompatible with benevolent humanistic activity, but largely rules out any *metaphysical* basis for such activity (the edicts of God, for example, or an assumption of godlike superiority over other men). It is essentially a hardheaded philosophy that faces up to the world as it *is*, rather than as it *ought* to be. I am therefore using a definition of the term that is much closer to the aesthetic program used by "realist" writers and painters of the nineteenth century like Zola or Courbet—an "accurate and detailed depiction of contemporary life and its problems," in the *Encyclopaedia Britannica* definition—than it is to the definition of "realism" that would be accepted by most philosophers: "the conception that objects of sense perception and cognition are real in their own right and exist independently of their being known or related to the mind" (once again, I am using the *Encyclopaedia Britannica* definition). In *this* light, Plato, for example, could be seen as a realist, whereas his concern with ideal forms (which, as far as he was concerned, *exist*, although we cannot perceive them) would have seemed utterly inimical to Zola or Courbet. I have chosen to define realism in an aesthetic rather than philosophical sense not because I believe Browning was uninterested in these sort of philosophical questions (he undoubtedly was), but because this book focuses

upon his, and Wordsworth's, attitude toward and participation in the sort of actively humanistic beliefs that pretty much *demand*, before anything else, that their followers be realists in the philosophical sense—since, if the outside world does not really exist at all, why trouble oneself about changing it?

2. See Shaw, "Browning's Intimations Ode," 9–10; Kramer, "Victorian Sexuality," 315–35; and Sharp, "Poet's Age," 86–91. The latter also suggests that Browning may have been making a mocking reference to Wordsworth's "Peter Bell": an interesting suggestion, but adversely colored by Sharp's overly simplistic account of Browning's relationship with Wordsworth, which he characterizes as almost entirely hostile. Browning's poem is in fact the product of long years of ambivalence and struggle.

3. Kramer, "Victorian Sexuality," 335.

4. Kelley and Coley, *Browning Collections*, 582.

5. I am indebted to Michael Meredith for this information.

6. Bate, *Burden of the Past*, passim.

7. Bloom, *Anxiety of Influence*, 25–26.

8. Ibid., 30.

9. Ibid., 31.

10. Ibid., 14.

11. Ibid., 15.

12. Bloom, *Poetry and Repression*, 195–96. Bloom, in discussing the prologue to *Asolando*, argues that Browning "overcomes" Wordsworth through fusing Shelley's "spark or ember," as demonstrated in *Alastor* and the "Hymn to Intellectual Beauty," with Wordsworth's "Intimations" Ode.

13. See, for example, Bloom, *Anxiety of Influence*, 128–32; Bloom, *Map of Misreading*, 106–22; and Bloom, *Poetry and Repression*, 175–204.

14. Bloom, *Poetry and Repression*, 177. See also chapter 6. I differ entirely from the conclusion drawn by Park Honan, who denies the importance of any influence of the romantic poets on Browning. He argues, instead, that Browning and the romantics were working in *parallel* ways: "Browning incidentally owes a little to Wordsworth, a little more to Shelley; but the direct debt is insignificant when weighed against the fact that he, Wordsworth and Shelley all respond to the prevailing new appreciation of the mind's processes" (Honan, "Robert Browning and Romanticism," 147–72). I believe Honan is mistaken, certainly in the case of Wordsworth's influence on Browning.

15. Allen, *Harold Bloom*, 38–39.

16. Bloom, *Anxiety of Influence*, 11.

17. Bloom, *Map of Misreading*, 9–10.

18. See chapter 2.

19. Woolford, *Browning the Revisionary*, 1–2.

20. See chapter 2.

21. See chapter 4.

22. Bloom, *Map of Misreading*, 80.

23. Ibid., 17.

24. Much more work has been done on the influence of Wordsworth upon Elizabeth Barrett Browning than on the relationship between Wordsworth and Robert Browning. See, for example, Blake, "Elizabeth Barrett Browning and Wordsworth," 387–98; Morlier, "Death of Pan," 131–55; and Woolford, "Elizabeth Barrett and the Wordsworthian Sublime," 36–56. Barrett Browning's attitude toward Wordsworth was more openly expressed and a good deal less ambivalent than that of her husband.

Chapter 2. Wordsworth and Browning's Rejection of Romanticism

1. Browning to Elizabeth Barrett, August 22, 1846, in Browning and Browning, *Brownings' Correspondence*, 12:280.

2. The relationship between Browning and Shelley has been exhaustively detailed. See, for example, Pottle, *Shelley and Browning*; Maynard, *Browning's Youth*, 193–237; Latane, "Shelley's 'Baleful Influence'," 31–36; Yetman, "Exorcising Shelley," 79–98; Martin, "Browning," 4–9; Tucker, *Browning's Beginnings*, 285–325; and Woolford, "Philosophy and Poetics," 1–21.

3. See Raymond, "Browning and the Shelley Letters," 184–92.

4. Bloom, *Anxiety of Influence*, 8.

5. Knight, *Retrospects*, 75.

6. Maynard, *Browning's Youth*, 168–69.

7. Browning to Elizabeth Barrett, February 16, 1846, in Browning and Browning, *Brownings' Correspondence*, 13:74.

8. Orr, *Life and Letters of Browning*, 88; and Griffin and Minchin, *Life of Robert Browning*, 77.

9. Miller, "This Happy Evening," 57.

10. Gosse, *Robert Browning*, 7.

11. Ibid., 41–42.

12. Irvine and Honan, *Book, the Ring and the Poet*, 64.

13. Duffy, *My Life*, 2:259.

14. Orr, *Life and Letters of Browning*, 105; and Irvine and Honan, *Book, the Ring, and the Poet*, 84.

15. Gosse, *Robert Browning*, 41–42.

16. Pinion, *Wordsworth Chronology*, 179, 182, 188–89, 195, 198–99, 208–9.

17. Ibid., 199.

18. Duffy, *My Life*, 2:259.

19. The most detailed discussion of Browning's 1830s radicalism comes in Armstrong, *Victorian Poetry*, 113–35. Armstrong demonstrates Browning's affinity to the "Benthamite" radicalism of W. J. Fox and the *Monthly Repository* circle around him, as displayed in *Pauline*, though she also argues that that poem displays an "agonistic and interrogative relationship" to this sort of radicalism (113). Unfortunately, she does not go on to discuss the literary radicalism of *Paracelsus* and *Sordello*.

20. Browning to W. J. Fox, April 16, 1835, in Browning and Browning, *Brownings' Correspondence*, 3:134–35.

21. Browning to Euphrasia Fanny Haworth, [May 1840], in Browning and Browning, *Brownings' Correspondence*, 4:269.

22. Armstrong, *Victorian Poetry*, 113.

23. For Armstrong's ingenious suggestion that the fragmentary nature of *Pauline* is taken from the new biblical criticism (the "Higher Criticism") that was being actively disseminated by the *Monthly Repository* at this period, see ibid., 120–21. The poem would thus be seen as open to the hermeneutic process and an unfixed "democratic" reading.

24. Armstrong, *Victorian Poetry*, 114.

25. Ibid., 119.

26. Wordsworth, *William Wordsworth*, 70–71, lines 423–25.

27. Ibid., 61, lines 131–33.
28. Ibid., 79, lines 657–63.
29. Primarily in *Fifine*, lines 1683–89, 1737–39.
30. Woolford, *Browning the Revisionary*, x.
31. Ibid., 29.
32. Ibid., 43–44.
33. Ibid., 35.
34. Martin, *Browning's Dramatic Monologues*, 151.
35. Ibid., 150–58.
36. Elizabeth Barrett to H. S. Boyd, July 7, 1842, in Barrett, *Elizabeth Barrett to Mr. Boyd*, 247.
37. Woolford, *Browning the Revisionary*, 55.
38. Ibid., 56.
39. Collins, *Robert Browning's Moral-Aesthetic Theory*, 29–30.
40. Interestingly, Browning condemns Shelley for his "low practical dexterity" in his "Essay on Shelley" (Browning, *Poetical Works*, 4:436). He attacks Shelley's early attempts to further the revolutionary cause, which he feels "left him pledged to the defence of a set of miserable little expedients, just as if they represented a set of great principles" (436). Browning seems to be taking this rather odd line as part of his attempt to persuade the reader that Shelley would, had he lived, have become a Christian and concentrated on the "sufficiency of the First Cause" rather than on practical—and revolutionary—opposition to oppression and poverty. By arguing in this way, Browning sounds strangely like the pietistic Festus in the later books of *Paracelsus*, but he does not return to this argument later in his career.
41. These critics include DeVane, in *Browning Handbook*, who declares that "the poem is thoroughly autobiographical, and in spite of his later declaration, Browning is the speaker, hardly disguised at all" (42). He also describes the poem as "Browning's autobiography to his twentieth year" (44). Betty Miller tries to equate Pauline herself with one or both of Browning's friends, the Flower sisters (Miller, *Robert Browning*, 27–34).
42. Shelley, *Poems*, 1:463, lines 33–36.
43. Ibid., line 38.
44. The misquotation is of *Excursion*, 1.500–502 (Shelley replaces "they" with "those").
45. *Pauline*'s earliest critics found the poem not merely confused, but incoherent and baffling; for a selection of scathing contemporary reviews, see Litzinger and Smalley, *Browning*, 34–38. Browning and Browning, *Brownings' Correspondence*, prints all of the reviews. Later works that point out the poem's confusion, though without the derision found in some early reviews, include Maynard, *Browning's Youth*, 212; de Ryals, *Becoming Browning*, 28–29; Honan, *Browning's Characters*, 16–17; and Tucker, *Browning's Beginnings*, 31–32.
46. Martin, *Browning's Dramatic Monologues*, 82–83.
47. Southey, *Vision of Judgement*, xx–xxi.
48. Hazlitt, *Spirit of the Age*, 159–81.
49. Knight, *Retrospects*, 87–88.

CHAPTER 3. *PARACELSUS*: THE PROBLEM SOLVED?

1. Woolford, *Browning the Revisionary*, 31.
2. Kelley and Coley, *Browning Collections*, 190.
3. Taylor, *Philip van Artevelde*, 1:xii.
4. Ibid., viii–ix.
5. Ibid., xii–xiii.
6. Ibid., xiv.

7. Ibid., xvi.
8. See chapter 5.
9. Taylor, *Philip van Artevelde*, 1:xxii–xxxiii.
10. Ibid., xxiii.
11. Ibid., xxv.
12. Ibid., xxv–xxvi.
13. Bloom, *Map of Misreading*, 12.
14. Ibid., 17.
15. Gill, *William Wordsworth*, 415.
16. John Keats to B. R. Haydon, January 10, 1818, in Keats, *Letters*, 1:203.
17. Browning to Elizabeth Barrett, April 8, 1846, in Browning and Browning, *Brownings' Correspondence*, 12:223.
18. Ryan, *Romantic Reformation*, 113.
19. Ibid., 114.
20. *Excursion*, 2.164–97.
21. See, for example, *Pauline*, lines 458–69; and *Paracelsus*, line 2.
22. John Keats to J. H. Reynolds, May 3, 1818, Keats, *Letters*, 1:281.
23. *Paracelsus*, 5.627–770; and *Fifine,* lines 1821–2226.
24. *Paracelsus*, 1.466–99, 1.618–30, and 4.290–93.
25. Wordsworth, *Prose Works*, 3:6, lines 57–58.
26. Tucker, *Browning's Beginnings*, 54.
27. Ibid., 65.
28. Griffin and Minchin, *Life of Robert Browning*, 66–67.
29. Browning, *Letters*, 159.
30. John Keats to Benjamin Bailey, October 8, 1817, in Keats, *Letters*, 1:170.
31. Hartman, *Wordsworth's Poetry*, 74.
32. Ibid., 75.
33. Ibid., 74.
34. Ibid., 138.
35. See chapter 6.
36. Bloom, *Anxiety of Influence*, 86.
37. There may be a glancing reference to Wordsworth's "Sonnet, Composed upon Westminster Bridge" in these lines; they are reminiscent of Wordsworth's "silent, bare, / Ships, towers, domes, theatres, and temples lie / Open unto the fields, and to the sky" (lines 5–7). Browning may be *rehumanizing* Wordsworth's lines, which present a city devoid of human activity, like Wordsworth's beloved mountains; unlike Wordsworth, Aprile perceives the beauty in a *populated* urban landscape.
38. I am thinking of the dramatic monologues in *Men and Women* and *Dramatis Personae*, as well as those of the speakers in *The Ring and the Book.*
39. *Paracelsus*, 2.458–519, and the note on this passage at Browning, *Poems*, 1:181.
40. Browning, *Poems*, 1:181.
41. Wordsworth, *William Wordsworth*, 59, lines 77–78 and 95–99.
42. Ibid., 59, lines 96–97, 99–101.
43. Ibid., 61, lines 127, 129–34.
44. Ibid., 64, line 238, and 65, line 246.
45. Ibid., 64, lines 210–12.
46. Browning, *Poems*, 1:113, lines 7–18.
47. See the 1802 "Preface" and many of the poems in the *Lyrical Ballads* with rustic subjects.
48. Shelley, *Poems and Prose*, 279, lines 1282–83.
49. This passage would be excised from all subsequent editions of Browning's poetry.

It is difficult to determine the reasons for this; one possible explanation is that, having dismissed Wordsworth in *Sordello*, Browning wanted his previous poetry to display as little evidence of an engagement with Wordsworth as possible.

50. Hartman, *Wordsworth's Poetry*, 15.
51. *Paracelsus*, 3.340–51.
52. See Keats, *Complete Poems*, 120n.
53. Maynard, *Browning's Youth*, 135, 432–33.
54. See chapter 4.
55. The details of this incident are murky. See Gittings, *John Keats*, 115–16; and Bate, *John Keats*, 137–40.
56. See, in particular, Browning to Elizabeth Barrett, February 16, 1846, in Browning and Browning, *Brownings' Correspondence*, 12:73–74.
57. Moorman, *William Wordsworth*, 2:421.
58. Irvine and Honan, *Book, the Ring, and the Poet*, 52.
59. Woolford, *Browning the Revisionary*, 3.
60. See *Sordello*, 6.353–84; "Fra Lippo Lippi"; and *Paracelsus*, 1.811–22.
61. See chapters 7 and 8.
62. *Paracelsus*, 3.1028–29; see also Browning, *Poems*, 1:238.
63. *Paracelsus* (Berg-1888 editions), 4.299–300.
64. Tucker, *Browning's Beginnings*, 82.
65. Woolford, *Browning the Revisionary*, 3.
66. Browning, *Poems*, 1:294. The translations into English are Woolford and Karlin's.
67. Orr, *Life and Letters of Robert Browning*, 67.
68. Browning, *Poems*, 1:297.
69. Tucker, *Browning's Beginnings*, 84.
70. "Prospectus" 33–35; and *Paracelsus*, 5.824.

Chapter 4. Wordsworth Rejected

1. Tucker, *Browning's Beginnings*, 3.
2. Martin, *Browning's Dramatic Monologues*, 26.
3. Ibid., 27.
4. Ibid.
5. Tucker, *Browning's Beginnings*, 61.
6. Martin, *Browning's Dramatic Monologues*, 160.
7. Ibid., 161.
8. Bloom, *Anxiety of Influence*, 69.
9. Wordsworth to Moxon, October 12, 1846, in Wordsworth and Dorothy Wordsworth, *Letters: Later Years*, 4:804.
10. Browning to Elizabeth Barrett, April 16, 1846, in Browning and Browning, *Brownings' Correspondence*, 12:252.
11. DeVane, "Harlot and the Thoughtful Young Man," 463–84.
12. The articles are reprinted in De Quincey, *Collected Writings*, 2:229–302.
13. Lindop, *Opium-Eater*, 305.
14. Baxter, *De Quincey's Art of Autobiography*, 75.
15. Ibid., 76.
16. Ibid., 79.
17. De Quincey, *Collected Writings*, 1:242.
18. Ibid., 2:283.
19. Ibid., 2:284.

20. Marshall, preface, xii.
21. De Quincey, *Collected Writings*, 1:289.
22. Ibid., 1:293.
23. Ibid., 1:292.
24. See chapter 3.
25. De Quincey, *Collected Writings*, 1:238–39, 298–99.
26. Ibid., 237.
27. Jordan, *De Quincey to Wordsworth*, 347.
28. Kelley and Coley, *Browning Collections*, 189.
29. Bloom, *Map of Misreading*, 69.
30. Browning, *Poems*, 1:424–25.
31. The two classes of poetic temperament are described in lines 462–566. The specific quotation is at lines 509–15.
32. *Sordello*, 1.467–69; and Wordsworth, *William Wordsworth*, 74–75, lines 522–23.
33. Browning, *Poems*, 1:425–26.
34. Arnold, *Complete Prose Works*, 3:121, lines 33–37.
35. Hazlitt, *Spirit of the Age*, 231–32.
36. Woolford ("Browning Rethinks Romanticism," 211–27) points out some additional passages at the start of book 3 of *Sordello* that seem to attack Wordsworth's concern with nature; he argues, in particular, that the "upheaval" described in lines 85–93, in its emphasis on the essentially alien status of nature, "anticipates Arnold's charge, put forward in 'Stanzas in Memory of the Author of "Obermann,"' that by immersing himself in nature and ignoring "half of human fate" Wordsworth effectively isolates himself from his kind, or, as Browning more severely puts it, is "lost" to them" (214–15).
37. Browning, *Poems*, 1:540.
38. De Quincey, *Complete Works*, 2:277.
39. See the running head above 3.730 of the revised 1863 *Sordello*: "would but suffering humanity allow!" Though Browning did not substantially rewrite *Sordello* for this edition, as he seems to have tried to do in the mid-1850s, he did try to make it easier to read by untangling some of the syntax and adding what he hoped would be helpful running heads. Unsurprisingly, this attempt to bring *Sordello* to the masses did not succeed.
40. Browning to Euphrasia Fanny Haworth, [May 1840], in Browning and Browning, *Brownings' Correspondence*, 4:269.
41. *Sordello* (1863 ed.), 3.717–21.
42. Keats to J. H. Reynolds, May 3, 1818, in Keats, *Letters*, 1:281.
43. Hazlitt, *Spirit of the Age*, 235.
44. Ibid..
45. Browning, *Poems*, 1:581.
46. *Sordello*, 4.296; and Browning, *Poems*, 1:611.
47. Wordsworth, *William Wordsworth*, 78, lines 631–33.
48. Wordsworth, *Prose Works*, 3:81, lines 744–45.
49. Browning, *Poems*, 1:697–98.
50. Bloom, *Anxiety of Influence*, 15.

Chapter 5. Wordsworth Erased

1. Browning, *Poems*, 2:482–83, lines 163–66.
2. Ibid., 484, lines 209–30.
3. Maynard, *Browning's Youth*, 169–78.
4. Browning, *Browning's Essay on Chatterton*, 140–41, 145.

5. The note is reprinted in Browning, *Poems*, 1:15–16.
6. Browning, *Poems*, 1:483, lines 199–203.
7. Wordsworth to Edward Moxon, October 12, 1846, in Wordsworth and Wordsworth, *Letters: Later Years*, 4:804.
8. For example, to A. B. Grosart in a letter of February 24, 1875 (Browning, *Letters*, 166–67), to Ruskin, and, in a letter of September 7, 1875, to a "Miss Lee" (Orr, *Life and Letters of Robert Browning*, 132–33).
9. Browning, *Letters*, 166–67.
10. Karlin, *Browning's Hatreds*, 37.
11. Woolford and Karlin, *Robert Browning*, 36.
12. Ibid., 36–37.
13. Ibid., 37.
14. Browning, *Poems*, 1:173.
15. Ibid.
16. Browning to Elizabeth Barrett, May 30, 1845, in Browning and Browning, *Brownings' Correspondence*, 10:206.
17. Browning to Elizabeth Barrett, February 16, 1846, in Browning and Browning, *Brownings' Correspondence*, 12:73–74.
18. De Quincey, *Collected Writings*, 2:248.
19. Bloom, *Map of Misreading*, 103.
20. Browning to Elizabeth Barrett, August 22, 1846, in Browning and Browning, *Brownings' Correspondence*, 13:280.
21. Woolford, *Browning the Revisionary*, viii.
22. Browning, *Poetical Works*, 4:427, lines 29–33.
23. Ibid., 246, lines 18–20.
24. Ibid., 4:431, lines 4–16.
25. Woolford, *Browning the Revisionary*, ix.
26. See chapter 7.
27. Browning, *Poetical Works*, 4:431, lines 26–30.
28. See chapter 8.
29. Browning, *Poetical Works*, 4:426, lines 18–24.
30. Wordsworth, "Immortality" Ode, lines 67–68, 4. This possible allusion has been pointed out by Ann Wordsworth in "Communication Different," 4–18.
31. See Altick, "Browning's 'Transcendentalism,'" 24–28.
32. Greg Cossan argues that Browning, like Coleridge in his own poem, is mounting a critique of the supposedly "Wordsworthian" virtues of "duty," "fortitude," "perseverance," "resolution," and "independence" in "The Last Ride Together." He sees Browning rebelling in the poem against Wordsworth's "conventional fixities and pieties" and his "constancy," and against his reputation as "sage and moralist" (Cossan, "Irresolution and Dependence," 41). His argument relies too much on a picture of Wordsworth as far more "constant" and conventionally pious than Browning could have envisioned in 1855, after the publication of *The Prelude* (which he would have certainly read, if not fully assimilated, by this time). It should also be remembered that the conclusion of *The Excursion*, which leaves the Solitary unconvinced, cannot be reconciled with Cossan's oversimplistic depiction of a "resolute" Wordsworth in this article. Browning would have had a far more complex and ambivalent attitude toward Wordsworth by this stage than Cossan implies.
33. Nichols, "Browning's Modernism," 81–99; and Kramer, "Victorian Sexuality," 399–410. For Isobel Armstrong's theory that Browning's Pauline "stands in for Dorothy Wordsworth," see Armstrong, *Victorian Poetry*, 125.
34. Kramer, "Victorian Sexuality," 403.
35. Poston, "Browning and the Altered Romantic Landscape," 426–39.

36. Ibid., 431, 433.
37. Ibid., 439.
38. Ibid., 435. See *Prelude*, 1.357–400; and "Childe Roland," line 166.
39. Collingwood, *Life and Work of Ruskin*, 1:200.
40. Tucker, *Browning's Beginnings*, 13–14.
41. See chapter 6.
42. Tucker, *Browning's Beginnings*, 15.
43. Woolford, *Browning the Revisionary*, 50–52.
44. Collingwood, *Life and Work of Ruskin*, 1:201.
45. A. Taylor, "Religious Readings of the Immortality Ode," 645–48.
46. Browning and Wedgwood, *Robert Browning and Julia Wedgwood*, 158–59.
47. See chapter 6.
48. Woolford, *Browning the Revisionary*, 150–51.
49. See chapter 6.
50. Browning and Wedgwood, *Robert Browning and Julia Wedgwood*, 158–59.
51. For a detailed examination of this rather silly business, see Whitla, "Browning and the Ashburton Affair," 12–41.
52. Plutarch, *Lives*, 3:309.
53. Browning tells the unfortunate rabbi's story in a letter of August 19, 1864 to Julia Wedgwood (Browning and Wedgwood, *Robert Browning and Julia Wedgwood*, 61–62) and in the grueling late poem "Jochanan Hakkadosh," lines 212–44.
54. Woolford, "Life—That's Venice!" 248–49.
55. *Sordello*, 6.1–5; *Prince Hohenstiel-Schwangau*, lines 517ff.; *Fifine*, lines 105–28; and *La Saisiaz*, lines 564–72.
56. Browning, *Letters*, 159.
57. Woolford, "Life—That's Venice!" 249.

Chapter 6. The Browning-Knight Correspondence: Wordsworth Disinterred

1. Gill, *Wordsworth and the Victorians*, 222.
2. Ibid., 223–24.
3. Knight, *Transactions of the Wordsworth Society*, 1:4.
4. Gill, *Wordsworth and the Victorians*, 236.
5. Matthew Arnold to Frances Arnold, May 2, 1883, in Arnold, *Letters*, 2:211.
6. Gill, *Wordsworth and the Victorians*, 238.
7. Raymond, "*Infinite Moment*," 236ff.
8. Knight, *Retrospects*, 75.
9. *Notes and Queries* 4, no. 12 (1873): 473, 519; and *Notes and Queries* 5, no. 1 (1874): 71–72, 138, 192, 213, 241–42.
10. Knight, *Retrospects*, 76.
11. Orr, *Life and Letters of Robert Browning*, 374, 396–97.
12. Domett, *Diary*, 46.
13. For the details of this meeting, at which, according to the queen, Browning made himself "very agreeable," see Irvine and Honan, *Book, the Ring, and the Poet*, 441.
14. Gill, *Wordsworth and the Victorians*, 206–11. See also Harris, "Romantic Bard and Victorian Commentators," 387–98, in which Harris argues that most Victorian criticism of Wordsworth lacks interest, because the critics had not thought hard enough about the *meaning* of Wordsworth's work, as opposed to its *significance*: the criticism rushes "to evaluate

Wordsworth's poetry in terms of certain stated or unstated criteria, or analyses it relative to some external structure of thought," rather than examining it on its own terms (457–58).

15. Gill, *Wordsworth and the Victorians*, 211.
16. Knight, *Retrospects*, 80.
17. For some speculations about Browning's shyness, see Miller, *Robert Browning*, 104–7.
18. Kelley and Coley, *Browning Collections*, 209–10.
19. Knight, *Retrospects*, 85.
20. Ibid., 85–86.
21. Ibid., 86.
22. Ibid.
23. Ibid., 85–86.
24. Ibid.
25. Ibid., 86.
26. Ibid.
27. Ibid.
28. Ibid., 210.
29. Browning to White, 24 August 1881 (Armstrong Browning Library).
30. Knight, *Retrospects*, 86–88.
31. Ibid., 88.
32. Arnold, *Poems of Wordsworth*, xii.
33. Knight, *Retrospects*, 88.
34. Browning is (mis)quoting John Dryden's *Aureng-Zebe*, 4.1.42; see Dryden, *Works*, 12:210.
35. Knight, *Retrospects*, 88–89.
36. Orr, *Life and Letters of Robert Browning*, 356.
37. Wordsworth, *Selections*, v.
38. Ibid.
39. Ibid., xiv.
40. Ibid., vi.
41. Ibid., 5.
42. Gill, *Wordsworth and the Victorians*, 239. Gill's book contains the most detailed account so far of William Knight's heroic labors on behalf of the Wordsworth Society, as well as a rather alarming photograph of him. Gill does not mention the Knight-Browning correspondence, but his book does contain a chapter (pp. 168–205) on the way Arnold and Tennyson struggled with Wordsworth's influence in a way that parallels Browning's own struggle with his predecessor.
43. Wordsworth, *Selections*, xiv.
44. Ibid., xii–xiii.
45. Ibid., xii.
46. Kelley and Coley, *Browning Collections*, 118.
47. Ibid.
48. Ibid.
49. See the uncompromising "To Edward Fitzgerald," in which an irate Browning expresses the wish to spit upon and kick the unfortunate (and dead) Fitzgerald.
50. Browning is said to have threatened to hurl "a bottle of claret" (the contents of which one suspects he had sampled extensively during the evening) at Forster if his friend dared offer any doubt concerning the veracity of a lady whom Browning was quoting. The threat led to a prolonged breach in their friendship, and they were reconciled only shortly before Forster's death in 1876. The rather ridiculous story appears in Lehmann, *Memories*, 112–14.

51. Brombert, *Edouard Manet*, 222–23.
52. Wordsworth, *Selections*, xiv.

Chapter 7. Browning's Wordsworth Selection

1. Wordsworth's relationship with Napoleon is discussed in some detail in Bainbridge, *Napoleon and English Romanticism*, 54–94. Bainbridge demonstrates how Wordsworth's earlier ambivalence toward Napoleon had turned into open hostility by 1802, as demonstrated in his sonnets "I griev'd for Bonaparte" and "Calais, August 15th, 1802"; Wordsworth also attacks the dictator in his sonnet "October, 1803." By the time he wrote "Rob Roy's Grave" Wordsworth was fully opposed to Napoleon and supported the war effort against him. He equated Napoleon's campaigns with those of the Conquistadors (Wordsworth to Captain Pasley, Royal Engineers, 28 March 1811, in Wordsworth and Wordsworth, *Letters: Middle Years*, 476) and called his government "tyrannical and immoral" (Wordsworth to Richard Sharp, 28 March 1811, in ibid., 483).
2. Herodotus, *Histories*, 15–16.
3. The reference to the "Orthian" lay is puzzling; Orthia was one of the names of a Dorian goddess worshipped by the Spartans, who has no connection with Arion. Pettigrew and Collins suggest that Browning confused Arion with Orion, who lived with Artemis; this sounds unlikely, since Browning evidently knew the story of Arion far too well to confuse him with Orion the hunter (Browning, *Poems*, 2:981n). Adam Roberts has suggested that "Orthian" may refer to Poseidon, one of whose names was Orthosios, in his guise of "Poseidon of the straight lines, or the Right way." In the context of what is about to happen to Arion, this seems the most likely explanation. I am indebted to Adam Roberts for this suggestion (private communication).
4. Plutarch, *Lives*, 6:117.
5. The lines appear only in editions of *Sordello* published between 1863 and 1888.
6. Johnston, *Hidden Wordsworth*, 243.
7. This "realistic" aspect of the poem would have appealed to the Browning who had written *Fifine*, a poem containing numerous exhortations that one should avoid dwelling in the comfortable realms of fantasy and face up to the real world. The poem's somber conclusion, too, in which "the mist and the river, the hill and the shade" fade away from Susan's vision, to be replaced with the bleak vista of the London streets, reminds one both of Wordsworth's "Immortality" Ode and Browning's response to it, his prologue to *Asolando*: Wordsworth and Susan feel desolate upon the withdrawal of a visionary quality from the world around them, while Browning feels himself to be redeemed by this very withdrawal. Browning may have been implying that in "Poor Susan" Wordsworth, in his recognition of the ultimately sterile nature of fantasy, was on the right track, but had failed to go far enough—unlike, by implication, Browning himself.
8. Honan, *Browning's Characters*, 104–5.
9. Ibid., 107.

Chapter 8. Browning and *The Prelude*

1. Cook, *Browning's Lyrics*, 236.
2. Harrison, *Victorian Poets and Romantic Poems*, 215.
3. Kelley and Coley, *Browning Collections*, 210.
4. "Elegaic Stanzas" (1820–27 revision), lines 14–16.

5. Woolford, *Browning the Revisionary*, 220.

6. The idea that one should seek a permanence that is somehow inherent in the world, despite its dazzling transience, is reminiscent of the "Simplon Pass" passage in book 6 of *The Prelude*, in which Wordsworth perceives the unitary presence of God both behind and within the continually changing world. As was shown in chapter 5, these lines may well have influenced Browning while writing the epilogue to *Dramatis Personae* in 1864; the passage discussed here differs in that its vision of "permanence" seems to be more profoundly rooted in human traditions and beliefs, and thus more humanistic generally.

7. Woolford, "Life—That's Venice!" 247.

8. Ibid.

9. Hartman, *Wordsworth's Poetry*, 228.

10. Woolford, "Browning Rethinks Romanticism," 220–21.

11. Woolford, "Life—That's Venice!" 247. See Woolford, "Browning Rethinks Romanticism," 225, for the suggestion that Browning found the idea of permanence amid change symbolized by an ancient monument in *The Prelude*, book 8: "monuments, erect, / Prostrate, or leaning towards their common rest / In earth, the widely scattered wreck sublime / Of vanished nations" (*Prelude*, 8.610–14).

12. King, *Focusing Artifice*, 184.

13. Wordsworth's "Simplon Pass" passage in book 6 of *The Prelude* describes a similar vision of permanence in change, but invests the permanence in a quasi-pantheistic God rather than in the more humanistic characteristics described here. Woolford suggests ("Browning Rethinks Romanticism," 222) that Wordsworth alludes to a similar vision in *Prelude*, 8.644–50, in which Wordsworth describes the way he perceives the essential integrity of "human nature" even amid the squalor of London. Woolford argues that this may have served to convince Browning of Wordsworth's essential humanism.

14. Woolford, "Browning Rethinks Romanticism," 247.

Chapter 9. Conclusion

1. Browning and Wedgwood, *Robert Browning and Julia Wedgwood*, 158–59.

2. Domett, *Diary*, 53.

3. "The Householder," line 18. The depiction in *Fifine*, lines 1979–84, of conventional morality as a "dame demure" seated behind her stall and displaying her wares like a shopkeeper may also be a swipe at the sort of prudish and unadventurous readers Browning despised—a swipe that few would notice, since, as Browning had ruefully predicted, few managed to digest such a "bold" and "metaphysical" poem.

4. *Othello*, 1.3.387.

Bibliography

Allen, Graham. *Harold Bloom: A Poetics of Conflict*. London: Harvester Wheatsheaf, 1994.

Altick, Richard Daniel. "Browning's 'Transcendentalism.'" *Journal of English and German Philology* 58 (1958): 24–28.

Armstrong, Isobel. *Victorian Poetry: Power, Politics and Poetics*. London: Routledge & Kegan Paul, 1993.

———, ed. *Writers and Their Background: Robert Browning*. London: Bell, 1974.

Arnold, Matthew. *The Complete Prose Works of Matthew Arnold*. Edited by R. H. Super. 11 vols. Ann Arbor: University of Michigan Press, 1962–77.

———. *Letters of Matthew Arnold*. Edited by George W. E. Russell. 2 vols. London: Macmillan, 1895.

———, ed. *Poems of Wordsworth, Chosen and Selected by Matthew Arnold*. London: Macmillan, 1879.

Bainbridge, Simon. *Napoleon and English Romanticism*. Cambridge: Cambridge University Press, 1995.

Barrett, Elizabeth. *Elizabeth Barrett to Mr. Boyd*. Edited by Barbara P. McCarthy. London: Murray, 1955.

Bate, Walter Jackson. *The Burden of the Past and the English Poet*. London: Chatto and Windus, 1971.

———. *John Keats*. Cambridge, MA: Harvard University Press; London: Oxford University Press, 1963.

Baxter, Edmund. *De Quincey's Art of Autobiography*. Edinburgh: Edinburgh University Press, 1990.

Blake, Kathleen. "Elizabeth Barrett Browning and Wordsworth: The Romantic Poet as a Woman." *Victorian Poetry* 24, no. 4 (1986): 387–98.

Bloom, Harold. *The Anxiety of Influence: A Theory of Poetry*. New York: Oxford University Press, 1973.

———. *A Map of Misreading*. New York: Oxford University Press, 1975.

———. *Poetry and Repression*. New Haven, CT: Yale University Press, 1976.

Brombert, Beth Archer. *Edouard Manet: Rebel in a Frock Coat*. London: Little, Brown, 1996.

Browning, Robert. *Browning's Essay on Chatterton*. Edited by Donald Smalley. Cambridge, MA: Harvard University Press, 1948.

———. *Letters of Robert Browning, Collected by T. J. Wise*. Edited by T. L. Hood. London: Murray, 1933.

———. *The Poems of Browning*. Edited by John Woolford and Daniel Karlin. London: Longman, 1991–.

———. *The Poetical Works of Robert Browning*. Edited by Ian Jack et al. Oxford: Clarendon Press, 1983–.

———. *Robert Browning: The Poems*. Edited by John Pettigrew and Thomas J. Collins. 2 vols. London: Penguin, 1981.

Browning, Robert, and Elizabeth Barrett Browning. *The Brownings' Correspondence*. Edited by Philip Kelley et al. Winfield, KS: Wedgestone Press, 1984–.

Browning, Robert, and Julia Wedgwood. *Robert Browning and Julia Wedgwood: A Broken Friendship as Revealed in Their Letters*. Edited by Richard Curle. London: Murray and Cape, 1937.

Collingwood, William Gershon. *The Life and Work of John Ruskin*. 2 vols. London: Methuen, 1893.

Collins, Thomas J. *Robert Browning's Moral-Aesthetic Theory, 1833–55*. Lincoln: University of Nebraska Press, 1967.

Cook, Eleanor. *Browning's Lyrics, an Exploration*. Toronto: University of Toronto Press, 1974.

Cossan, Greg. "Irresolution and Dependence: The Defeat of Wordsworthian Idealism in Coleridge's 'The Picture' and Browning's 'The Last Ride Together.'" *AUMLA (Journal of the Australian Universities Language and Literary Association)* 71 (1989): 30–44.

De Quincey, Thomas. *The Collected Writings of Thomas De Quincey*. Edited by David Masson. 14 vols. London: Black, 1896–97.

de Ryals, Clyde. *Becoming Browning: The Poems and Plays of Robert Browning, 1833–46*. Columbus: Ohio State University Press, 1983.

DeVane, William Clyde. *A Browning Handbook*. 2nd ed. New York: Appleton Century Crofts, 1955.

———. "The Harlot and the Thoughtful Young Man." *Studies in Philology* 29 (1932): 463–84.

Domett, Alfred. *The Diary of Alfred Domett, 1872–1885*. Edited by Ernest Alan Horsman. London: Oxford University Press, 1953.

Dryden, John. *The Works of John Dryden*. Edited by Edward Niles Hooker et al. 20 vols. Berkeley and Los Angeles: University of California Press, 1956–96.

Duffy, Charles Gavan. *My Life in Two Hemispheres*, 2 vols. London: Fisher Unwin, 1890.

Gill, Stephen. *William Wordsworth: A Life*. Oxford: Oxford University Press, 1989.

———. *Wordsworth and the Victorians*. Oxford: Clarendon Press, 1998.

Gittings, Robert. *John Keats*. London: Heinemann, 1968.

Gosse, Edmund. *Robert Browning: Personalia*. London: Fisher Unwin, 1890.

Griffin, W. Hall, and Harry Christopher Minchin. *The Life of Robert Browning*. 2nd ed. London: Methuen, 1938.

Harris, Wendell. "Romantic Bard and Victorian Commentators: The Meaning and Significance of Meaning and Significance." *Victorian Poetry* 24, no. 4 (1986): 455–69.

Harrison, Antony H. *Victorian Poets and Romantic Poems: Intertextuality and Ideology*. Charlottesville: University Press of Virginia, 1990.

Hartman, Geoffrey H. *The Unremarkable Wordsworth*. London: Methuen, 1987.

———. *Wordsworth's Poetry, 1787–1814*. New Haven, CT: Yale University Press, 1964.

Hazlitt, William. *The Spirit of the Age, or Contemporary Portraits*. London: Colburn, 1825.

Herodotus. *The Histories*. Translated by George Rawlinson. London: Everyman, 1997.

Honan, Park. *Browning's Characters: A Study in Poetic Technique*. New Haven, CT: Yale University Press, 1961.

———. "On Robert Browning and Romanticism." *Browning Institute Studies* 1 (1973): 147–72.

Irvine, William, and Park Honan. *The Book, the Ring, and the Poet: A Biography of Robert Browning*. London: Bodley Head, 1974.

Johnston, Kenneth Richard. *The Hidden Wordsworth: Poet, Lover, Rebel, Spy*. New York: Norton, 1998.

Jordan, John Emory. *De Quincey to Wordsworth: A Biography of a Relationship*. Berkeley: University of California Press, 1962.

Karlin, Daniel. *Browning's Hatreds*. Oxford: Clarendon Press, 1993.

Keats, John. *The Complete Poems*. Edited by Miriam Allott. London: Longman, 1970.

———. *The Letters of John Keats*. Edited by Hyder Edward Rollins. 2 vols. Cambridge, MA: Harvard University Press, 1958.

Keenan, Richard C. "Browning and Shelley." *Browning Institute Studies* 1 (1975): 119–45.

Kelley, Philip, and Betty A. Coley, eds. *The Browning Collections: A Reconstruction with Other Memorabilia*. Winfield, KS: Wedgestone Press, 1984.

King, Roma A., Jr. *The Focusing Artifice: The Poetry of Robert Browning*. Athens: Ohio University Press, 1968.

Knight, William Henry. *Retrospects*. London: Smith, Elder, 1904.

———, ed. *Transactions of the Wordsworth Society*. 8 vols. Edinburgh: Edinburgh University Press, 1882–87.

Knoepflmacher, U. C., and G. B. Tennyson, eds. *Nature and the Victorian Imagination*. Berkeley: University of California Press, 1977.

Kramer, Lawrence. "The Intimations Ode and Victorian Romanticism." *Victorian Poetry* 18 (1980): 315–35.

———. "Victorian Sexuality and Tintern Abbey." *Victorian Poetry* 24, no. 4 (1986): 399–410.

Latane, David. "Shelley's 'Baleful Influence.'" *Studies in Browning and His Circle* 11, no. 2 (1983): 31–36.

Lehmann, Frederick. *Memories of Half a Century: A Record of Friendships*. Edited by R. C. Lehmann. London: Smith, Elder, 1908.

Lindop, Grevel. *The Opium-Eater: A Life of Thomas De Quincey*. Oxford: Oxford University Press, 1985.

Litzinger, Boyd, and Donald Smalley. *Browning: The Critical Heritage*. London: Routledge & Kegan Paul, 1970.

Marshall, Donald G. Preface to *The Unremarkable Wordsworth*, by Geoffrey H. Hartman. London: Methuen, 1987.

Martin, Loy D. "Browning: The Activation of Influence." *Victorian Newsletter* 53 (1978): 4–9.

———. *Browning's Dramatic Monologues and the Post-Romantic Subject*. Baltimore: Johns Hopkins University Press, 1985.

Maynard, John. *Browning's Youth*. Cambridge, MA: Harvard University Press, 1977.

Miller, Betty. *Robert Browning: A Portrait*. London: Murray, 1952.

———. "This Happy Evening: The Story of *Ion*." *Twentieth Century* 154 (1953): 53–61.

Moorman, Mary. *William Wordsworth: A Biography*. 2 vols. Oxford: Clarendon Press, 1957–65.

Morlier, Margaret M. "The Death of Pan: Elizabeth Barrett Browning and the Romantic Ego." *Browning Institute Studies* 18 (1990): 131–55.

Nichols, Ashton. "Browning's Modernism: The Infinite Moment as Epiphany." *Browning Institute Studies* 11 (1983): 81–99.

Orr, Alexandra Sutherland. *Life and Letters of Robert Browning*. 2nd ed. London: Smith, Elder, 1891.

Peterson, William S. "An Unpublished Memoir of Robert Browning." *Victorian Poetry* 7 (1969): 147–51.

Pinion, F. B. *A Wordsworth Chronology*. Basingstoke, U.K.: Macmillan, 1988.

Plutarch. *Lives*. Translated by Bernadotte Perrin. 11 vols. London: Loeb Classical Library, 1914–26.

Poston, Lawrence, III. "Browning and the Altered Romantic Landscape." In *Nature and the Victorian Imagination,* edited by U. C. Knoepflmacher and G. B. Tennyson, 426–39. Berkeley: University of California Press, 1977.

Pottle, Frederick Albert. *Shelley and Browning: A Myth and Some Facts*. 2nd ed. Hamden, CT: Archon Books, 1965.

Raymond, William Odber. "Browning and the Harriet Westbrook Shelley Letters." *University of Toronto Quarterly* 32 (1963): 184–92.

———. *"The Infinite Moment" and Other Essays*. 2nd ed. Toronto: University of Toronto Press, 1965.

Ryan, Robert M. *The Romantic Reformation*. Cambridge: Cambridge University Press, 1997.

Sharp, Philip D. "The Poet's Age Is Sad: Browning's Late Reference to Wordsworth." *Studies in Browning and His Circle* 9, no. 2 (1981): 86–91.

Shaw, William David. "Browning's Intimations Ode: The Prologue to *Asolando*." *Browning Society Notes* 8, no. 1 (1978): 9–10.

Shelley, Percy Bysshe. *Poems and Prose of Percy Bysshe Shelley*. Edited by Timothy Webb. London: Dent, 1995.

———. *The Poems of Shelley*. Edited by Geoffrey Matthews and Kelvin Everest. London: Longman, 1989–.

Southey, Robert. *A Vision of Judgement*. London: Longman, 1821.

Taylor, Anya. "Religious Readings of the Immortality Ode." *Studies in English Literature* 26 (1986): 633–54.

Taylor, Henry. *Philip van Artevelde, A Dramatic Romance*. 2 vols. London: Moxon, 1834.

Thomas, Charles Flint. *Art and Architecture in the Poetry of Robert Browning: An Illustrated Compendium of Sources*. Troy, NY: Whitson Publishing Company, 1991.

Tucker, Herbert F., Jr. *Browning's Beginnings: The Art of Disclosure*. Minneapolis: University of Minnesota Press, 1980.

———. "Memorabilia: Mnemonic Imagination in Shelley and Browning." *Studies in Romanticism* 19 (1980): 285–325.

Whitla, William. "Browning and the Ashburton Affair." *Browning Society Notes* 2 (1972): 12–41.

Woolford, John. "Browning Rethinks Romanticism." *Essays in Criticism* 43, no. 3 (1993): 211–27.

———. *Browning the Revisionary*. London: Macmillan, 1988.

———. "Elizabeth Barrett and the Wordsworthian Sublime." *Essays in Criticism* 45 (1995): 36–56.

———. "Life—That's Venice! Browning's Romanticism in *Fifine*." Florence: Olschki, 1991.

———. "The Philosophy and Poetics of Power in Browning's Early Work." *Browning Society Notes* 14, no. 2 (1984): 1–21.

Woolford, John, and Daniel Karlin. *Robert Browning*. London: Longman, 1996.

Wordsworth, Ann. "Communication Different." *Browning Society Notes* 13, no. 1 (1983): 4–18.

Wordsworth, William. *The Poetical Works of William Wordsworth*. Edited by Ernest De Selincourt and Helen Darbishire. 5 vols. Oxford: Clarendon Press, 1940–49.

———. *The Prose Works of William Wordsworth*. Edited by W. J. B. Owen and Jane Worthington Smyser. 3 vols. Oxford: Clarendon Press, 1974.

———. *Selections from Wordsworth, by William Knight and Other Members of the Wordsworth Society*. Edited by William Henry Knight. London: Kegan Paul, Trench, 1888.

———. *William Wordsworth: Lyrical Ballads*. Edited by Michael Mason. London: Longman, 1992.

Wordsworth, William, and Dorothy Wordsworth. *The Letters of William and Dorothy Wordsworth: The Middle Years, 1806–11*. Edited by Ernest De Selincourt. Revised by Mary Moorman. Oxford: Clarendon Press, 1969.

———. *The Letters of William and Dorothy Wordsworth: The Later Years, 1821–53*. Edited by Ernest De Selincourt. Revised by Alan G. Hill. 4 vols. Oxford: Clarendon Press, 1978–88.

Worton, Michael, and Judith Still, eds. *Intertextuality: Theories and Practices*. Manchester: Manchester University Press, 1990.

Yetman, Michael G. "Exorcising Shelley Out of Browning: *Sordello* and the Problem of Poetic Identity." *Victorian Poetry* 13, no. 2 (1975): 79–98.

Index